MW01006093

Heroes, Horror, and Happenstance

Stories from This Day in History

by

Thomas E. Keefe

First Edition
~Kincora Press~
Denver, Colorado

Heroes:

Man becomes great exactly in the degree in
which he works for the welfare of his
fellow-men.

Gandhi

~~~

Horrors:

Man is nature, nature man, and all crude
and raw, stinking, vicious, evil. And
holding that evil lightly because the
collective mind refuses to recall the spring
of mountains, the vault of seas and, of
course, besides that, the puny murder of
millions.

John A. Williams

The Man Who Cried I Am

Also, by Tom Keefe

My Journey: A Life According to God (2016)

This Day in Genocide (2016)

Reflections: Catholic Education in RI (2016)

This Day in Donald Trump (2017)

This Day in Peace (2017)

Are You Listening? (2017)

This Day in Black and Blue (2017)

Remembering the Unforgettable (2017)

This Day in Rhode Island (2018)

This Day in Ireland (2018)

Dedication

This book is a collage of significant events in the history of genocide. Told in an almost diary format, *Heroes, Horrors, and Happenstance* is like a "This Day in This Day Favorites" and weaves together an overview of my favorite stories in history.

In the way, each entry catches a sense of choice and the human capacity to do good or evil. *Heroes, Horrors, and Happenstance* is dedicated to the women and men who do their best to fight for justice against discrimination and crimes against humanity. In addition, special recognition goes out to those whose stories aren't told or the stories that aren't told enough…

Forward

Reactions from A Reader

"Great... Tom 'wrote' another book."

Robb Fladry

Denver, Colorado

Preface

To say that history fascinates me if the understatement of the century. For the past couple of years, I have been editing these "This Day in…" books of history and current events.

I created a 366-day template and, as I begin each book, I add in the most famous persons or biggest events into the template. Sometimes I add people sometimes by their birth date and sometimes by their death date; the goal is to have an entry for each of the 366 days of the year. I had to layer the history into the template. Of course, some days are more plentiful than others in terms of eventful people or stories. As a result, some of the day's entries are essentially fillers and can be a bit less interesting at times than other dates in history.

In *Heroes, Horrors, and Happenstance*, I have gleaned the best of the stories from my other books. Essentially, this is a "Greatest Hits" album of historical events and interesting people in history. Some of the narratives in the book are inspirational tales of heroism, while other stories reflect the depraved nature of some questionable characters in history. Some days in history are remarkable in the seeming randomness of unfolding the events.

After all, how could Jonathan Edward Back have known that at 2:29 p.m. on June 6, 1889, he would set into motion events that would lead to the burning of the whole city of Seattle? Random chance, twist of fate, or predestination, it all seems like happenstance.

And, who would have imagined that FDR is in twice as a 'horror' while disgraced former Illinois Governor George Ryan and Vietnam-escalater LBJ are included in the anthology as a 'heroes'? Truly, this is a collection of "Any Given Sunday," meaning that we each hold the capacity to choose good or evil at any moment. My hope is that *Heroes, Horrors, and Happenstance* inspires us all to choose good.

Thomas E. Keefe

Tom

Lakewood, Colorado
July 2018

Acknowledgements

I wish to thank my friends, family, and former teachers who have inspired my love of history and helped me maintain the passion for history as well. At Bishop Hendricken High School, I was fortunate to have three tremendous history teachers: Br. Kiernan, Mike Quigley, and Dennis Mullen. I am the teacher I am today because of these three gentlemen.

Thank you to all of those who have participated in Wikipedia, edited by volunteers around the world and hosted by the Wikimedia Foundation. This project would have been even more of an endeavor without the of Wikipedia and other public domain sources. More specifically, I am indebted to Stacy Conradt of *Mental Floss* for the piece on "29 Unforgettable Epitaphs" (July 30, 2015). I also followed up on Conradt's article by using the website https://www.findagrave.com for more information on the famous epitaphs. Finally, thank you to Blake Wolf of the Associated Press for capturing that iconic moment of Mallory Holtman and Liz Wallace carrying Sara Tucholsky around the bases at the Western Oregon University v Central Washington game on April 26, 2008.

Table of Contents

Introduction

Heroes, Horrors, and Happenstance is an attempt to bring together an anthology of stories from history in an easily accessible almost diary format. Most of the book borrows from my earlier books, specifically *This Day in Genocide*, *This Day in Peace*, *This Day in Black and Blue*, *This Day in Rhode Island*, and *This Day in Ireland*.

In *This Day in Genocide*, I argue that genocide is ordinary, not extra-ordinary. Each event may see extraordinary, but sadly genocide had been an ordinary, or common, occurrence in human history. It is certainly not my intent to devaluing the victims of genocide by calling such atrocities ordinary. Perhaps common or prevalent would be a better word choice, but it is my intent to shock us out of our complacency and self-absorption.

But there are the Righteous Among the Nations and others who have stood up to evil too. *This Day in Peace* weaves together an overview of the women and men of peace. In the way, each entry catches a sense of choice and the human capacity to do good or evil. *This Day in Peace* contains remarkable stories of the women and men who do their best to fight discrimination, war crimes and crimes against humanity.

My interest in R.I. history a natural extension of my passion for history and all things Rhodey. I'm a homer. I was born in Wakefield and raised in nearby Peace Dale, R.I. I went to Nursey School in the basement of Prout Memorial School at Lilly Pads with Sr. Mary and Mrs. Pat. Later I attended Msgr. Clarke School and then Bishop Hendricken High School. At Saint Joseph's University in Philadelphia, P.A., I earned the Lyndon Baines Johnson Award for Congressional Internships, and worked at the U.S. House of Representatives in the office of (then) U.S. Representative Jack Reed (2-RI). I have taught English, Religion, and History at Espirito Santo School in Fall River, M.A., LaSalle Academy in Providence, R.I., and The Prout School in Wakefield, R.I. Like I said, I'm a homer. So, I put together *This Day in Rhode Island* and *This Day in Rhodey* as a way to brag about the awesomeness that is Rhode Island. I've also had the opportunity to be a regular guest on the Lil' Rhody Sport Report on 89.9 FM The Juice in Providence, Rhode Island. This weekly sports talk show is hosted by Ron Robert and Eric Levy.

I think that is one of the themes of all my *This Day in...*" books: whether it be *This Day in Genocide* or, more recently, *This Day in Ireland*, I am hoping to show that there are few "innocents" in the world.

To me, one of the limitations of the human condition is our propensity to dwell on the sins of others, without seeing our own sins. From a macroscopic perspective, people tend to remember history as a series of ethnic or national accomplishments and defeats. People easily remember the attacks upon their ethnicity, nationality, religion, culture, ideology, or identity. If only we remembered history from the perspective of those "other" ethnicities, nationalities, races, religions, cultures, ideologies, or identities that "our" demographic tribes attacked. Rarely do we self-examine our own national, ethnic, or religious culpability in the persecution of others. We, humans, have a complicated victim mentality and a short memory when it comes to our own perpetrations.

For example, in *This Day in Ireland*, is a day collection of events -both positive and negative- that shaped the history of a small island in the North Atlantic. It is not a Green Irish Catholic Gaelic history of Ireland. Remember, the Anglo-Normans were invited to Ireland by an Irish king. The plantations of Ireland in Ulster were created, to a degree, to pacify the province that was constantly rebelling against the government. And violence begets violence: The Irish leaders in the 16th and 17 Centuries, in particular, seem quite quick to resort to violent rebellion.

Penal Laws and United Irishmen. Reforms and Emancipation. Partition and Sectarianism. The so-called Loyalist organizations of Northern Ireland are as responsible for The Troubles as the Irish so-called nationalist organizations. Violence is violence. No, This Day in Ireland is not just a Green Irish Catholic Gaelic history of Ireland. To paraphrase John Donne, as no man is an island, no one owns the Emerald Island or Irish history.

Ireland belongs to all the children of Erin: kings and soldiers, bards and boxers, druids and distance runners, actors and actresses, priests and patriots, nationalists and unionists... Irish history is the history of the Irish Gaelics, the Anglo-Normans and the Norman-Irish, and the Scots-Irish Unionists. And it's a history filled with rich stories, some of which are included here in *Heroes, Horrors, and Happenstance.*

Of course, there is the issue of writer bias. Did I mention that I'm a homer yet? Yes, there are probable more references to Ireland and Rhode Island in this history anthology than you might expect, but that's what makes it unique. Please forgive me if any of my inclusions offend and my omissions of your favorite stories from history. This is *my* collection of stories of history, heroes, horrors, and happenstance. I hope you enjoy!

Heroes,

Horrors,

and

Happenstance

The people we surround ourselves with either raise or lower our standards. They either help us to become the-best-version-of-ourselves or encourage us to become lesser versions of ourselves. We become like our friends. No man becomes great on his own. No woman becomes great on her own. The people around them help to make them great.

We all need people in our lives who raise our standards, remind us of our essential purpose, and challenge us to become the-best-version-of-ourselves.

Matthew Kelly

The Rhythm of Life

~January 1~

"Sugihara Jews"

On this day, January 1, 1900, Chiune Sugihara (杉原 千畝) was born in Mino, Gifu Prefecture, Japan. Sugihara (January 1, 1900 – July 31, 1986) was a Japanese diplomat who served as Vice-Consul for the Empire of Japan in Lithuania. During World War II, he helped between 10,000 and 40,000 Jews leave the country by issuing transit visas so that they could travel to Japanese territory, risking his career and his family's lives. The Jews who escaped were refugees from German-occupied Western Poland or Russian-occupied Eastern Poland, as well as residents of Lithuania. In 1985, Israel named him to the Righteous Among the Nations for his actions.

~~~~~

"İsmail Necdet Kent"

On this day, January 1, 1911, İsmail Necdet Kent was born Constantinople, Ottoman Empire. Necdet Kent (January 1, 1911 – September 20, 2002) was a Turkish diplomat who risked his life to save Jews during World War II. While vice-consul in Marseilles, France between 1941 and 1944, he gave documents of citizenship to dozens of Turkish Jews living in France who did not have proper identity papers, to save them from deportation to the Nazi gas chambers. At one point, he entered an Auschwitz-bound train at enormous personal risk to save 70 Jews, to whom he had granted Turkish citizenship, from deportation.

~January 2~

"The Reconquista"

On this day, January 2, 1492, the Emirate of Granada, the last Moorish stronghold in Spain surrendered. The surrender of Granada completed the Spanish Catholic Reconquista and setting in motion the Inquisition as well as the Conquest of the Americas. With a centuries old culture of warfare and a newly homogeneous nation-state, it was an easy transition for the Reconquista to become colonization, crusaders to become conquistadors, and a Church used to the forced conversion of Muslims and Jews to bring the Inquisitions brand of Christianity to the natives of the alleged "New World."

~January 3~

"William Tucker"

On this day, January 3, 1624 (or possibly 1621), William Tucker was born in the Colony of Virginia. William Tucker was the first person of African ancestry born in the 13 colonies and was the son of two African indentured servants, "Antoney and Isabell." He was named after his parents' master, captain William Tucker. Per the 1624-1625 Virginia Census, 22 Africans lived in Virginia at the time of Tucker's birth. The first Africans arrived in 1619, and all of them worked under indentured servitude contracts. Though they were not treated as equals of European indentured servants. (See August 18th.)

~~~

"Father Damien"

On this day, January 3, 1840, Jozef De Veuster was born in Tremelo, Brabant, Belgium. Fr. Damien was a Roman Catholic priest from Belgium who ministered from 1873 to 1889 in the Kingdom of Hawai'i. People with leprosy, who were required to live under a government-sanctioned medical quarantine on the island of Moloka'i on the Kalaupapa Peninsula. Father Damien worked for sixteen years in Hawaii providing comfort for the lepers of Kalaupapa. He gave the people not only faith but also homes and his medical expertise. He would pray at the cemetery of the deceased and comfort the dying at their bedsides. In December 1884 while preparing to bathe, Damien inadvertently put his foot into the scalding water, causing his skin to blister. He felt nothing and realized he had contracted leprosy after 11 years of working in the colony. Father Damien (January 3, 1840 – April 15, 1889) died of leprosy at 8:00 a.m. on 15 April 1889, aged 49.

~January 4~

"The Arab Spring"

On January 4, 2011, Tarek el-Tayeb Mohamed Bouazizi محمد البوعزيزي died in Tunis, Tunesia. Bouazizi (March 29, 1984 – January 4, 2011) was a Tunisian street vendor who set himself on fire on December 17, 2010, in response to the confiscation of his wares and the harassment and humiliation that he said was inflicted on him by Faida Hamdi and her aides. His act became a catalyst for the Tunisian Revolution and the wider Arab Spring, inciting demonstrations and riots throughout Tunisia in protest of social and political issues in the country. Simmering public anger and sporadic violence intensified following Bouazizi's death, leading then-president Zine El Abidine Ben Ali to step down on January 14, 2011, after 23 years in power.

In 2011, Bouazizi was posthumously awarded the Sakharov Prize jointly along with four others for his and their contributions to "historic changes in the Arab world." The Tunisian government honored him with a postage stamp, and *The Times* of the United Kingdom named Bouazizi as "Person of 2011."

~January 5~

"Protestant on Protestant Martyrdom"

On this day, January 5, 1527, Felix Manz (c. 1498 – January 5, 1527) was executed by the Zürich council of Switzerland and the first Swiss Anabaptist to be martyred at the hands of other Protestants. Manz was a co-founder of the original Swiss Brethren Anabaptist congregation in Zürich, Switzerland, and the first martyr of the Radical Reformation. Manz was executed for preaching adult baptism and contradicting Huldrych Zwingli. Ironically the method of execution proscribed for violating Zwingli's teaching on infant baptism was death by drowning.

It is a sad testament to the human tendency toward institutionalization that Protestants, who were executed by Catholics for practicing their religious beliefs, turned on other Protestants and executed them for professing their beliefs.

~~~~~

"The Good Nazi"

On this day, January 5, 1950, John Heinrich Detlev Rabe (b. November 23, 1882) died of a stroke. Rabe had been a German businessman and Nazi Party member. He is best known for his efforts to stop the atrocities of the Japanese army during the Nanking Occupation and his work to help the Chinese civilians during the event. He used his official capacity as Germany's representative and as senior chief of the European–American establishment in Nanjing, to protect Chinese civilians.

As the Japanese army approached the Chinese capital of Nanking (now Nanjing) and initiated bombing raids on the city, all but 22 foreigners fled the city.

On November 22, 1937, as the Japanese Army advanced on Nanking, Rabe and the other foreign nationals, organized the International Committee for the Nanking Safety Zone and created the Nanking Safety Zone to provide Chinese refugees with food and shelter from the impending Japanese slaughter. The Nanking Safety Zone, which he helped to establish, sheltered approximately 200,000 Chinese people from slaughter during the massacre. Rabe and his zone administrators also tried to stop the atrocities. His attempts to appeal to the Japanese by using his Nazi Party membership credentials only delayed the Japanese offensive, but that delay allowed hundreds of thousands of refugees to escape.

After the war, Rabe was arrested first by the Soviet NKVD and then by the British Army. Both, however, let him go after intense interrogation. He worked but was later denounced for his Nazi Party membership by an acquaintance and lost his meager income. In 1948, the citizens of Nanking learned of the very dire situation of the Rabe family in occupied Germany, and they quickly raised a very large sum of money, equivalent to $2000 ($20,000 in 2016). The mayor of Nanjing went to Germany, bought a large amount of food for the Rabe family, and delivered it in person. From mid-1948 until the communist takeover of China, the people of Nanking sent a food package each month to the Rabe family.

On January 5, 1950, John Heinrich Detlev Rabe died of a stroke. In 1997 his tombstone was moved from Berlin to Nanjing (as it is now) where it received a place of honor at the massacre memorial site. In 2005, Rabe's former residence in Nanking (as it then was) was renovated and now accommodates the "John Rabe and International Safety Zone Memorial Hall," which opened in 2006.

~January 6~

"Danny Thomas"

On this day, January 6, 1912, Amos Muzyad Yakhoob Kairouz was born in Deerfield, Michigan. Known professionally by his stage name Danny Thomas, Kairouz (January 6, 1912 – February 6, 1991) was an American nightclub comedian, singer, actor, and producer. His legacy includes a lifelong dedication to fundraising for charity and, specifically, his founding of St. Jude Children's Research Hospital.

~~~

"Nelson Mandela of Asia"

On this day, January 6, 1912, Kim Dae-jung was born in Sābu-do, Sin'an, Zenra-nandō, Japanese Korea. Kim (January 6, 1924 – August 18, 2009) was elected to parliament, but Park Chung-hee led a military coup, voided the elections and assumed dictatorial powers. In 1973, Kim was kidnapped in by KCIA agents in response to his criticism of President Park's Yushin program, which had granted near-dictatorial powers. Kim recalled,

"I have lived, and continue to live, in the belief that God is always with me. I know this from experience. In August of 1973, while exiled in Japan, I was kidnapped from my hotel room in Tokyo by intelligence agents of the then military government of South Korea. The news of the incident startled the world. The agents took me to their boat at anchor along the seashore. They tied me up, blinded me, and stuffed my mouth. Just when they were about to throw me overboard, Jesus Christ appeared before me with such clarity. I clung to him and begged him to save me. At that very moment, an airplane came down from the sky to rescue me from the moment of death.

~January 7~

"The Enemy of My Enemy is Still My Enemy?"

On this day, January 7, 1979, Vietnam ended the Cambodian Genocide. Vietnamese forces had entered Phnom Penh, and the genocidal Khmer Rouge leadership was forced to flee to western Cambodia. Vietnam, operating out of the Soviet sphere-of-influence alienated China even further as the Khmer government had been in the Chinese sphere-of-influence.

Ironically, the US sanctioned Vietnam for their invasion of Cambodia, even though the Vietnamese performed a service to the international community by ending the genocide. Crimes Against Humanity were certainly viewed within the lens of the Cold War.

~January 8~

"Maximilian Kolbe"

On this day, January 8, 1894, Maximilian Maria Kolbe was born in Zduńska Wola, Kingdom of Poland, Russian Empire. Kolbe was a Polish Conventual Franciscan friar. After the outbreak of WWII, Kolbe was one of the few who remained in the monastery, where he organized a temporary hospital. After the town was captured by the Germans, he was briefly arrested on September 19, 1939, but was later released. He refused to sign the Deutsche Volksliste, which would have given him rights similar to those of German citizens in exchange for recognizing his German ancestry. Instead, he continued work at his monastery, where he and others provided shelter to refugees including 2,000 Jews whom he hid at the friary in Niepokalanów.

The monastery was also a publishing house, issuing a number of anti-Nazi German publications, and on February 17, 1941, the monastery was shut down by the German authorities. Kolbe was arrested by the German Gestapo and imprisoned in the Pawiak prison. On May 28th, he was transferred to Auschwitz as prisoner #16670. Kolbe was subjected to violent harassment, including beating and lashings, and once had to be smuggled to a prison hospital by friendly inmates.

At the end of July 1941, three prisoners disappeared from the camp, prompting SS-Hauptsturmführer Karl Fritzsch, the deputy camp commander, to pick 10 men to be starved to death in an underground bunker to deter further escape attempts. When one of the selected men, Franciszek Gajowniczek, cried out, "My wife! My children!" Kolbe volunteered to take his place.

According to an assistant janitor, Kolbe led the prisoners from the cell, and each time the guards checked on him, he was standing or kneeling in the middle of the cell looking calmly at all who entered. After two weeks of dehydration and starvation, only Kolbe remained alive. The guards gave Kolbe a lethal injection of carbolic acid. Kolbe is said to have raised his left arm and calmly waited for the deadly injection. He died on August 14, 1941.

~January 9~

"Rigoberta Menchú"

On this day, January 9, 1959, Rigoberta Menchú Tum was born in Laj Chimel, Quiché, Guatemala. Menchú is a K'iche' political activist who has dedicated her life to publicizing the rights of Guatemala's indigenous feminists during and after the Guatemalan Civil War (1960–1996), and to promoting indigenous rights in the country. She received the Nobel Peace Prize in 1992 and is the subject of the testimonial biography *I, Rigoberta Menchú* (1983) and the author of the autobiographical work, Crossing Borders. Menchú is a UNESCO Goodwill Ambassador.

~~~

"Ascanio Arosemena"

On this day, January 9, 1964, Ascanio Arosemena was shot while trying to evacuate wounded protesters during the Flag Pole Incident of 1964. Witnesses state that Arosemena was shot from behind, through the shoulder and thorax. The eyewitness accounts and a photograph of Arosemena supporting an injured man corrobaorate the account. The former Balboa High School, one of the buildings of the Panama Canal Authority and the site of the Flag Pole Incident, has been renamed in memory of Ascanio Arosemena. Martyrs' Day is a Panamanian Day of National Mourning which commemorates the January 9, 1964, Riots over sovereignty of the Panama Canal Zone. The riot started after a Panamanian flag was torn and Panamanian students were killed during a conflict with Canal Zone Police officers and Canal Zone residents.

~January 10~

"Rabbi Yekusiel Yehudah Halberstam"

On this day, January 10, 1905, Rabbi Yekusiel Yehudah Halberstam was born in Rudnik nad Sanem is a town in Nisko County, Subcarpathian Voivodeship, Poland. Halberstam (January 10, 1905 – June 18, 1994) was an Orthodox rabbi and the founding Rebbe of the Sanz-Klausenburg Hasidic dynasty. Halberstam became one of the youngest rebbes in Europe, leading thousands of followers in the town of Klausenburg, Romania, before WWII. When the war began, the Jews of Hungary and Romania were not immediately affected like the Polish and Lithuanian Jewry. In 1941, a new law required all Jews living in Hungary to prove that their family had lived in and paid taxes in Hungary back to 1851. Suddenly thousands of Jews, including the Rebbe, were placed in jeopardy. The Rebbe, his wife, and eleven children were arrested and brought to Budapest, where the family was separated. The Rebbe was jailed with other leaders who were eventually sent directly to Auschwitz. Through the intercessions of others, Rebbe was released, but in 1944 the Germans invaded Hungary, and Gestapo chief Adolf Eichmann immediately organized the round-up, ghettoization, and deportation of Hungarian Jews to Auschwitz.

Knowing that the Gestapo targeted community leaders, the Rebbe hid in an open grave in a cemetery for several weeks. He then fled to the town of Banya, where he was conscripted into a forced-labor camp along with other Hungarian Jews. As the war wound down in spring 1945, the Germans disbanded the Muldorf camp and sent the inmate population on yet another death march, chasing them from place to place without food or rest. Sometimes they were loaded aboard rail cars and driven to and fro.

On Friday, April 27, 1945, the train suddenly stopped in a small town, and SS officers jumped aboard, declaring, "You are free!" Many prisoners believed them and jumped off the train. But Halberstam told the people around him, "Today is the eve of Shabbat. Where will we go?" Then he added, "My heart tells me that not everything here is as it should be." Suddenly, SS soldiers rode in on bicycles from all directions, firing machine guns and killing hundreds of people. At the same time, American bombers dove in, strafing the field. Only Halberstam and those who stayed with him on the train escaped injury. Two days later, their real liberation came when the train stopped near a village, and the Nazi guards deserted them. American soldiers boarded the train with smiles, candy, and chocolates.

~~~

"Maria Mandl"

On this day, January 10, 1912, Maria Mandl was born in Münzkirchen, Upper Austria, then part of Austria-Hungary.
She went on to become the most famous female SS guard. She controlled all the female Auschwitz camps and female subcamps including at Hindenburg, Lichtewerden, and Raisko. She oversaw the inmate lists, sending an estimated half a million women and children to their deaths in the gas chambers at both Auschwitz I and Auschwitz II.

Mandl was arrested by the US Army on August 10, 1945, handed over to Poland in November 1946, tried in the Auschwitz Trial (1947) and executed on January 24, 1948, at the age of 36. (See also February 1st and August 10th).

~January 11~

"George Ryan"

On this day, January 11, 2003, Governor George Homer Ryan (R-IL) commuted the death sentences of 167 prisoners on Illinois' death row. Ryan helped to renew the national debate on capital punishment when, as governor, he declared a moratorium on his state's death penalty in 2000. "We have now freed more people than we have put to death under our system," he said. "There is a flaw in the system, without question, and it needs to be studied."

Clearly, George Ryan is an imperfect person, as are we all, but that does not negate the fact that on January 11, 2003, Ryan swas on the right side of history.

~January 12~

"Christiane Amanpour"

On this day, January 12, 1958, Christiane Amanpour was born in London, England, United Kingdom. Raised in Tehran, Iran, Amanpour moved to the United States to study journalism at the University of Rhode Island.

During her time at URI, Amanpour worked in the news department at WBRU-FM in Providence, Rhode Island. She also worked for NBC affiliate WJAR in Providence, Rhode Island, as an electronic graphics designer. In 1983, Amanpour graduated from the university summa cum laude and Phi Beta Kappa with a B.A. degree in journalism.

In 1995, Amanpour received an honorary doctorate from the University of Rhode Island. Amanpour, CNN's chief international correspondent, has earned every major television journalism award, including 11 News and Documentary Emmy Awards and four Peabody Awards. In addition, the URI alumna has endowed The Christiane Amanpour Lecture Series at URI, which brings renowned journalists to campus.

~January 13~

"Zola"

On this day, January 13, 1898, Émile Zola published *J'accuse....!* And exposed the Dreyfus affair. Émile Zola was convicted and imprisoned.

Coined "The Dreyfus Affair," the French government was aware of Dreyfus' innocence as well as Esterhazy's guilt but chose to cover-up both. Zola is credited with bringing the truth to light in his libel trial and ultimately justice for Dreyfus.

~January 14~

"Selahattin Ülkümen"

On this day, January 14, 1914, Selahattin Ülkümen was born in Antakya, Turkey. Ülkümen (January 14, 1914 – June 7, 2003) was a Turkish diplomat and consul in Rhodes during   the Second World War, who assisted many local Jews to escape the Holocaust. In 1989, Israel recognized him as among the Righteous Among the Nations and listed his name at Yad Vashem. Turkish and Greek Jews were deported to death camps from the island of Corfu. But on the island of Rhodes, Turkey's Consul, Selahattin Ülkümen, saved the lives of close to 50 people, among a Jewish community of some 2,000 after the Germans took over the island.

~~~~~

"Brigadier General Elisha Rhodes"

On this day, January 14, 1917, Elisha Hunt Rhodes died in Providence, Rhode Island. Rhodes (March 21, 1842 – January 14, 1917) was an American soldier who served in the Union Army of the Potomac for the entire duration of the American Civil War. Rhodes' illustrative diary of his war service was quoted prominently in Ken Burns' PBS documentary *The Civil War*. He enlisted as a corporal in the 2nd Rhode Island Volunteers Company and, by the end of the war, was promoted to Colonel. From June 25, 1879, until March 21, 1892, he served as the commander of the Brigade of Rhode Island Militia with the rank of brigadier general.

~January 15~

"The Great Molasses Flood"

On this day, January 15, 1919, the Great Molasses Flood, also known as the Boston Molasses Disaster or the Great Boston Molasses Flood, occurred in the North End neighborhood of Boston, Massachusetts. A large molasses storage tank burst and a wave of molasses rushed through the streets at an estimated 35 mph, killing 21 and injuring 150. The event entered local folklore, and for decades afterwards, residents claimed that on hot summer days the area still smelled of molasses.

~~~

"The Witch of Buchenwald"

On this day, January 15, 1951, Ilse Koch, the wife of the commandant of the Buchenwald concentration camp, was sentenced to life imprisonment by a court in West Germany. She was accused of numerous acts of dehumanization, including taking souvenirs from the skin of murdered inmates with distinctive tattoos. At least four separate witnesses for the prosecution testified that they had seen Koch choose tattooed prisoners, who were then killed, and then made into human-skin lampshades. Koch committed suicide by hanging herself at Aichach women's prison on September 1, 1967.

~~~

"Pope John Paul II"

On this day, January 15, 1981, Pope John Paul II welcomed Lech Wałęsa and members of Solidarity to the Vatican. Four months later, May 13, 1981, the Pope was shot by Mehmet Ali Ağca in St. Peter's Square. The Bulgarian Secret Service was allegedly instructed by the KGB to assassinate the Pope because of his support of Solidarity. The Pope later forgave Ağca for the assassination attempt. Following the shooting, Pope John Paul II asked people to "pray for my brother [Ağca] ... whom I have sincerely forgiven." In 1983, he and Ağca met and spoke privately at Rome's Rebibbia Prison, and Ağca kissed the Pope's ring at the conclusion of their visit. The Pope was also in touch with Ağca's family over the years, meeting his mother in 1987 and his brother, Muezzin Agca, a decade later. Ağca was eventually pardoned by Italian President Carlo Azeglio Ciampi at the Pope's request and was deported to Turkey in June of 2000.

~January 16~

"Jefferson's Epitaph"

On this day, January 16, 1786, the Commonwealth of Virginia passed into law the Statute for Religious Freedom authored by Thomas Jefferson. The statute disestablished the Church of England in Virginia and guaranteed freedom of religion to people of all religious faiths, including Christians of all denominations, Jews, Muslims, and Hindus. The statute was a notable precursor of the Establishment Clause and Free Exercise Clause of the First Amendment to the United States Constitution. The Statute for Religious Freedom was one of only three accomplishments Jefferson instructed to be put in his epitaph.

~~~

"Jan Palach"

On this day, January 16, 1969, Czech student Jan Palach committed suicide by self-immolation in Prague, Czechoslovakia, in protest against the Soviets' crushing of the Prague Spring the year before.

~~~

"A Democratically Elected Female African Leader"

On this day, January 16, 2006, Ellen Johnson Sirleaf was sworn in as Liberia's new president. She became Africa's first female elected head of state. Opposition leader George Weah was elected President of Liberia in the 2017 election, defeating the incumbent Vice President Joseph Boakai; this is a noteworthy peaceful transfer of power in Liberian and African history.

~January 17~

"The Committee of Public Safety"

On this day, January 17, 1893, Lorrin Thurston, along with the Citizens' Committee of Public Safety, led the coup d'état in the Kingdom of Hawaii. The anti-monarchical insurgents, composed largely of United States citizens, engineered the overthrow of its native monarch, Queen Lili'uokalani. America's "Committee of Public Safety" was as ironic of a name as the "Committee of Public Safety" of the French Revolution and its Reign of Terror. The coup is undoubtedly illegal by today's moral and legal standards and makes US criticism of Russian annexation of South Ossetia and Crimea sound a bit tin to international ears.

~~~

"Mercy Brown"

On this day, January 17, 1892, Mercy L. Brown died in Exeter, Rhode Island. In one of the best documented cases of the exhumation of a corpse in order to perform rituals to banish an undead manifestation, her body was exhumed three months later to determine whether Mercy Brown was a vampire.

~January 18~

"The First Fleet"

On this day, January 18, 1788, the HMS *Supply* arrived in Botany Bay Australia as the lead ship of the First Fleet.

The HMS *Alexander*, HMS *Friendship*, and HMS *Scarborough* arrived the next day, and the rest of the fleet arrived January 20th. The First Fleet was one of the world's greatest sea voyages – eleven vessels carrying about 1,487 people and stores had traveled for 252 days for more than 15,000 miles without losing a ship.

The Cadigal people of the Botany Bay area witnessed the Fleet arrive. First contacts, however, were made with the local indigenous people, the Eora, who seemed curious but suspicious of the newcomers. In retrospect and at best, this began the end of their cultural autonomy. At worst, it was the beginning of their cultural genocide and the genocide of Australia's aboriginal people.

Eddie Mabo (c. June 29, 1936 – January 21, 1992) was an Indigenous Australian man from the Torres Strait Islands known for his role in campaigning for Indigenous land rights and for his role in a landmark decision of the High Court of Australia which overturned the legal doctrine of *terra nullius* ("nobody's land") which characterized Australian law with regard to land and title.

Today, Australia celebrates National Reconciliation Week as an attempt to mend those "rabbit-proof fences." It is held between May 27th and June 3rd of each year, with the dates holding special historical significance: the former marks the anniversary of the 1967 referendum in Australia and the latter marks the anniversary of High Court of Australia judgement on the Mabo v Queensland of 1992.

~ ~ ~

"John Hume"

On this day, January 18, 1937, John Hume was born in Derry, Northern Ireland. Hume was founding member of the Social Democratic and Labour Party. He was a prime negotiator in the Belfast (Good Friday) Agreement of April 1998 and is regarded as one of the most important figures in the recent political history of Ireland. Hume received the 1998 Nobel Peace Prize with David Trimble. He was also a recipient of the Gandhi Peace Prize and the Martin Luther King Award, as well as several other peace awards.

~January 19~

"Operation Paper Clip"

On this day, January 19, 1983, Nazi war criminal Klaus Barbie was arrested in Bolivia. It is curious how outraged that many Americans are that Klaus Barbie, Joseph Mengele, Adolf Eichmann, and so many others escaped to South America. After all, the US government had an entire plan for brings Nazis into the United States. Operation Paperclip helped former Nazis find new lives, so long as the Nazis were deemed useful to the US government.

~~~

"Coach"

On this day, January 19, 1924, Nicholas Colasanto was born in Providence, Rhode Island. Colasanto (January 19, 1924 – February 12, 1985) was an American actor and television director, known for his role as "Coach" Ernie Pantusso in the American sitcom *Cheers*. He served in the United States Navy during World War II, and later attended the American Academy of Dramatic Arts in the 1950s. He was diagnosed with heart disease in the mid-1970s. By 1984 his worsening symptoms forced him to stop working on *Cheers*, and he filmed his last full episode in November 1984. He died of a heart attack at his home on February 12, 1985, at age 61.

~January 20~

"Bill Kugle"

On this day, January 20, 1925, William Herrell Kugle, Jr., was born in Fort Worth, Texas. I'm sure Bill Kugle (January 20, 1925 – December 27, 1992) was an interesting man, did lots of interesting things, and both loved and was loved by lots of other, equally, interesting people. However, what is perhaps most interesting is the epitaph engraved upon Bill Kugle's gravestone:

"He never voted for Republicans and had little to do with them"

~~~

(See also April 16th)

~January 21~

"The National League Providence Grays"

On this day, January 21, 1878, the Providence Grays applied for membership in the National League and was officially approved on February 6, 1878. In a break with tradition, the League's newest addition adopted gray flannel instead of white for their home uniform and the team became known as the 'Grays.'

~January 22~

"U Thant"

On this day, January 22, 1909, Thant was born in Pantanaw, British Burma, British India. Thant, known honorifically as U Thant, was appointed as Secretary-General in 1961, after Dag Hammarskjöld, died in an air crash. In his first term, Thant facilitated talks between U.S. President John F. Kennedy and Soviet premier Nikita Khrushchev during the Cuban Missile Crisis (1962), helping to avert a global catastrophe.

~~~

"Congressman Lyndon B. Johnson"

On this day, January 22, 1973, Lyndon B. Johnson (b. August 27, 1908) died in Stonewall, Texas. As a Congressman, Lyndon Johnson (Texas-10th) helped Austrian conductor Erich Leinsdorf gain permanent residency in the United States in 1938. Johnson later helped Jews enter the U.S. through Latin America and become workers on National Youth Administration projects in Texas.

~~~

"First Indigenous Head of Government or State"

On this day, January 22, 2006, Evo Morales was inaugurated as President of Bolivia, becoming the country's first indigenous president and the first indigenous head of state in the world. For Bolivia's poor and indigenous communities who felt marginalized from Bolivian politics, Morales has invoked a sense of dignity and destiny in a way that no other politician has done for the indigenous people.

~January 23~

"Zulu!"

On this day, January 23, 1879, the Battle of Rorke's Drift ended. This battle was famously portrayed in the (1964) film *Zulu*. The real result of the Anglo-Zulu War, however, was not as entertaining. The Anglo-Zulu War resulted in the subjugation of the independent Zulu kingdom and Boer's Republic alike. Ultimately, the suppression of the Zulus and other indigenous tribes paved the way for the Afrikaner years of apartheid (1948-1994).

~~~

"The Piegan Massacre"

On this day, January 23, 1870, U.S. cavalrymen killed 173 Piegan Blackfeet, mostly women, and children, in what became known as the Marias Massacre (also known as the Baker Massacre or the Piegan Massacre). Major Eugene Baker had been tasked by General Sheridan to suppress Mountain Chief's band of Piegan Blackfeet, but mistakenly attacked a Piegan Blackfeet band led by Chief Heavy Runner, an ally of the United States.

As a result, President Grant insisted that the Bureau of Indian Affairs be kept under the Department of the Interior (at a time with the War Department was trying to regain control) and he appointed a significant number of pacifist Quakers as "Indian Agents," hoping they would be free of corruption and militancy in BIA.

~January 24~

"Thurgood Marshall"

On this day, January 24, 1993, Thurgood Marshall died in Bethesda, Maryland. Marshall (July 2, 1908 – January 24, 1993) was an Associate Justice of the Supreme Court of the United States. Marshall was the Court's 96th justice and its first African-American justice. Before becoming a judge, Marshall was a lawyer who was best known for his high success rate in arguing before the Supreme Court and for the victory in *Brown v. Board of Education*, a 1954 decision that ruled that segregated public schools were unconstitutional.

~~~

"Hey, its 2015, Let's Attack Kids for Being Native America?"

On this day, January 24, 2015, Native American fourth-through eighth-graders from American Horse School (Allen, SD) were subjected to beer baths and racial slurs while attending a Rapid City Rush hockey game. Trace O'Connell, 41, of Philip SD was charged with violating Rapid City's municipal disorderly conduct ordinance but was later acquitted on September 1, 2015.

~~~

"J. Joseph Garrahy"

On this day, January 24, 2012, John Joseph Garrahy died in West Palm Beach, Florida. Governor Garrahy (November 26, 1930 – January 24, 2012) is most well-known for his red plaid shirt that he wore during the 1978 Blizzard.

~January 25~

"March to the Sea"

On this day, January 25, 1945, approximately 3000-5000 prisoners from the Stutthof concentration camp began their forced march into the Baltic Sea and were subsequently machined gunned to death.

The death march began on January 25, ended on January 30th and 31st. Survivors of the camp were marched in the direction of Lauenburg in eastern Germany to keep away from the advancing Soviet Army. When this column of prisoners and their German guards were then cut off by advancing Soviets, the Germans forced the surviving prisoners back toward Stutthof. Marching in severe winter conditions and brutal treatment by SS guards led to thousands of more deaths.

Evidence also exists of small-scale soap production of soap made from human corpses in the Stutthof concentration camp.

~January 26~

"Israel Meir Kagan"

On this day, January 26, 1839, Israel Meir (HaKohen) Kagan was born in Dzyatlava, Grodno Governorate, Russian Empire (today Belarus).

Kagan (January 26, 1839 – September 15, 1933), known popularly as the Chofetz Chaim חפץ חיים, was an influential rabbi of the Musar movement, a Halakhist, posek, and ethicist whose works continue to be widely influential in Jewish life. Kagan initially refused to become personally involved Zionism but refrained from publicly denouncing the movement. When his views became known, he cautioned his students about joining the Zionists and declared its political aims as being contrary to the Torah. During his lifetime, he was venerated by Jews and non-Jews alike. Orthodox Jews across the world viewed him as one of the 36 saints, and Polish farmers were said to have lured him into their fields believing his feet would bring blessing to their crops.

~January 27~

"The Portuguese Schindler"

On this day, January 27, 1902, Alberto Carlos de Liz-Texeira Branquinho was born. De Liz-Texeira Branquinho (January 27, 1902, in Viseu, Portugal – †1973) was a Portuguese diplomat credited with saving the lives of 1,000 Jews in Nazi-occupied Hungary during the Holocaust from Hungarian Fascists and the Nazis during the later stages of World War II. While serving as Portugal's Chargé d'Affaires in Budapest in 1944.

~~~

"A 'Peace People' Person"

On this day, January 27, 1944, Mairead Maguire (also known as Mairead Corrigan Maguire and formerly as Mairéad Corrigan) was born in Belfast, Northern Ireland. Maguire co-founded, with Betty Williams and Ciaran McKeown, the Women for Peace, which later became the Community for Peace People, an organization dedicated to encouraging a peaceful resolution of The Troubles in Northern Ireland. Maguire and Williams were awarded the 1976 Nobel Peace Prize.

~January 28~

"A Life of Pi"

On this day, January 28, 1540, Ludolph van Ceulen was born in the Bishopric of Hildesheim. Van Ceulen (January 28, 1540 – December 31, 1610) was a German-Dutch mathematician who spent his life calculating the numerical value of π, using essentially the same methods as those employed by Archimedes. He published a 20-decimal value in his 1596 book Van den Circkel (On the Circle), and he later expanded this to 35 decimals. After his death, the Ludolphine number was engraved on his tombstone:

3.14159265358979323846264338327950288...

~~~

"We Are the World"

On this day, January 28, 1985, the supergroup United Support of Artists (USA) for Africa recorded the song "We Are the World" written by Michael Jackson and Lionel Richie.

~~~

"Challenger"

On this day, January 28, 1986, the NASA shuttle orbiter mission STS-51-L and the tenth flight of Space Shuttle Challenger (OV-99) broke apart 73 seconds into its flight, killed all seven crew members (which consisted of five NASA astronauts and two payload specialists). The spacecraft disintegrated over the Atlantic Ocean, off the coast of Cape Canaveral, Florida, at 11:39 EST. The disintegration of the vehicle began after a joint in its right solid rocket booster (SRB) failed at liftoff. The failure was caused by the fact that O-ring seals used in the joint were not designed to handle the unusually cold conditions that existed at this launch. The seals' failure caused a breach in the SRB joint, allowing pressurized burning gas from within the solid rocket motor to reach the outside and impinge upon the adjacent SRB aft field joint attachment hardware and external fuel tank. This led to the separation of the right-hand SRB's aft field joint attachment and the structural failure of the external tank. Aerodynamic forces broke up the orbiter.

~~~

"Buddy"

On this day, January 28, 2016, Vincent Albert "Buddy" Cianci Jr. died in Providence, Rhode Island. Cianci (April 30, 1941 – January 28, 2016) was an American lawyer, convicted felon, radio talk show host, politician, and political commentator who served as the mayor of Providence, Rhode Island (1975–84, 1991–2002). Cianci was the longest-serving mayor of Providence and one of the longest-serving "big city" mayors in United States history, having held office for over 21 years.

~January 29~

"Bear Creek Massacre"

On this day, January 29, 1863, the United States Army attacked Shoshone gathered at the confluence of the Bear River and Beaver Creek. After about two hours, the Shoshone had run out of ammunition. [According to some later reports, some Shoshone were seen trying to cast lead ammunition during the middle of the battle and died with the molds in their hands.] After the Shoshone ran out of ammunition, the battle quickly turned ugly, and the event became known as the Bear Creek Massacre.

~~~

"Full Circle"

On this day, January 29, 1984, Yad Vashem recognized Mustafa and Zejneba Hardaga, Izet and Bachriya Hardaga and Ahmed Sadik as Righteous Among the Nations. Established in 1953, Yad Vashem is Israel's official memorial to the victims of the Holocaust as well as to non-Jews who, at personal risk and without a financial or evangelistic motive, chose to save their Jews from the Shoah. The greatest honor Yad Vashem can bestow is to recognize a person (or persons) as Righteous Among the Nations. When Yad Vashem recognized the Hardaga family, they recognized a relationship that has transcended faith, generations, and multiple genocides. Mustafa and Zejneba Hardaga, Izet and Bachriya Hardaga and Ahmed Sadik all worked to save Jews when the Germany Wehrmacht invaded Yugoslavia. After the Hardaga family had worked to save the Kabiljo family in the 1940s, karma came full circle during the Bosnian Genocide when the Karbiljo family -in turn- saved the Hardaga family from the evils of genocide as well.

~January 30~

This day, January 30th is recognized as Fred Korematsu Day in California and Virginia, United States of America.

~~~

"Sunday, Bloody Sunday"

On this day, January 30, 1972, soldiers of the British Army shot 26 civil rights protesters and bystanders. Vehicles of the 1st Battalion, Parachute Regiment, also drove over two civilians. The event became known as Bloody Sunday (and the Bogside Massacre) and was immortalized in US's song, "Sunday, Bloody Sunday."

The Saville Inquiry, chaired by Lord Saville of Newdigate, was established in 1998 to reinvestigate the events. Following a 12-year inquiry, Saville's report was made public in 2010 and found that all those civilians shot were unarmed and that the killings were both "unjustified and unjustifiable." On the publication of the Saville report the British prime minister, David Cameron made a formal apology on behalf of the United Kingdom.

~January 31~

"Giorgio Perlasca"

On this day, January 31, 1910, Giorgio Perlasca was born in Como, Italy. Perlasca (January 31, 1910 – August 15, 1992) fought as an Italian volunteer in the Spanish Civil War and, as a result of his service to Spain, he received the gratitude of Francisco Franco and a guarantee of cooperation of Spanish embassies.

When Italy surrendered to the Allied forces, Italians had to choose whether to join Benito Mussolini Italian Social Republic or stay loyal to the King and join the Allies' side. Perlasca chose the latter. As a result, he was arrested while in Budapest and confined to a castle reserved for diplomats. After a few months, he used a medical pass that allowed him to travel within Hungary and, taking advantage of his status as a veteran of the Spanish war, fled to the Spanish Embassy to claim political asylum. Perlasca worked with the Spanish Chargé d'Affaires, Ángel Sanz Briz, and other diplomats of neutral states to smuggle Jews out of Hungary. The system he devised consisted of furnishing 'protection cards' which placed Jews under the guardianship of various neutral states. He helped Jews find refuge in protected houses under the control of various embassies, which had extraterritorial conventions that gave them an equivalent to sovereignty.

When Sanz Briz was removed from Hungary to Switzerland in November 1944, he invited Perlasca to accompany him to safety. However, Perlasca chose to remain in Hungary. However, the new Hungarian government suddenly ordered the Spanish Embassy and extraterritorial houses where the Jews took refuge to be abandoned.

Perlasca immediately claimed that Sanz Briz had appointed
Perlasca as his deputy and that Sanz Briz would soon return to
handle the situation. Throughout the winter, Perlasca hid and fed
thousands of Jews in Budapest. He continued to arrange safe
conduct passes on the basis of a Spanish law passed in 1924 that
granted citizenship to Jews of Sephardi origin (descendants of
Iberian Jews expelled from Spain in the late 15th century).

In December 1944, Perlasca even rescued two boys from being
herded onto a freight train in defiance of a German lieutenant
colonel on the scene. Swedish diplomat Raoul Wallenberg, also
present, later told Perlasca that the officer who had challenged
him was Adolf Eichmann. In a period of some forty-five days
(December 1, 1944, to January 16, 1945), Perlasca helped save
more than 5,000 Jews.

~~~

"Thomas Merton"

On this day, January 31, 1915, Thomas Merton was born in
Prades, Pyrénées-Orientales, France. Merton (January 31, 1915 –
December 10, 1968) was an American Catholic writer, theologian,
and mystic. A Trappist monk of the Abbey of Gethsemani,
Kentucky, he was also a poet, social activist, and student of
comparative religion. In 1949, he was ordained to the priesthood.
Merton wrote more than 70 books, including his autobiography
The Seven Storey Mountain (1948). Merton was a keen proponent
of interfaith understanding. He pioneered dialogue with
prominent Asian spiritual figures, including the Dalai Lama and
the Vietnamese monk Thich Nhat Hanh, and authored books
on Zen Buddhism and Taoism.

~~~

"Family Guy and the Superman Building"

On this day, January 31, 1999, *Family Guy* debuted on the Fox Broadcasting network.

The series, created by Rhode Island School of Design graduate Seth MacFarlane, is set in the fictional city of Quahog, Rhode Island. The downtown Providence building and its neighbors are displayed prominently on the skyline of the fictional City of Quahog, Rhode Island, the setting of the American adult animated sitcom Family Guy.

The Industrial National Bank Building is often seen behind the Griffin family's home on fictional Spooner Street. The Industrial National Bank Building, also known as the Superman Building, is the tallest building in the city of Providence, Rhode Island, the tallest in the state of Rhode Island, and currently the 28th tallest in New England. Commissioned by Samuel P. Colt), the building designed in the Art Deco style and opened for tenants on October 1, 1928.

Bessie Braddock, MP: "Winston, you are drunk, and what's more you are disgustingly drunk."

WSC: "Bessie, my dear, you are ugly, and what's more, you are disgustingly ugly. But tomorrow I shall be sober, and you will still be disgustingly ugly."[1]

---

[1] https://www.winstonchurchill.org/publications/churchill-bulletin/bulletin-031-jan-2011/drunk-and-ugly-the-rumor-mill

~February 1~

"Therese Brandl"

On this day, February 1, 1902, Therese Brandl was born in Staudach-Egerndach, Bavaria, Germany. Brandl took part in the selection of women and children to the gas chambers as well as physically abusing prisoners, including children, as Andreas Larinciakos, a nine-year-old boy from Cles, Hungary, recalled:

"While in the camp, Doctor Mengele took my blood many times. In November 1944, all children were transferred to Camp A, the gypsy camp. When they counted us, one was found missing, so [Maria] Mandl, the manageress of the women's camp and her assistant, [Therese] Brandl, drove us out into the street at one in the morning and made us stand there in the frost until noon the next day."

Therese Brandl was convicted of crimes against humanity after the war during the Auschwitz Trial in Kraków and executed. (See also January 10th).

~~~

"Another Execution"

On this day, February 1, 1968, Eddie Adams photographed the execution of Viet Cong officer Nguyễn Văn Lém by South Vietnamese National Police Chief Nguyễn Ngọc Loan. The photograph and accompanying videotape further erodes the argument that there is are good guys and bad guys in the Vietnam Conflict, let alone any war. Adams won the 1969 Pulitzer Prize for Spot News Photography and a World Press Photo award for the photograph (captioned 'General Nguyen Ngoc Loan executing a Viet Cong prisoner in Saigon') but later lamented its notoriety.

~February 2~

"Samuel Whittemore"

On this day, February 2, 1793, Samuel Whittemore died in Cambridge, Massachusetts. Whittemore (July 27, 1696 – February 2, 1793) was an American farmer and one-time soldier. He was at least 78 years of age (or older) when he became the oldest known colonial combatant in the American Revolutionary War.

A monument in Arlington, Massachusetts, on Massachusetts Avenue near Pleasant Street, reads:

"Near this spot, Samuel Whittemore, then 80 years old,
killed three British soldiers, April 19, 1775.
He was shot, bayoneted, beaten and left for dead, but recovered
and lived to be 98 years of age."

~~~

"The Other Guy"

On this day, February 2, 1990, F. W. de Klerk (born March 18, 1936) announced the unbanning of the African National Congress and promised to release Nelson Mandela.

In some of his first speeches after assuming the party leadership in the fall of 1989, de Klerk called for a non-racist South Africa and for negotiations about the country's future. De Klerk also opened the way for the negotiations of the government with the anti-apartheid-opposition about a new constitution for the country.

I have often thought about the *other guy* in those watershed moments of human history. I know I exaggerate, but to an extent, there is no President Thomas Jefferson, without John Adams. There is no Martin Luther King, Jr., without Lyndon Johnson. There is no Ronald Reagan, without Mikhail Gorbachev. There is no Nelson Mandela, without F. W. de Klerk.

To be sure, the primary actors are charismatic catalysts of immense courage and accomplishment. My point is just that these great men were greatly helped by the facilitation, or at least the indifference, of other men and often their rivals. (See also February 11th.)

~February 3~

"Woodrow Wilson"

On this day, February 3, 1924, US President (Thomas) Woodrow Wilson died in Washington, D.C. Wilson strongly articulated the concepts of self-determination and territorial integrity. These tension has been the source of most 20th and 21st century ethnic-conflicts. Wilson pushed for "a general association of nations" which became first the League of Nations and later the United Nations. He also argued for international disarmament and, specifically, the disarmament of Germany. This disarmament greatly contributed to the rise of Hitler. By no means are either WWII or the corresponding genocides the fault of Woodrow Wilson, but the inherent contradiction between the theory of self-determination and the theory of territorial integrity espoused in the Fourteen Points, have never been resolved. This greatly contributed to the Bosnian genocide in particular, but, regardless, Wilsonianism certainly advanced important concepts in international law.

~~~

"Bishop Belo"

On this day, February 3, 1948, Carlos Filipe Ximenes Belo was born in Baucau, Portuguese Timor (now East Timor). Belo vehemently protested against the brutalities of the Kraras Massacre and condemned the many Indonesian arrests. In February 1989, he wrote to the Pope and the UN Secretary-General, calling for a UN referendum on the future of East Timor and for international help for the East Timorese, who were "dying as a people and a nation." Bishop Belo, along with José Ramos-Horta, he was awarded the Nobel Peace Prize in December 1996.

~February 4~

"Slobodan Milošević"

On this day, February 4, 1997, Serbian President Slobodan Milošević recognized the opposition victories in some local elections, after mass protests lasting 96 days. This was the beginning of the end for the Balkan despot.

This is also significant because the Serbian people themselves ultimately rejected the jingoistic policies of their genocidarian president. The protests started November 17, 1996, in Niš where thousands of opposition supporters gathered against the election fraud. Even more beautifully, the protests were then joined and later led by the university students of Serbia.

The protests lasted even after February 11, 1997, when Milošević signed the *lex specialis*, accepting the opposition victory and installed a local government in several cities.

This was truly one of the best examples of grassroot, democratic protests. Within four years, Milošević was defeated in national elections, lost the support of the military and ultimately extradited to International Criminal Tribunal for Yugoslavia.

~February 5~

"Paris is worth a Mass"

On this day, February 5, 1576, Henry of Navarre abjured Catholicism at the French city of Tours and joined the Protestant Huguenot forces in the French Wars of Religion. The most famous massacre in this series of wars is the St. Bartholomew's Day massacre, in which Henry barely escaped assassination. Five to ten thousand Huguenots were slaughtered.

After both Henry of Guise and Henry III of France died during the War of the Three Henrys, Henry of Navarre won by default: he was the only one left. Then, thirteen years after abjuring Catholicism, Henry abjured his Calvinist Huguenot faith and became Catholic again as he ascended the throne of France as Henry IV. Referring to his own religious fickleness, he is said to have declared that

"Paris vaut bien une messe"

~~~

"Roger Williams"

On this day, February 5, 1631, Roger Williams emigrated from England to Boston. Ultimately moving to the wilderness of what would become Rhode Island, Roger Williams is unique in the seventeenth century for his views on religious toleration and respect for Native Americans (Rhode Island is the only state in the US to be mostly purchased from Native Americans, rather than taken by force or bullied treaty). In my opinion, the world is a slightly better place because of Roger Williams.

~February 6~

"The Frontier Gandhi"

On this day, February 6, 1890, Khan Abdul Ghaffār Khān was born in Utmanzai, Hashtnagar, Frontier Tribal Areas of Punjab Province, British India (in present-day Charsadda District, Khyber Pakhtunkhwa, Pakistan).

Bacha Khan (February 6, 1890 – January 20, 1988) was a Pashtun independence activist against the rule of the British Raj. He was a political and spiritual leader known for his nonviolent opposition, and a lifelong pacifist and devout Muslim. A close friend of Mohandas Gandhi, Bacha Khan, was nicknamed the "Frontier Gandhi" in British India. Bacha Khan founded the Khudai Khidmatgar ("Servants of God") movement in 1929, whose success triggered a harsh crackdown by the British Empire against him and his supporters, and they suffered some of the most severe repression of the Indian independence movement.

~February 7~

"The Mother of the Arab Spring"

On this day February 7, 1979, Tawakkol Abdel-Salam Karman was born in Taiz, Taiz Governorate, Yemen Arab Republic.

Karman is a Yemeni journalist, politician, and human rights activist. During the beginnings of the Arab Spring, Tawakkol's voice became a common sound over the loudspeaker in Yemen's Change Square, where she urged Yemeni youth to stand up against human rights abuses. To many, Karman is known as the "Mother of the Revolution." She is known for her nonviolent work to secure the safety of women and her struggle for women's rights in Yemen. Karman leads the group "Women Journalists Without Chains," which she co-founded in 2005. She is the 2011 recipient of the Nobel Peace Prize.

~February 8~

"The Dawes Act"

On this day, February 8, 1887, the Dawes Allotment Act was signed into law by US President Grover Cleveland. The Act authorized American Indian tribal land to be divided into allotments for individual Indians. Those, who accepted allotments and lived separately from the tribe, were then granted US citizenship. US Senator Henry Dawes was chairman of the Committee on Indian Affairs and believed the law would assimilate Native Americans by breaking up tribal governments and communal lands. The Dawes Act, coupled with Indian Boarding Schools, based on the Carlisle Indian Industrial School model, was sadly successful at forcing assimilation. Later, the Coolidge Administration studied the effects of the Dawes Act and in what is known as the Meriam Report, completed in 1928. It found that the Dawes Act had been used illegally to deprive tribes of their land rights.

The Dawes Act broke up tribes as a social unit and forced European notions of ownership and inheritance. The primary motivation for the Dawes Act was economic; 'free land to be squatted and homesteaded was disappearing, so tribal lands were desired for European-American settlement. Certainly, some of those who supported the law were well-intentioned; they said that they were 'helping' Native Americans become more 'civilized,' but from our 21st perspective we recognize that the US had no right to 'civilize' Native Americans by force, nor did the US have the legal right to abridge so many treaties. The displacement of Native Americans from their lands is eerily similar to other displacements of people in history: the Jewish Diaspora by the Romans, the Penal Laws (Irish) imposed by Britain, the Palestinian Diaspora by Israel, and indigenous people throughout the world including the Americas, Africa, and Australia/Oceania.

~February 9~

"The Regent of Hungary"

On this day, February 9, 1957, Miklós Horthy, the Regent of Hungary died in exile in Portugal. Horthy is a complicated and controversial figure in Hungarian history.

Horthy took the title of Regent of Hungary to serve as a Head of State in lieu of the deposed Habsburgs. After the end of World War I, the Habsburgs were deposed, and the Austro-Hungarian Empire became four independent countries, Austria, Hungary, and the newly formed Czechoslovakia and State of Slovenes, Croats and Serbs. Emperor Charles and Empress Zita left for exile in Switzerland and later Madeira, where Charles died in 1922. After her husband's death, Otto became Emperor in-exile. Thus Horthy's title was a nod to Otto's claim and a symbol of past glory.

It can be agreed upon by both defenders and detractors alike, however, that under Horthy, Hungarian Jews were spared the worst of the Holocaust until 1944. In that year, Horthy was forced by Germany to appoint General Döme Sztójay as Prime Minister. Contrary to Horthy's hopes, Sztójay's government eagerly proceeded to participate in the Holocaust.

Horthy was finally deposed by Hitler on October 15, 1944, after Horthy tried to surrender to the Allies. He remained under house arrest in Bavaria (Germany) until the war in Europe ended. On April 29th, his SS guardians fled in the face of the Allied advance. On May 1st, Horthy was first liberated and then arrested, by elements of the U.S. 7th Army. (See also December 26th.)

~February 10~

"Tricky Fish"

On this day, February 10, 1935, James Poisson was born in the Twin Cities, Minnesota. A laicized Crosier priest, Tricky Fish, has taught, nurtured, and mentored generations of young men and women. From Minnesota to Archbishop Stepinac, to Iona College in New Rochelle, NY, to Bishop Hendricken High School in Warwick, RI. Jim Poisson is the epitome of Catholic, intellectual mysticism.

~~~

"Kathleen Johnson"

On this day, February 10, 1945, Kathleen Rita Grace Johnson was born in New Britain, Connecticut. Entering the Sisters of Notre Dame de Namur after high school, Miss Johnson taught in Springfield, MA, Warwick, RI, Bristol, CT, Waterbury, CT, and West Hartford, CT. She has always been the model of Catholic discipleship and a role model for all women and men. She also happens to be my Godmother, Confirmation sponsor, and maternal aunt.

~February 11~

"Tom Lantos"

On this day, February 11, 2008, Thomas Peter Lantos was born in Budapest, Hungary. In WWII, Lantos (February 1, 1928 – February 11, 2008) Lantos joined Wallenberg's network; his fair hair and blue eyes, which to the Nazis were physical signs of Aryanism, enabled him to serve as a courier and deliver food and medicine to Jews living in other safe houses.

In 1946, Lantos enrolled at the University of Budapest. As a result of his fluent English, he wrote an essay about FDR, and he was awarded a scholarship by the Hillel Foundation to study in the United States.

In 1980, he was elected to the US House of Representatives. A Hungarian-American, Lantos was the only Holocaust survivor to have served in the United States Congress. Bono, the lead singer of U2 (see May 10th), called Lantos a "prizefighter," whose stamina would make him go "any amount of rounds, with anyone, anywhere, to protect human rights and common decency." (see March 27th and July 31st)

~~~

"Mandela Freed!"

On this day, February 11, 1990, Nelson Mandela was released from Victor Verster Prison outside Cape Town, South Africa after 27 years as a political prisoner. (See also February 1st.)

~February 12~

"Carl Lutz"

On this day, February 12, 1975, Carl Lutz died in Bern, Helveti Confederation. Lutz (March 30, 1895 – February 12, 1975) was the Swiss Vice-Consul in Budapest, Hungary from 1942 until the end of World War II. He is credited with saving over 62,000 Jews, the largest rescue operation of Jews of during WWII.

Appointed in 1942 as Swiss vice-consul in Budapest, Hungary, Lutz soon began cooperating with the Jewish Agency for Palestine. He issued Swiss safe-conduct documents that enabled almost 10,000 Hungarian Jewish children to emigrate. Once the Nazis took over Budapest in 1944, they began deporting Jews to the death camps. Lutz negotiated a special deal with the Hungarian government and the Nazis. He gained permission to issue protective letters to 8,000 Hungarian Jews for emigration to Palestine.

Lutz deliberately interpreted his permission for 8,000 letters as applying to families rather than individuals and proceeded to issue tens of thousands of additional protective letters, all of them bearing a number between one and 8,000. He also set up some 76 safe houses around Budapest, declaring them annexes of the Swiss legation and thus off-limits to Hungarian forces or Nazi soldiers (according to the Vienna Convention on Diplomatic Relations). Among the safe houses was the now well known "Glass House" (Üvegház) at Vadász Street 29. About 3,000 Hungarian Jews found refuge at the Glass House and in a neighboring building.

In one incident, fascist Arrow Cross militiamen fired at Jews; Carl Lutz jumped in the Danube River to save a bleeding Jewish woman along the quay.

With water up to his chest and covering his suit, the consul swam back to the bank with her and asked to speak to the Hungarian officer in charge of the firing squad. Declaring the wounded woman to be a foreign citizen protected by Switzerland and quoting international covenants, the Swiss consul brought her back to his car in front of the stunned fascists and left quietly. No one dared to stop him.

Together with other diplomats of neutral countries, such as Raoul Wallenberg, appointed at the Swedish embassy; Carlos de Liz-Texeira Branquinho and Sampaio Garrido at the Portuguese Embassy, Angelo Rotta, the Apostolic nuncio of the Holy See; Angel Sanz Briz, the Spanish Minister; later followed by Giorgio Perlasca, an Italian businessman working at the Spanish embassy; and Friedrich Born, the Swiss delegate of the International Committee of the Red Cross, Lutz worked relentlessly for many months to prevent the planned deaths of innocent people. He and his colleagues dodged the actions of their German and Hungarian counterparts. Thanks to his diplomatic skills, Lutz succeeded in persuading Hungarian and Nazi-German officials, among them Adolf Eichmann, to tolerate, at least in part, his formal protection of Hungarian Jews. Lutz's efforts to undermine the Nazi genocide were so bold and so extensive that, in 1944, Proconsul Edmund Veesenmayer, the German representative in Hungary, asked permission to assassinate the Swiss Consul; Berlin never answered. Due to the actions of Lutz and others, it is estimated that half of the Jewish population of Budapest survived and was not deported to Nazi extermination camps during the Holocaust.

In 1965, Lutz was recognized as one of the Righteous Among the Nations by Yad Vashem.

~February 13~

"Kenneth MacAlpin"

On this day, February 13, 858, Kenneth MacAlpin died in Scotland. MacAlpin was a king of the Picts who, according to national myth, was the first king of Scots. He was thus later known by the posthumous nickname of An Ferbasach, "The Conqueror." His dynasty that ruled Scotland through the Medival Ages claimed descent from him. The current British Royal Family is descended from MacAlpin through Malcolm III, Robert the Bruce, and James VI and I of Scotland and England.

The Contention of the Bards (Iomarbhágh na bhFileadh) was a literary controversy of early 17th century Gaelic Ireland that lasted from 1616 to 1624 and peaked in 1617. The principal bardic poets of the country wrote polemical verses against each other and in support of their respective patrons. The Bards debated the two halves of Ireland: the north, dominated by the Eremonian descendants of the Milesians, and the south, dominated by the Eberian descendants.

Throughout the Contention, each side had eagerly and jealously claimed James I of Ireland as a descendant in its Milesian lineage (being descended from Robert the Bruce and the Gaelic kings of Scotland such as Kenneth McAlpine). The Contention proved to be the last flourish of Dán Díreach.

~February 14~

"Julian Huxley"

On this day, February 14, 1975, Julian Sorell Huxley died in London, England, United Kingdom of Great Britain and Northern Ireland. Julian Sorell Huxley (June 22, 1887 – February 14, 1975) was a British evolutionary biologist, eugenicist, and internationalist. His brother was the writer Aldous Huxley, and his half-brother a fellow biologist and Nobel laureate, Andrew Huxley; his father was the writer and editor Leonard Huxley; and his paternal grandfather was Thomas Henry Huxley, a friend and supporter of Charles Darwin and proponent of evolution. Julian Huxley was a proponent of natural selection and a leading figure in the mid-twentieth century modern evolutionary synthesis. While several of his comments on social class and eugenics are controversial, he distanced himself from extreme eugenics.

Huxley, a lifelong internationalist with a concern for education, got involved in the creation of the United Nations Educational, Scientific and Cultural Organization (UNESCO), and became the organization's first director-general in 1946. In the 1950s Huxley also played a role in publicizing the work of Pierre Teilhard de Chardin, S.J., to the English-speaking world.

Huxley is included in this anthology of because, in 1961, he founded the World Wide Fund for Nature (WWF). The World Wide Fund is an international non-governmental organization founded in 1961, working in the field of the wilderness preservation, and the reduction of humanity's footprint on the environment. It publishes the Living Planet report every two years and is the world's largest conservation organization with over five million supporters working in more than 100 countries, supporting around 1,300 conservation and environmental projects.

~February 15~

"Remember the *Maine!*"

On this day, February 15, 1898, the USS Maine exploded in Havana Bay, Cuba. In the (literal) textbook definition of *yellow journalism*, William Randolph Hearst and Joseph Pulitzer used their publications the *New York Journal* and *New York World* to bully President William McKinley into a declaration of war against Spain, though the reason for the mysterious explosion was not known. From that perspective, it is pathetic that the highest award and recognition for outstanding journalism is called the Pulitzer Prize, isn't it?

~~~

"Death by a Thousand Kisses?"

On this day, February 15, 1909, George Spencer Millet died from kisses on the day after Valentine's Day. Millet (February 15, 1894 – February 15, 1909) worked as office boy for the Met Life insurance company in Manhattan, New York, New York. To celebrate his 15th birthday, a pack of female stenographers apparently teased Millet and threatened the boy a birthday kissing spree. Later, when the stenographers tried to kiss Millett, he dodged the women and fell on the floor, crying "I'm stabbed" before he collapsed, unconscious in a pool of his own blood. His gravestone reads:

"Lost life by stab in falling on ink eraser, evading six young women trying to give him birthday kisses in office Metropolitan Life Building."

~~~

"The Serbian Trump?"

On this day, February 15, 1952, Tomislav Nikolić was born in Kragujevac, Serbia. Nikolić was the 4th President of Serbia. He is well-known for his statements on politically sensitive topics. As recently as 2004, he spoke dreamily about the Virovitica-Karlovac-Karlobag line which would eliminate Bosnia and make Croatia a rump-state. In his presidential campaign of 2012, he stated that was no longer his opinion. In May 2012, Nikolić said the Croatian city of "Vukovar was a Serb city and Croats have nothing to go back to there." The next day he denied making the statement, even though an audio recording exists. He is like Trump, before Trump was Trump, right?

Perhaps the worst of his statements and retractions occurred just one month later in 2012. On June 2, 2012, Nikolić stated on Montenegrin television that "there was no genocide in Srebrenica." More recently, Nikolić has apologized for the crimes committed by any individual in the name of Serbia and asked for forgiveness for Serbia for the crime committed in Srebrenica.

~~~

"Mohamed Shalgham"

On this day, February 15, 2011, the Libyan Ambassador to the UN, Mohamed Shalgham, publicly denounced Libyan dictator Muammar Gaddafi at a UN Security Council meeting. In doing so, Shalgham not only broke ranks with a close political associate but put his entire family still in Libya in danger.

And he did it anyway.

~February 16~

"Ivan the Terrible"

On this day, February 16, 1987, the trial of John Demjanjuk, accused of being a Nazi guard dubbed "Ivan the Terrible" in Treblinka extermination camp, started in Jerusalem.

Demjanjuk was born in Ukraine on April 3, 1920. In 1941, after Germany's attack on Soviet Occupied Poland, Demjanjuk was drafted into the Red Army. In Eastern Crimea, he was captured and became a German prisoner of war and was moved to a Nazi German concentration camp for Soviet POWs where he volunteered to be a "Trawniki" or "Hiwi" collaborator and work as a Nazi guard.

Demjanjuk later allegedly served in Majdanek, Sobibor and Flossenbürg camps as well as during the Warsaw Ghetto Uprising. Demjanjuk was convicted in 2011 in Germany for war crimes as an accessory to the murder of 27,900 Jews while acting as a guard named Ivan Demjanjuk at the Nazi extermination camp near Sobibór in occupied Poland.

~February 17~

"The Brazilian Schindler"

On this day, February 17, 1876, Luiz Martins de Souza Dantas was born in Rio de Janeiro, Brazil. De Souza (February 17, 1876 – April 14, 1954) was a Brazilian diplomat who was awarded the Righteous Among the Nations by the Israeli Supreme Court in June 2003 for his participation during the Holocaust in helping Jews in France escape. It is estimated he saved 80025 confirmed to be Jewish. His actions were not limited to saving Jews but others, such as communists and homosexuals.

~~~

"American Patriots?"

On this day, February 17, 2016, Ammon Bundy and his armed militants desecrated sacred Native American lands by defecating and urinating on the site. The anti-government militants were illegally occupying the Malheur National Wildlife Refuge which was also sacred to the Burns Paiute Tribe who had lived on the land for 6000 years.

The same thugs (who dress in Stars and Stripes and profess their love for this country, while demanding respect for states' rights and ranchers' rights) were apparently incapable of recognizing or respecting the rights of Native Americans.

Not really my kind of American patriotism.

~February 18~

"Huck Finn"

On this day, February 18, 1885, Mark Twain (November 30, 1835 – April 21, 1910) first published the *Adventures of Huckleberry Finn* in the United States. Perhaps no other book, with the possible exception of Harper Lee's *To Kill a Mockingbird* (1960), has done more to expose the sin of racism and the "peculiar institution" of American racially-based, inherited slavery.

~~~

"Sook Ching Massacre"

On this day, February 18, 1942, Japanese secret military police (Kempetai) began the Sook Ching massacres of ethnic Chinese in Singapore.

In Chinese, Sook Ching means "purge through cleansing" and, in Japanese, the operation is known as Kakyōshukusei or "purging of Chinese." The "great inspection" as it is also known in Japanese (Daikenshō) was also replicated in Malaysia as well. Between 50,000 and 100,000 are believed to have been killed in the Singapore Sook Ching massacres. Eventually, Japanese General Tomoyuki Yamashita was charged with war crimes, which included responsibility for the Sook Ching massacre, convicted by a US military court, and executed.

When we think of war crimes and crimes against humanity, we most often think of the Holocaust. Even in the history of Japanese early 20th Century expansionism, the Rape of Nanking and the treatment of Korean "comfort women" is far more well-known than the Japanese massacre of ethnic Chinese in southeast Asia

~February 19~

"Order 9066"

On this day, February 19, 1942, FDR signed Executive Order 9066. Clearly one of the saddest days in American history, this action resulted in more than 120,000 men, women, and children of Japanese ancestry were evicted from the West Coast of the United States and held in internment camps across the country.

The University of California JARDA project suggests that although the Japanese American population in Hawaii was nearly 40% of the population of Hawaii itself, only a few thousand people were detained there, suggesting that their mass removal on the West Coast was motivated by other reasons than "military necessity."

In August 1988, President Reagan signed the Civil Liberties Act, apologizing to the Japanese American internees and offering $20,000 in reparations to the survivors of the internment camps.

On August 1, 1993, President Clinton sent each survivor or the camps a personal apology and, in January 1998, he gave Fred Korematsu received the Presidential Medal of Freedom. (Korematsu was arrested for remaining in his home and not reporting to the local Assembly Center. He was convicted of violating E.O. 9066. The judgment was later overturned.)

Many Japanese-Americans have still not received just compensation for properties taken during the internment process.

~February 20~

"Frederick Douglass"

On this day, February 20, 1895, Frederick Douglass died in Washington, D.C. Douglass (c. February 1818 – February 20, 1895) was born into slavery on the Eastern Shore of the Chesapeake Bay in Talbot County, Maryland, and named Frederick Augustus Washington Bailey. After escaping from slavery in Maryland on September 3, 1838, Douglass became a national leader of the abolitionist movement in Massachusetts and New York, while also gaining notoriety for his oratory skills and incisive antislavery writings. In his time, he was considered a living counter-example to slaveholders' arguments that slaves lacked the intellectual capacity to function as independent American citizens. Many Northerners too found it difficult to believe that such a great orator had once been a slave. On July 4, 1852, Douglass gave a speech in Rochester, New York, in which he declared:

"Whether we turn to the declarations of the past, or to the professions of the present, the conduct of the nation seems equally hideous and revolting. America is false to the past, false to the present, and solemnly binds herself to be false to the future."

~~~

"The Bulgarian Schindler"

On this day, February 20, 1973, Dimitar Peshev died in Sophia, Bulgaria. Peshev (June 25, 1894 – February 20, 1973) was the Deputy Speaker of the National Assembly and Minister of Justice before WWII. He rebelled against the pro-Nazi cabinet and prevented the deportation of Bulgaria's 48,000 Jews and was bestowed the title of Righteous Among the Nations.

~February 21~

"What's in a language?"

On this day, February 21, 1952, students of the University of Dhaka and other political activists defied the 1948 Pakistani law which established Urdu as the sole national language of Pakistan. This law was seen as cultural genocide in East Pakistan (or East Bangal, or Bangledesh as it is known now) where Urdu is not the common language.

The movement reached its climax when police killed student demonstrators on that day. The deaths provoked widespread civil unrest. After years of conflict, the central government relented and granted official status to the Bengali language in 1956.

The Language Movement catalyzed the assertion of Bengali national identity in East Bengal (East Pakistan) and is the forerunner to Bengali nationalist movements, including the 6-Point Movement and subsequently the Bangladesh Liberation War and Indo-Pakistani War of 1971.

[In 1999, UNESCO declared February 21st as International Mother Language Day, in tribute to the Language Movement and the ethno-linguistic rights of people around the world.]

~February 22~

"White Rose"

On this day, February 22, 1943, Sophie Scholl, Hans Scholl, and Christoph Probst were executed in Nazi Germany.
These three pacifists were members of the White Rose, a resistance group in Nazi Germany, consisting of students from the University of Munich and their philosophy professor. The group became known for an anonymous leaflet and graffiti campaign, lasting from June 1942 until their capture in February 1943.

~~~

"Paul Grüninger"

On this day, February 22, 1972, Paul Grüninger died in the Helveti Confederation. Grüninger (October 27, 1891 - February 22, 1972) was a Swiss police commander in St. Gallen, and football player. Following the Austrian Anschluss, Grüninger saved about 3,600 Jewish refugees by backdating their visas and falsifying other documents to indicate that they had entered Switzerland at a time when legal entry of refugees was still possible. He was dismissed from the police force, convicted of official misconduct, and fined 300 Swiss francs. Ostracized and forgotten, Paul Grüninger lived for the rest of his life in difficult circumstances. Despite the difficulties, he never regretted his action on behalf of the Jews. In 1954, he explained his motives: "It was basically a question of saving human lives threatened with death. How could I then seriously consider bureaucratic schemes and calculations." He received no pension and died in poverty. In 1971, Grüninger was recognized as one of the Righteous Among the Nations by the Yad Vashem Holocaust memorial foundation.

~~~

"The Miracle on Ice"

On this day, February 22, 1980, USA defeated "evil" Soviets.

The "Miracle on Ice" refers to a medal-round game during the men's ice hockey tournament at the 1980 Winter Olympics in Lake Placid, New York, played between the hosting United States, and the four-time defending gold medalists, the Soviet Union.

The Soviet Union had won the gold medal in five of the six previous Winter Olympic Games and were the favorites to win once more in Lake Placid. The team consisted primarily of professional players with significant experience in international play. By contrast, the United States' team consisted exclusively of amateur players and was the youngest team in the tournament and in U.S. national team history. In the group stage, both the Soviet and U.S. teams were unbeaten. For the first game in the medal round, the United States played the Soviets. Finishing the first period tied at 2–2, and the Soviets leading 3–2 following the second, the U.S. team scored two more goals to take their first lead during the third and final period, winning the game 4–3 in a major upset against the Cold War rival.

~February 23~

"J'Accuse!"

On this day, February 23,1898, Émile Zola is convicted and imprisoned in France after writing "J'Accuse" which accused the French government of antisemitism and wrongfully imprisoning Captain Alfred Dreyfus (who was Jewish).

Coined "The Dreyfus Affair," the French government was aware of Dreyfus' innocence as well as Esterhazy's guilt but chose to cover-up both. Zola is credited with bringing the truth to light in his libel trial and ultimately justice for Dreyfus.

~~~

"Russia's 'Trail of Tears'"

On this day, February 23, 1944, the Soviet Union began Operation Lentil ("Chechevitsa"), the forced deportation of the Chechen and Ingush people from their homelands in North Caucasus to the Kazakh and Kirghiz SSRs in Central Asia.

The deportation encompassed their entire nations, well over 500,000 people, as well as the complete liquidation of the Chechen-Ingush Autonomous Soviet Socialist Republic. Tens of thousands of Chechens and Ingushes died or were killed during the round-ups and the transportation, and in their early years in exile. [At least one-quarter and perhaps half of the entire Chechen population perished.] The survivors could not return to their native lands until 1957.

Many in Chechnya and Ingushetia classify it as an act of genocide, as did the European Parliament in 2004.

~February 24~

"Shocking… another broken treaty"

On this day, February 24, 1831, the Treaty of Dancing Rabbit was proclaimed between the Choctaw and the United States Government.

Article 22 was never honored by the US government; it could have and should have, been a model for US-Tribal relations.
This was the first removal treaty under the Indian Removal Act. The treaty ceded about 11 million acres of the Choctaw Nation (now Mississippi) in exchange for about 15 million acres in the Indian territory (now the state of Oklahoma). With ratification by the U.S. Congress in 1831, the treaty allowed those Choctaw who chose to remain in Mississippi to become the first major non-European ethnic group to gain recognition as U.S. citizens.
In 1831, tens of thousands of Choctaw walked the 800-kilometer journey to Oklahoma, and many died. This is known as the Choctaw Trail of Tears. Late twentieth-century estimates are that between 5,000–6,000 Choctaws remained in Mississippi in 1831 after the first removal. For the next ten years, they were objects of increasing legal conflict, harassment, and intimidation. The removals continued well into the early 20th century. In 1903, three hundred Mississippi Choctaws were persuaded to move to the Nation in Oklahoma. The name of Oklahoma comes from the Choctaw language meaning "red people."

The Choctaw Nation thrived until Oklahoma was created as a U.S. state. Their government was dismantled under the Curtis Act, along with those of other Native American nations in the former Indian Territory. Their communal lands were divided and allotted to individual households under the Dawes Act, and the US declared communal land remaining after allotment to be surplus and sold it to American settlers.

~February 25~

"Demobilization of the Armenians"

On this day, February 25, 1915, Ottoman Minister of War Enver Pasha sent the order to all Imperial military units that Armenians in the active Ottoman forces were to be demobilized and assigned to the unarmed Labour Battalion.

Demobilization of Armenians in the Ottoman military strongly illustrates pre-planning for the massacres of the Armenian civilian population. Armenia officers and soldiers certainly would have been less likely to follow orders, or passively watch, the slaughter of their fellow Armenians.

In addition, the creation of labor battalions effectively removed males of fighting age from the Armenia civilian populations, thus increasing the vulnerability of those populations to attacks by Turkish nationalists. Armenian businessmen who were conscripted into these battalions also could not operate their business, which increased the bankruptcy of Armenian businesses and facilitated the confiscation of Armenian property and assets.

~~~

"Amnesty International"

On this day, February 25, 2005, Peter Benenson died in Oxford, England. Benenson (July 31, 1921 – February 25, 2005) was a British lawyer and the founder of human rights group Amnesty International. Benenson refused all honors, but in his 80s, largely to please his family, Benenson accepted the Pride of Britain Award for Lifetime Achievement in 2001.

~February 26~

"Skittles and Iced Tea"

On this day, February 26, 2012, George Zimmerman fatally shot Trayvon Benjamin Martin in Sanford, Florida, United States. Trayvon Martin (February 5, 1995 – February 26, 2012) was a 17-year-old African American from Miami Gardens, Florida. Martin had gone with his father on a visit to his father's fiancée at her townhouse at The Retreat at Twin Lakes in Sanford. On the evening of February 26th, Martin was walking back alone to the fiancée's house after buying Skittles and iced tea from a nearby convenience store. The neighborhood had suffered several robberies that year and had developed a community watch. Zimmerman saw Martin and reported him to the Sanford Police as suspicious. Moments later, an altercation between Martin and Zimmerman occurred, and Zimmerman fatally shot Martin in the chest; Zimmerman claimed self-defense in the confrontation.

~~~

"Gerald Kaufman"

On this day, February 26, 2017, Sir Gerald Bernard Kaufman died in office as the Father of the House. Kaufman (June 21, 1930 – February 26, 2017) was a British MP. In January 2009, during the Gaza War, he gave a speech to the House of Commons where he stated:

"The present Israeli government ruthlessly and cynically exploits the continuing guilt from Gentiles over the slaughter of Jews in the Holocaust as justification for their murder of Palestinians… My grandmother was ill in bed when the Nazis came to her home town. A German soldier shot her dead in her bed. My grandmother did not die to provide cover for Israeli soldiers murdering Palestinian grandmothers in Gaza."

~February 27~

"I Wonder Why the Chechens Hate the Russians?"

On this day, February 27, 1944, Soviet forces led by Colonel Mikhail Maksimovich Gveshianihe of the NKVD executed the Chechen civilian population of the aul (village) Khaibakh. More than 704 villagers (including "non-transportable" elderly, women and children) were locked in a stable fortified with dry hay and burned alive; those who broke from burning stable were shot.

After the slaughter, Gveshiani was reportedly congratulated for his success and good work by Lavrenty Beria, who promised him a medal. In 2014, the Russian Ministry of Culture stated that it had searched three Russian state archives, and that "as a result of the investigation, no documents were discovered proving the fact of the mass burning of residents" and finally, "This allows us to conclude that claims of this 'event' are a historical falsification."

"And Modi is Elected Prime Minister?"

On this day, February 28, 2002, the Gulbarg Society Massacre took place during the Gujarat riots. The massacre occurred when a Hindu mob attacked the Gulbarg Society, a Muslim neighborhood in Chamanpura, Ahmedabad. Most of the homes were burnt, and at least 35 victims (including a former Congress Member of Parliament Ehsan Jafri) were burnt alive, while 31 others went missing, bringing the total deaths to 69.

The 14th Prime Minister of India, Narendra Modi, was the Gujarat Chief Minister during the riots. His responsibility and/or negligence has never been fully clarified.

~~~

"And what of the Kurds?"

On this day, February 28, 2015, Yaşar Kemal (born Kemal Sadık Gökçeli died in İstanbul, Turkey. Kemal (October 6, 1923 – February 28, 2015) was a Turkish writer and human rights activist of Kurdish origin. He was one of Turkey's leading writers. He received 38 awards during his lifetime and had been a candidate for the Nobel Prize in Literature on the strength of *Memed, My Hawk*. An outspoken intellectual, he often did not hesitate to speak about sensitive issues, especially those concerning the plight of the Kurdish people. He was tried in 1995 under anti-terror laws for an article he wrote for the German magazine *Der Spiegel* accusing the Turkish army of destroying Kurdish villages.

~February 29~

"Tutu"

On this day, February 29, 1988, South African Archbishop Desmond Tutu was arrested along with 100 clergymen during a five-day anti-apartheid demonstration in Cape Town.

"We are not defying the law… we are obeying God."

Desmond Tutu

South African Archbishop
February 29, 1988

~March 1~

"Where Have All the Huguenots Gone?"

On this day, March 1, 1562, twenty-three Huguenots were massacred by Catholics in Wassy, France, marking the start of the French Wars of Religion.

The massacre of Wassy occurred when Francis Duke of Guise, stopped in Wassy ostensibly to attend Mass. He found a large congregation of Huguenots holding religious ceremonies in a barn that was their church. Some of the Duke's party attempted to push their way inside and were repulsed. Events escalated, stones began to fly, and the Duke was struck. Outraged, he ordered his men to fortify the town and set fire to the church, killing 63 unarmed Huguenots and wounding over a hundred.

It is worth pointing out that there are no Huguenots today. The French Catholic repression and persecution of Huguenots is perhaps one of the more "successful" persecutions in history.

~March 2~

"Gorby"

On this day, March 2, 1931, Mikhail Sergeyevich Gorbachev was born in Stavropol, USSR, into a mixed Russian-Ukrainian family of migrants from Voronezh and Chernigov Governorates. Gorbachev is undoubtedly one of the most influential persons of the 20th century. While he is widely popular in the West for ending the Cold War, he has a more nuanced reputation in Russia. As his policies of non-intervention led to the end of the Warsaw Pact, they also inadvertently led to ethnic nationalist movements within the Soviet Union and secessionist movements. Thus, in many ways, Gorbachev can be credited with recognizing the right of self-determination of those peoples who had been ruled by Moscow, but he is also responsible for the manner in which ethnic rivalries were dealt with by the state apparatus.

During Gorbachev's tenure as leader, ethnic tensions led to riots in Kazakhstan, the Nagorno-Karabakh War, nationalist demonstrations in Georgia, pro-Romanian riots in Moldova, as well as the Lithuanian declaration of independence and subsequent (temporary) suppression.

~~~

"USA PATRIOT Act"

On this day, March 2, 1953, Russ Feingold was born. Feingold was the only senator to vote against the Patriot Act saying that its provisions infringed upon citizens' civil liberties. Feingold was also one of only 23 senators to vote against H.J. Resolution 114, which authorized President George W. Bush to use force against Iraq in 2002.

~March 3~

"The Roar of the Lion"

On or about this day, March 3, 1995, in an undated entry, I wrote on Page 60 of my diary:

The more time one spends with the lion,
The more reasonable roaring sounds.

~Winston Churchill~

~March 4~

"Omar al-Bashir"

On this day, March 4, 2009, the International Criminal Court (ICC) issued an arrest warrant for Sudanese President Omar Hassan al-Bashir for war crimes and crimes against humanity in Darfur. The genocide in Darfur has caused the death of 200-400,000 persons as well as more than two million displaced persons.

Al-Bashir is the first sitting head of state to be indicted by the ICC since its establishment in 2002. [In 2011, Libyan head of state Muammar Gaddafi was indicted and, in 2014, Kenyan head of state Uhuru Kenyatta appeared before the ICC to answer to charges stemming from 2010 before his ascension to the Kenyan presidency.

Slobodan Milošević also had been indicted in May 1999 for crimes against humanity in Kosovo but by the UN's precursor International Criminal Tribunal for the Former Yugoslavia. Milošević also died before his trial and appeals were completed.]

~March 5~

"Katyn"

On this day, March 5, 1940, Lavrentiy Beria wrote the proposal to execute all captive members of the Polish Officer Corps.

The approximately 22,000 victims included not only military POWs but also Poles from across the spectrum of Polish intelligencia. These executions became known as the Katyn Massacre, named after the Katyn Forest where bodies of the executed officers were first found, and the most number of bodies were discovered. Later, Lavrentiy Beria was executed after a "trial" on orders from Nikita Khrushchev for participation in the Purge of the Red Army and Counter-revolutionary activity during the Russian Civil War in Azerbaijan. Notably, his trial did not include any charges for his genocidal acts against Poles, Chechnyans, Ingush or Crimean Tatar peoples. After denying responsibility for fifty years accusing the Nazis of the massacres, the Soviets acknowledged responsibility in 1990. In 2010, legislation by the Russian Duma officially blamed Stalin.

~~~

"Lynch v Donnelly"

On this day, March 5, 1976, *Lynch v. Donnelly* (1984), was decided by the US Supreme Court concerning the legality of Christmas decorations on municipal property. The Court held that the crèche did not violate the Establishment Clause based on *Lemon v. Kurtzman* (1971), ruling that the crèche is a passive representation of religion. More importantly, the Court also stated that the Constitution "affirmatively mandates accommodation, not merely tolerance of all religions, and forbids hostility toward any."

~March 6~

"First, They Came"

On this day, March 6, 1984, Martin Niemöller died in Wiesbaden, West Germany. His poem, "First They Came…" is a provocative indictment of inaction and complacency in the face of injustice (See also March 15th):

First, they Came…

First, they came for the Socialists, and I did not speak out—
Because I was not a Socialist.
Then they came for the Trade Unionists, and I did not speak out—
Because I was not a Trade Unionist.
Then they came for the Jews, and I did not speak out—
Because I was not a Jew.
Then they came for me—and there was no one left to speak for me.

~~~

"What a funny husband!"

On this day, March 6, 2011, Herman Harband was born in Vienna, Austria. Harband (March 6, 1918 – December 29, 2011) became "Internet famous" when the cenotaph which he had prepared as a gravestone was revealed:

"My wife Eleanor Arthur of Queens, NY lived like a princess for 20 years traveling the world with the best of everything. When I went blind, she tried to poison me, took all my money, all my medication and left me in the dark alone and sick. It's a miracle I escaped. I won't see her in heaven because she's surely going to hell!"

Strangely, when Harband died, his widow had the stone removed.

~March 7~

"Stephen Hopkins"

On this day, March 7, 1707, Stephen Hopkins was born in Providence, Rhode Island. Hopkins (March 7, 1707 – July 13, 1785) was a governor of the Colony of Rhode Island and Providence Plantations, a Chief Justice of the Rhode Island Supreme Court, and a signer of the Declaration of Independence.

~~~

"Selma"

On this day, March 7, 1965, "Bloody Sunday" occurred in Selma, Alabama. Approximately 600 civil rights marchers departed Selma on U.S. Highway 80, heading east to the capital of Montgomery.

After they passed over the crest of the Edmund Pettus Bridge and left the boundaries of the city six blocks away, they were confronted by state troopers and county sheriff's deputies, who attacked them using tear gas and billy clubs and drove them back to Selma. Because of the brutal attacks, this became known as "Bloody Sunday."

~March 8 ~

"Gnadenhutten Massacre"

On this day, March 8, 1782, ninety-six Native Americans in Gnadenhutten, Ohio, who had converted to Christianity were killed by Pennsylvania militiamen.

The militia tied the Indians, stunned them with mallet blows to the head, and killed them with fatal scalping cuts. In all, the militia murdered and scalped 28 men, 29 women, and 39 children. The bodies were piled in the settlement buildings and burned to the ground. Two Indian boys, one of whom had been scalped, survived to tell of the massacre.

~ ~ ~

"Juvénal Habyarimana"

On this day, March 8, 1937, Juvénal Habyarimana was born in Rwanda and later went on to become the third President of Rwanda. His death, 57 years and one month later, sparked the Rwandan Genocide. An estimated one million Rwandans died in just three months of genocidal chaos.

~March 9~

"The March Incident"

On this day, March 9, 1956, rallies recognizing the third anniversary of Stalin's death and protests of Khrushchev's denunciation of Stalin quickly evolved into an uncontrollable mass demonstration and rioting which paralyzed the city of Tbilisi.

These pro-Stalin rallies eventually took on more of a pro-Georgian nature. Students made demands and took to the streets. The Soviet response was to bring in troops and tanks from non-Georgian units. Soldiers opened fire on the crowds and tanks later pushed demonstrators out of city squares.

Several dozens, if not hundreds, died in this crackdown. As no official report exists, various estimates put the number of casualties from 106 to 800. Hundreds were wounded and injured. Over 200 were arrested in the ensuing reprisals, and many were subsequently deported to labor camps in Siberia.

Seven months later, the Hungarian Revolution of 1956 would bring renewed ethnic resistance to Russian oppression as well as another round of Russian suppression of ethnic self-determination.

~March 10~

"Tibet"

On this day, March 10, 1959, more than 300,000 Tibetans surrounded the Dalai Lama's palace in Lhasa, Tibet, to prevent the Chinese abduction of the Dalai Lama.

This was a significant even of the Tibetan Uprising of 1959 (though violence has begun as early as 1956). This peaked on March 15th, as plans for the Dalai Lama's evacuation were set in motion, with Tibetan troops being employed to secure an escape route from Lhasa. On March 17, two artillery shells landed near the Dalai Lama's palace, triggering his flight into exile. Then on March 19th, Chinese forces started to shell the Norbulingka, prompting the full force of the Uprising. The combat lasted only about two days, with Tibetan rebel forces being badly outnumbered and poorly armed.

China has controlled Tibet ever since and practiced a policy of Hanification.

~March 11~

"Ryūkyū"

On this day, March 11, 1879, Shō Tai formally abdicated his position as King of Ryūkyū, under orders from Tokyo, ending the Ryukyu Kingdom.

The Ryūkyū people are a distinct ethnic, religious and linguistic people southeast of Japan. The Ryūkyū were centered on Okinawa (Uchinaa) but spread their kingdom to the Amami Islands as well as the Sakishima Islands.

Subjugated by the Japanese in the late 19th century, the Ryūkyū have significant hostility towards both the Japanese as well as Americans. The Ryūkyū believe they suffered during WWII because the Japanese used them geographically and literally as human shields against the American forces. Today, they believe they disproportionately pay for the Japanese-American Alliance. Hostility towards Americans stems from the large American military presence on the home island of Okinawa and related social and criminal issues.

The Ryūkyū language has slowly died out, with only elderly Ryūkyū, or Okinawans, speaking the old language. The Ryūkyū people, it seems, are slowly being absorbed into Japanese history and disappearing.

~March 12~

"Czeslawa Kwoka"

On this day, March 12, 1942, Czeslawa Kwoka died in Auschwitz. Czeslawa was a Polish Catholic child who died in the Auschwitz concentration camp at the age of 14. She was one of the thousands of child victims of German World War II crimes and is among those memorialized in the Auschwitz-Birkenau State Museum indoor exhibit called Block no. 6: Exhibition: The Life of the Prisoners.

Photographs of Kwoka and others were taken by the "famous photographer of Auschwitz," Wilhelm Brasse, from 1940 to 1945, displayed in that Museum photographic memorial.

~~~

"LeRoy Collins"

On this day, March 12, 1991, former Florida Governor LeRoy Collins died. On March 20, 1960, Collins called lunch counter segregation "unfair and morally wrong." Collins (March 10, 1909 – March 12, 1991) was the first governor of the South to promote the moral necessity of ending segregation. Counseling "progress under law," he took a moderate course during the civil rights movement and is remembered as a voice for civil rights.

Perhaps one of the least well-known heroes of the Civil Rights Era, it is my hope that this book will help spread the story of his moral courage and inspire more women and men to transcend their own demographic tribes and seek justice for all.

~~~

"The Butcher of Bosnia"

On this day, March 12, 1943, Ратко Младић, better known as General Ratko Mladić was born in Božanovići, then part of Croatia but now part of Bosnia-Herzegovina. Mladić is best known as the commander of Serbian forces during the Siege of Sarajevo and the Srebrenica Massacre. Both he and the Bosnian-Serb political leader Radovan Karadžić are known as the "Butchers of Bosnia," and were indicted by the ICTY for their actions during the Bosnian War. Mladić was sentenced to life imprisonment on 10 counts of genocide, war crimes and crimes against humanity by the International Criminal Court on November 22, 2017.

~~~

"A Saintly Apology"

On this day, March 12, 2000, Saint Pope John Paul II defied warnings from some theologians that the unprecedented apology would undermine the church's authority and asked God to forgive the persecution of the Jews:

"We are deeply saddened by the behavior of those who in the course of history have caused these children of yours to suffer, and asking your forgiveness we wish to commit ourselves to genuine brotherhood."

Pope Francis canonized John Paul II on April 27, 2014.

~March 13~

"The Girl in the Red Dress"

On this day, March 13, 1943, the final liquidation of the Krakow Ghetto began. Eight thousand Jews deemed able to work were transported to the Płaszów labor camp. Those deemed unfit for work – some 2,000 Jews – were killed in the streets of the ghetto with the use of Trawniki (Eastern European collaborators from the POW camps) police auxiliaries. Any remaining were sent to Auschwitz. The final liquidation of March 13th and 14th was immortalized in the film *Schindler's List*. The liquidation of the ghetto was carried out under the command of SS-Untersturmführer Amon Göth.

It is interesting that Ralph Fiennes was cast to portray the embodiment of evil in both historical and fantasy films: Fiennes is the Nazi war criminal Amon Göth in Schindler's List (1993) as well Lord Voldemort in the films *Harry Potter and the Goblet of Fire*, *Harry Potter and the Order of the Phoenix*, *Harry Potter and the Half-Blood Prince*, and both *Harry Potter and the Deathly Hallows* – Part 1 and Part 2.

~~~

"And now for something completely different..."

On this day, March 13, 1943, Fran Dederich Thatcher died in Dane County, Wisconsin, after a long struggle with breast cancer. Frances Eileen Dederich Thatcher (January 19, 1945 -March 13, 2006) had one last thing to say, which she had engraved onto her gravestone:

"Damn, Its Dark Down Here!"

~March 14~

"Attempted Assassination of Gerry Adams"

On this day, March 14, 1984, John Gregg severely wounded Sinn Féin president Gerry Adams in an attack supposedly ordered as a response to the earlier killings of Ulster Unionist Party politicians Robert Bradford and Edgar Graham.

Gregg, a UDA commando in Rathcoole, led a team that pulled up alongside Adams' car near Belfast City Hall and opened fire injuring Adams and his three fellow passengers, who nonetheless escaped to seek treatment at the Royal Victoria Hospital, Belfast. Gregg and his team were apprehended almost immediately by a British Army patrol. The attack had been known in advance by security forces due to a tip-off from informants within Rathcoole; Adams and his co-passengers had survived in part because Royal Ulster Constabulary officers, acting on the informants' information, had replaced much of the ammunition in the UDA's Rathcoole weapons dump with low-velocity bullets.

Gregg was jailed for 18 years; however, he only served half his sentence and was released in 1993. When asked by the BBC in prison if he regretted anything about the shooting, his reply was, "Only that I didn't succeed."

On February 1, 2003, Gregg was shot dead on Nelson Street, in the old Sailortown district near the Belfast docks. Ironically, his death was arranged not by Catholic paramilitaries, but by a loyalist rival, Alan McCullough.

On a personal note, I met Gerry Adams on September 24, 1994. Adams was the guest speaker at The World Affairs Council luncheon at the Doubletree Hotel in Philadelphia, Pennsylvania.

~March 15~

"An American Problem"

On this day, March 15, 1965, Lyndon B. Johnson offered the "The American Promise," in which he stated:

"At times history and fate meet at a single time in a single place to shape a turning point in man's unending search for freedom. So it was at Lexington and Concord. So it was a century ago at Appomattox. So it was last week in Selma, Alabama... There is no Negro problem. There is no southern problem. There is no northern problem. There is only an American problem... There is no moral issue. It is wrong — deadly wrong — to deny any of your fellow Americans the right to vote in this country. There is no issue of States rights or national rights. There is only the struggle for human rights."

~~~

"The New America?"

On this day, March 15, 2006, I wrote a parody of Martin Niemöller's famous poem (See also March 6th):

In America, they came first for the Mexicans,
And I didn't speak up because I wasn't a Mexican;

And then they came for the Muslims,
And I didn't speak up because I wasn't a Muslim;

And then they came for the African-Americans,
And I didn't speak up because I wasn't an African-American;

And then they came for me...
And there was no one left to speak for me...

~March 16~

"Rachel Corrie"

On this day, March 16, 2003, during the height of the Second Palestinian Intifada, Rachel Corrie killed by an Israel Defense Forces (IDF) armored bulldozer in a combat zone in Rafah, in the southern part of the Gaza Strip.

Rachel was in Rafah with other International Solidarity Movement (ISM) activists in efforts to prevent the Israeli army's demolition of Palestinian houses in operations to eliminate weapons smuggling tunnels. Fellow ISM protesters said that the Israeli soldier operating the bulldozer deliberately ran over Corrie, and Israeli eyewitnesses saying that it was an accident since the bulldozer operator could not see her.

~March 17~

"US Senator John O. Pastore"

On this day, March 17, 1907, John Orlando Pastore was born in Providence, Rhode Island. Pastore (March 17, 1907 – July 15, 2000) was an American lawyer and politician. A member of the Democratic Party, he served as United States Senator from Rhode Island from 1950 to 1976. He previously served as the 61st Governor of Rhode Island from 1945 to 1950. He was the first Italian American to be elected as a senator.

On May 1, 1969, Mr. Rogers addressed the Senate to argue that $20 million in funding for PBS should not be cut. John Pastore, the Senator from Rhode Island who led the hearing, had never seen nor heard of Mr. Rogers' television show. It took Mr. Rogers just six minutes to convince the gruff and impatient Senator from Rhode Island that the $20 million was well worth it.

~~~

"Judge Frank Johnson"

On this day, March 17, 1965, Judge Frank Johnson ordered that civil rights protesters be granted a permit for the march from Selma to Montgomery:

"The law is clear that the right to petition one's government for the redress of grievances may be exercised in large groups...and these rights may be exercised by marching, even along public highways."

~U.S. District Judge Frank Johnson~

~March 18~

"Appeasement"

On this day, March 18, 1869, Neville Chamberlain was born in Edgbaston, Birmingham, England. He went on to become Prime Minister of the United Kingdom and is most famously remembered for his appeasement policy toward Adolf Hitler.

At the Munich Conference in 1938, Chamberlain conceded the German speaking Sudetenland region of Czechoslovakia to Germany. Upon returning to 10 Downing Street, Chamberlain spoke to Britain and said:

"My good friends, for the second time in our history, a British Prime Minister has returned from Germany bringing peace with honour. I believe it is peace for our time. We thank you from the bottom of our hearts. Go home and get a nice quiet sleep"

While this is often, and understandably noted as a mistake (at least in hindsight), the issue provides an interesting historical example of the inherent contradiction in two major tenets of international law: the right of people to self-determination, and the right of nation-states to territorial integrity.

~March 19~

"From my autobiography, *Are You Listening?*"

On this day, March 19th, I annually post on Facebook:

> The U.S. Constitution is a lot like the Bible; more people tell you what it says than have actually read either.

~~~

On this day, March 19, 2017:

> Happy St Joseph's Day!! My mom, Mimi, often made orange Jell-O for my green Irish Gaelic dad!!

~~~

On this day, March 19, 2017:

> I have often wondered, considering how careful JK Rowling was in naming her characters [Draco (King Draco of Athens), Remus Lupin (Romulus and Remus and the wolf), etc.], what does it mean that Rowling named Longbottom, "Neville"? A sort of redemption of Neville Chamberlain, or a historical, what if the Munich deal had worked?

~March 20~

"Catholic Relief Services"

On this day, March 20, 1903, Edward E. Swanstrom, the titular Bishop of Arba, Auxiliary Bishop of New York, was born in New York City. Swanstrom (March 20, 1903 - August 10, 1985) was the Assistant Diocesan Director of Catholic Charities from 1933 to 1943, Assistant Executive Director of Catholic Relief Services from 1943 to 1947, and finally as Executive Director of CRS from 1947 to 1976. Catholic Relief Services was originally intended as a temporary effort of the U.S. bishops to assist World War II refugees and POWs, but by 1955 the organization became permanent and assisted victims of natural disasters as well as victims of war. In its earlier years, CRS concentrated on resettling refugees and sending supplies of food, clothing, and medicine to areas of need. Later, CRS began efforts to foster economic development in the areas it serves, particularly in the Third World.

~~~

"Hungarian-Romanian Ethnic Violence"

On this day, March 20, 1990, Mihăilă Cofariu, an ethnic Romanian from Ibăneşti was severely beaten until unconsciousness during the ethnic clashes of Târgu Mureş. Mihăilă Cofariu fell into a coma and, ultimately, became neurologically disabled. One of the perpetrators, ethnic Hungarian Pál Cseresznyés, was tried, convicted, and sentenced to 10 years in prison, but later released in 1996 by President Emil Constantinescu of Romania, as an act of ethnic reconciliation. The other convicted perpetrator, ethnic Hungarian Ernő Barabás, emigrated to Hungary to avoid a 10-year imprisonment sentence *in absentia*. The Hungarian authorities denied all extradition requests from the Romanian government.

~March 21~

"Let there be light!"

On this day, March 21, 1773, David Melville was born in Newport, Rhode Island. A pewterer by trade and manufacturer of housewares, Melville experimented with hydrogenous gas, made from burning coal and wood. In 1805, he illuminated his house and sidewalk on the corner of Thames and Pelham Streets with gas. Melville received the first American gas light patent, granted on March 24, 1810.

~~~

"Benito Juárez"

On this day, March 21, 1806, Benito Pablo Juárez García was born in Oaxaca, Mexico. Benito Pablo Juárez García (March 21, 1806 – July 18, 1872) was a Mexican lawyer and liberal politician of Zapotec. Benito Pablo Juárez García was of poor, rural, indigenous origins, but he became a well-educated, urban professional and politician, who married a socially prominent white woman of Oaxaca City. In 1858 as head of the Supreme Court, he became President of Mexico by the succession mandated by the Constitution of 1857 when moderate liberal President Ignacio Comonfort was forced to resign by Mexican conservatives. Juárez remained in the presidential office until his death by natural causes in 1872. He weathered the War of the Reform (1858–60), a civil war between Liberals and Conservatives, and then the French invasion (1862–67), which was supported by Mexican Conservatives. Never relinquishing office although forced into exile in areas of Mexico not controlled by the French, Juárez tied Liberalism to Mexican nationalism and maintained that he was the legitimate head of the Mexican state, rather than Emperor Maximilian.

When the French-backed Second Mexican Empire fell in 1867, the Mexican Republic with Juárez as president was restored to full power. In his success in ousting the European incursion, Latin Americans considered his a "second struggle for independence, a second defeat for the European powers, and a second reversal of the Conquest."

~~~

"Corporal Rhodes"

On this day, March 21, 1842, Elisha Hunt Rhodes was born in Pawtuxet, Rhode Island. Rhodes (March 21, 1842 – January 14, 1917) was an American soldier who served in the Union Army of the Potomac for the entire duration of the American Civil War, rising from corporal to colonel of his regiment by war's end. Rhodes' illustrative diary of his war service was quoted prominently in Ken Burns' PBS documentary *The Civil War*. He enlisted on June 5, 1861, and was appointed to the rank of corporal in the 2nd Rhode Island Volunteer Company.

~~~

"The First Nazi Camp"

On this day, March 21, 1933, construction of the first Nazi concentration camp was completed. The Dachau camp system grew to include nearly 100 sub-camps, which were mostly work camps or Arbeitskommandos and were located throughout southern Germany and Austria. There were 32,000 documented deaths at the camp and thousands that are undocumented.

~~~

"The Winship Massacre"

On this day, March 21, 1937, 21 Puerto Ricans were killed, and more than 235 were wounded in what became known as the Ponce Massacre. The protesters were shot by Puerto Rican police. An investigation led by the United States Commission on Civil Rights put the blame for the massacre squarely on the U.S.-appointed Governor of Puerto Rico, Blanton Winship.

~~~

"Sharpsville Massacre"

On this day, March 21, 1960, the Sharpeville Massacre occurred in Sharpeville, South Africa. The Sharpeville Massacre was an event which occurred at the police station in the South African township of Sharpeville in Transvaal (today part of Gauteng). After a day of demonstrations against pass laws, a crowd of about 5,000 to 7,000 black African protesters went to the police station. The South African Police opened fire on the crowd, killing 69 people. Sources disagree as to the behavior of the crowd; some state that the crowd was peaceful, while others state that the crowd had been hurling stones at the police and that the shooting started when the crowd started advancing toward the fence around the police station.

In present-day South Africa, the 21st of March is celebrated as a public holiday in honor of human rights and to commemorate the Sharpeville massacre.

~March 22~

"The Best Epitaph"

On this day, March 22, 1991, Edith Christine Jackson Barlow died in Portland, Cumberland County, Maine. In perhaps the least loquaciously written and most succinctly worded epitaph, Barlow's gravestone simply states:

"Shit Happens"

~March 23~

"Patrick Henry"

On this day, March 23, 1775, Patrick Henry gave an impassioned speech in support of the resolution from his pew in a Richmond church:

"Is life so dear, or peace so sweet, as to be purchased at the price of chains and slavery? Forbid it, Almighty God! — I know not what course others may take; but as for me, give me liberty or give me death!"

~~~

"Enabling Hitler"

On this day, March 23, 1933, Germany passed the Ermächtigungsgesetz (*Enabling Act*), allowing Adolf Hitler to become dictator of Germany. It passed in both the Reichstag and Reichsrat and was signed by President Paul von Hindenburg.

~~~

"Desmond Doss"

On this day, March 23, 1919, Desmond Thomas Doss was born in Lynchburg, Virginia. Doss (February 7, 1919 – March 23, 2006) was a United States Army corporal who served as a combat medic with an infantry company in World War II. After distinguishing himself in the Battle of Okinawa, he became the first conscientious objector to receive the Medal of Honor for actions above and beyond the call of duty.

~~~

"Being a *True* Christian"

On this day, March 23, 1943, Archbishop Damaskinos of the Greek Orthodox Church, along with 27 prominent leaders of cultural, academic, and professional organizations wrote an official letter of protest against the deportation of Greek Jews to the Nazi concentration camps. The document, written in a very sharp language, refers to unbreakable bonds between Christian Orthodox and Jews, identifying them jointly as Greeks, without differentiation. It is noteworthy that such a document is unique in the whole of occupied Europe, in character, content, and purpose.

Archbishop Damaskinos Papandreou (March 3, 1891 – May 20, 1949) was the archbishop of Athens and All Greece from 1941 until his death. The Archbishop of Athens was the spiritual leader of the Greek Orthodox people of Athens and All Greece, and Damaskinos worked very hard to live up to his position during those hard times. He frequently clashed with the German authorities and the quisling government. In 1943, the Germans began the persecution of the Jews of Greece and their deportation. He was also the regent of Greece between the pull-out of the German occupation force in 1944 and the return of King George II to Greece in 1946. His tenure as Archbishop was between the liberation of Greece from the German occupation during World War II and the Greek Civil War.

~March 24~

"How Christian of the Hiram, Ohio, townsfolk"

On this day, March 24, 1832, a group of men beat as well as tar and feathered Mormon leader Joseph Smith in Hiram, Ohio.

In retrospect, this attack is a clear violation of the modern understanding of human rights found in the US Bill of Rights and UN Universal Declaration of Human Rights.

It is worth noting that, as opposed to Zoroaster, Siddhartha, and Moses (that Moses was attacked militarily as the political leader of Hebrews) many Founders of religious traditions were persecuted during their ministries, such as Jesus, Paul, Mohammed, Bahá'u'lláh, Joseph Smith and others.

~~~

"Óscar Romero"

On this day, March 24, 1980, Óscar Arnulfo Romero y Galdámez was assassinated by soldiers of El Salvador. Romero (August 15, 1917 – March 24, 1980) was a prelate of the Catholic Church in El Salvador, who served as the fourth Archbishop of San Salvador. He spoke out against poverty, social injustice, assassinations, and torture. In 1980, Romero was assassinated while offering Mass in the chapel of the Hospital of Divine Providence.

On October 14, 2018, Pope Francis canonized Óscar Romero in Saint Peter's Square.

~March 25~

"The Priest Hunter"

On this day, March 25, 1710, all Catholic priests in Ireland had been required to take an Oath of Abjuration. The Penal Law of 1709 stated, "*Sec. 22. All registered popish priests shall take the oath of abjuration before the 25th of March, 1710, or incur the penalties as a popish regular.*" According to *The Penal Laws*, by Maureen Wall, only 33 priests took this oath. In the face of such widespread defiance, it was rarely enforced. However, John Mullowney (c. 1690 – 1726) was a talented rogue and excelled at the activity of hunting clergy.

Born in Derrew, near Ballyheane, County Mayo, Mullowney began his career as a horse thief. Mullowney was captured near Castlebar, arrested, and sentenced to death; but he agreed to turn in priests to escape the hangman's noose; and thus, John Mullowney became Seán na Sagart (John of the Priests). According to legend, Mullowney received £100 for the capture of an archbishop or bishop, £20 for a priest, and £10 for obtaining a hedge school teacher, and £5 for a priest in training. Mullowney used the money to fund his heavy drinking and expensive tastes.

According to legend, Mullowney would pretend to be sickly close to death, then call for a priest to confess his sins. When a priest arrived for Last Rites, Mullowney would capture or kill his confessor. Eventually, there were just two priests left. The priests lived in disguise, but Mullowney discovered one of the last two and killed him. As expected the last remaining priest appeared at the funeral of his fellow clergyman. Although the priest was dressed as a woman, the disguise did not fool Mullowney, who attacked him. Unlike other priests who had been ambushed by someone whom they thought was dying, this priest was expecting an attack and fought back. He held off Mullowney until a man known as McCann to stabbed and killed Seán na Sagart.

~~~

"Ishi"

On this day, March 25, 1916, the man known as Ishi died.

He was the last member of the Yahi, a group of the Yana of the U.S. state of California. Known as the "last wild Indian," Ishi lived most of his life completely outside modern culture.

At approximately 50 years of age, in 1911, he emerged out of the undeveloped area of Butte County, California. He spent the last five years of his life as a research subject at the University of California, San Francisco.

~March 26~

"Malcolm X and MLK, Jr."

On this day, March 26, 1964, the two famous African-American leaders met randomly on Capitol Hill, attending Senate debate on the Civil Rights Act of 1964.

~~~

"From my diary, *Are You Listening?*"

On this day, March 26, 2014, I reminded the world:

Silence is golden. Unless you're a puppy. Then silence is suspicious. Very, very suspicious.

~March 27~

"Dexter King"

On this day, March 27, 1997, Dexter Scott King met with James Earl Ray, the man imprisoned for his father's murder. When meeting, King asked, "I just want to ask you, for the record, did you kill my father?" and Ray replied, "No-no I didn't." King then told Ray that he along with the rest of the King family believed him.

~~~

"Vrba Jews"

On this day, March 27, 2006, Rudolf Vrba died. "Rudi" was known for his escape from the Auschwitz concentration camp during World War II and for co-writing the Vrba–Wetzler report. The Vrba–Wetzler report provided some of the most detailed information about the mass murder taking Auschwitz. Material from the Vrba–Wetzler appeared in newspapers and radio broadcasts in the United States and Europe throughout June and into July 1944, prompting world leaders to appeal to Hungarian regent Miklós Horthy to halt the deportations. On July 7th, Horthy ordered an end to the deportations, fearing he would be held responsible after the war. While 437,000 Jews had been deported, constituting almost the entire Jewish population of the Hungarian countryside, but another 200,000 living in Budapest were saved. In many ways, these are the "Vrba Jews" as much as the German Jews saved by Oscar Schindler are known as Schindler Jews or Schindlerjuden. Other Hungarian Jews are equally known as "Wallenberg Jews" due to the heroic efforts of the Swedish diplomat to Hungary, Raoul Wallenberg.

US Congressman Tom Lantos is one of the more famous survivors of the Hungarian deportations (see February 11th).

~~~

"Irving R. Levine, NBC News..."

On this day, March 27, 2009, Irving Raskin Levine died in Washington, D.C. Levine (August 26, 1922 – March 27, 2009) was born in Pawtucket, Rhode Island, and had graduated from Brown University. He was an American journalist and longtime correspondent for NBC News. During his 45-year career, Levine reported from more than two dozen countries. He was the first American television correspondent to be accredited in the Soviet Union. He wrote three non-fiction books on life in the USSR, each of which became a bestseller.

~March 28~

"Free Tibet"

On this day, March 28, 1959, the State Council of the People's Republic of China announced the dissolvement of the government of Tibet.

Mao's Great Leap Forward (1959–1962) had led to famine in Tibet. In 1959, China's socialist land reforms and military crackdown on rebels in Kham and Amdo led to the 1959 Tibetan uprising. In an operation launched in the wake of the National Uprising of March 10, 1959, in Lhasa, 10,000 to 15,000 Tibetans were killed within three days. "As a result of this and other Chinese policies, in many parts of Tibet people have starved to death... In some places, whole families have perished, and the death rate is very high. This is very abnormal, horrible and grave," according to a confidential report by the Panchen Lama sent to Chinese Premier Zhou Enlai in 1962.

In 1960, the western-based nongovernmental International Commission of Jurists (ICJ) gave a report titled Tibet and the Chinese People's Republic to the United Nations. The report was prepared by the ICJ's Legal Inquiry Committee, composed of eleven international lawyers from around the world. This report accused the Chinese of the crime of genocide in Tibet, after nine years of full occupation, six years before the devastation of the cultural revolution began. The ICJ also documented accounts of massacres, tortures and killings, the bombardment of monasteries, and extermination of whole nomad camps. Declassified Soviet archives provided data that Chinese communists, who received great assistance in military equipment from the USSR, broadly used Soviet aircraft for bombing monasteries and other punitive operations in Tibet.

The ICJ examined evidence relating to human rights within the structure of the Universal Declaration of Human Rights as announced by the General Assembly of the United Nations. After considering the human, economic and social rights, they found that the Chinese communist authorities had violated Article 3, 5, 9, 12, 13, 16, 17, 18, 19, 20, 21, 22, 24, 25, 26 and 27 of the Universal Declaration of Human Rights in Tibet.

The Tibetans were not allowed to participate in the cultural life of their own community, a culture which the Chinese have set out to destroy, according to the ICJ. The ICJ discovered that Chinese allegations that the Tibetans enjoyed no human rights before the entry of the Chinese were based on distorted and exaggerated accounts of life in Tibet. Accusations against the Tibetan "rebels" of rape, plunder, and torture were found in cases of plunder to have been deliberately fabricated and in other cases unworthy of belief for this and other reasons.

Under the Seventeen Point Agreement the Central People's Government of the Chinese People's Republic gave several undertakings, among them: promises to maintain the existing political system of Tibet, to maintain the status and functions of the Dalai Lama and the Panchen Lama, to protect freedom of religion and the monasteries and to refrain from compulsion in the matter of reforms in Tibet. The ICJ found that these and other undertakings had been violated by the Chinese People's Republic and that the Government of Tibet was entitled to repudiate the Agreement as it did on March 11, 1959.

~March 29~

"The Hyphen War"

On this day, March 29, 1990, in the aftermath of the Velvet Revolution, the Hyphen War erupted in Czechoslovakia.

Under Communism, the official name of the country was Czechoslovak Socialist Republic. In December 1989, President Václav Havel announced that the word *Socialist* would be dropped from the country's official name. Instead of calling the country the "Czechoslovak Republic," the Slovak politicians felt this diminished Slovakia's equal stature and demanded that the country's name be spelled with a hyphen (e.g. "Republic of Czecho-Slovakia" or "Federation of Czecho-Slovakia"). Havel then changed his proposal to "Republic of Czecho-Slovakia," but Czech politicians who saw reminders of the 1938 Munich Agreement, in which Nazi Germany annexed a part of that territory.

As a compromise, on March 29, 1990, the name was changed to the Czechoslovak Federative Republic, explicitly acknowledging that the country was a federation. The name was to be spelled without a hyphen in Czech (Československá federativní republika), but with a hyphen in Slovak (Česko-slovenská federatívna republika).

This solution was found to be unsatisfactory, and on April 20, 1990, the parliament changed the name again, to the "Czech and Slovak Federative Republic" and explicitly listed the long-form names in both languages and stated they were equal.

While the Hyphen War was not deserving of the name "war," it demonstrated that there were differences between Czechs and Slovaks regarding the identity of their shared country. Over the following two years, more substantial disputes arose between the two halves of the federation. In 1992, Czech and Slovak politicians agreed to split the country into the two states of the Czech Republic and the Slovak Republic. The Velvet Divorce became effective on January 1, 1993.

~~~

"James Stephens"

On this day, March 29, 1901, James Stephens died in Blackrock, County Dublin, Ireland.

Stephens (January 26, 1825 – March 29, 1901) had founded the Irish Republican Brotherhood and organized the Éirí Amach na bhFíníní. However, the Fenian Rising of 1867 was poorly organized and infiltrated by British spies. The brief rebellion included an uprising in County Kerry, followed by an attempt at nationwide insurrection and an attempt to take Dublin.

Most of the leaders were arrested, but Stephens escaped to France where he worked as a journalist and an English teacher. He spent years in France, Belgium, and the United States. In 1890 Charles Stewart-Parnell used his influence to allow Stephens to return to Ireland and Stephens returned home to Ireland in 1891. He spent the remainder of his life in seclusion in Blackrock, County Dublin, avoiding political intrigue.

~March 30~

"Fred Korematsu"

On this day, March 30, 2005, Fred Korematsu died of respiratory failure at his home in California.

He had said at the vacating of his immoral conviction: "I would like to see the government admit that they were wrong and do something about it so this will never happen again to any American citizen of any race, creed, or color." He also said, "If anyone should do any pardoning, I should be the one pardoning the government for what they did to the Japanese-American people."

On his deathbed: "I'll never forget my government treating me like this. And I really hope that this will never happen to anybody else because of the way they look if they look like the enemy of our country...Protest, but not with violence, and don't be afraid to speak up. One person can make a difference, even if it takes forty years."

Gee, I wonder what would Korematsu think of the decision in *Trump v. Hawaii* (2018)?

~March 31~

"St. Bernard of Clairvaux"

On this day, March 31, 1146, St. Bernard of Clairvaux called for a crusade in his famous sermon in a field at Vézelay. Louis VII of France and other monarchs then led the Second Crusade. In addition to encouraging religious warfare, the Crusades led to the sacking of Lisbon and Constantinople as well as countless battles in the Holy Land. (See also November 27th)

Bernard is well known as a Saint of the Catholic Church, a primary founder of the reforming Cistercian Order, and now even a Doctor of the Church. Illuminating the complexity of the human condition, as well as the phenomenon in which we are all limited by and products of our times, Bernard of Clairvaux is both a saint as well as a religious warmonger.

On the Assassination of MLK, Jr

Martin Luther King dedicated his life to love and to justice between fellow human beings. He died in the cause of that effort. In this difficult day, in this difficult time for the United States, it's perhaps well to ask what kind of a nation we are and what direction we want to move in. For those of you who are black -- considering the evidence evidently is that there were white people who were responsible -- you can be filled with bitterness, and with hatred, and a desire for revenge.

We can move in that direction as a country, in greater polarization -- black people amongst blacks, and white amongst whites, filled with hatred toward one another. Or we can make an effort, as Martin Luther King did, to understand, and to comprehend, and replace that violence, that stain of bloodshed that has spread across our land, with an effort to understand, compassion, and love.

For those of you who are black and are tempted to fill with -- be filled with hatred and mistrust of the injustice of such an act, against all white people, I would only say that I can also feel in my own heart the same kind of feeling. I had a member of my family killed, but he was killed by a white man.

~RFK~

~April 1~

"Putsch"

On this day, April 1, 1924, Adolf Hitler was sentenced to five years in jail for his participation in the Beer Hall Putsch. He only served nine months in jail at Landsberg Prison and, while there, wrote *Mein Kampf.*

~~~

"Srebrenica Apology"

On this day, April 1, 2005, the Serbian Parliament apologized for the Srebrenica Massacre, saying:

"The Srebrenica Declaration sharply condemns the crime committed against the Bosnian population in Srebrenica in July 1995, expresses condolences to families of victims and extends apologies to them for lack of measures that could have prevented the tragedy."

The massacre was committed by soldiers and paramilitaries under the command of General Ratko Mladić, who was on trial at The Hague. On March 24, 2016, the political leader Radovan Karadžić was found guilty of genocide in Srebrenica, war crimes and crimes against humanity, 10 of the 11 eleven charges in total, and sentenced to 40 years' imprisonment

On November 22, 2017, General Ratko Mladić was sentenced to life imprisonment on 10 counts of genocide, war crimes and crimes against humanity by the International Criminal Court.

~April 2~

"Anthony Lake"

On this day, April 2, 1939, Anthony Lake was born in New York City. He was also the Executive Director of UNICEF.

Lake served in the State Department service in Vietnam during the 1960s. After working under U.S. Secretary of State Henry Kissinger, Lake significantly disagreed with Kissinger's policies in Africa, and so Lake resigned from the State Department.

In the 1990s, Lake had significant influence ending two ethnic/religious conflicts. First, as National Security Advisor, Lake is credited as being one of the individuals who developed the policy that led to the resolution of the Bosnian Genocide (*Newsweek*, Feb 22, 1993). Later in the decade, as Special Envoy, Lake mediated the drafting of the Algiers Agreement, ending the Eritrean-Ethiopian War.

~April 3~

"Susan B. Anthony"

On this day, April 3, 1873, Susan B. Anthony (February 15, 1820 – March 13, 1906) toured the in 29 towns and villages of Monroe County, New York, giving a speech entitled, "Is it a crime for a US citizen to vote?"

"The preamble of the Federal Constitution says: "We, the people of the United States, in order to form a more perfect union, establish justice, insure domestic tranquility, provide for the common defence, promote the general welfare, and secure the blessings of liberty to ourselves and our posterity, do ordain and establish this Constitution for the United States of America."

It was we the people-not we white male citizens-nor yet we male citizens-but we the whole people, who formed this Union; and we formed it, not to give the blessings of liberty, but to secure them-not to the half of ourselves and the half of our posterity, but to the whole people, women as well as men. And it is downright mockery to talk to women of their enjoyment of the blessings of liberty while they are denied the use of the only means of securing them provided by this democratic-republican government.

…Clearly, then, if the 14th amendment was not to secure to black men their right to vote, it did nothing for them, since they possessed everything else before. But if it was meant to be a prohibition of the states to deny or abridge their right to vote, which I fully believe, then it did the same for "all persons"-white women included-"born or naturalized in the United States"; the amendment does not say all "male" persons of "African" decent, but all persons are citizens.

…Clearly, then, the national government must not only define the rights of citizens, but it must stretch its power and protect them in every state in this union."

~~~

"I've Been to the Mountaintop"

On this day, April 3, 1968, Martin Luther King Jr. delivered his "I've Been to the Mountaintop" speech. King spoke at the Mason Temple (Church of God in Christ Headquarters) in Memphis, Tennessee. On the following day, King was assassinated.

The speech primarily concerns the Memphis Sanitation Strike. King calls for unity, economic actions, boycotts, and nonviolent protest while challenging the United States to live up to its ideals.

At the end of the speech, he discusses the possibility of a sudden death. Toward the end of the speech, King refers to threats against his life and uses language that seems to foreshadow his impending death, but reaffirming that he was not afraid to die:

"Well, I don't know what will happen now. We've got some difficult days ahead. But it really doesn't matter with me now, because I've been to the mountaintop. And I don't mind. Like anybody, I would like to live - a long life; longevity has its place. But I'm not concerned about that now. I just want to do God's will. And He's allowed me to go up to the mountain. And I've looked over. And I've seen the Promised Land. I may not get there with you. But I want you to know tonight, that we, as a people, will get to the Promised Land. So I'm happy, tonight. I'm not worried about anything. I'm not fearing any man. Mine eyes have seen the glory of the coming of the Lord."

~April 4~

"The Assassination of MLK, Jr."

On this day, April 4, 1968, Martin Luther King, Jr., was shot while standing on the balcony at the Lorraine Motel in Memphis, Tennessee. He was rushed to St. Joseph's Hospital and was pronounced dead at 7:05 p.m. CST.

President Lyndon B. Johnson planned a meeting in Hawaii with Vietnam War military commanders, but after being informed of the assassination, he canceled the trip. LBJ assigned Attorney General Ramsey Clark to investigate the assassination; he made a personal call to King's wife, Coretta Scott King, and declared April 7th a national day of mourning, ordering the U.S. flag flown at half-staff.

The night of the assassination, Senator Robert F. Kennedy spoke about the assassination in a predominantly black neighborhood of the city. RFK urged Americans to continue King's practice of nonviolence.

James Earl Ray, a fugitive from the Missouri State Penitentiary, was arrested on June 8, 1968, in London at Heathrow Airport, extradited to the United States, and charged with the assassination. On March 10, 1969, he pleaded guilty and was sentenced to 99 years in the Tennessee State Penitentiary. He later made many attempts to withdraw his guilty plea and be tried by a jury but was unsuccessful; he died in prison on April 23, 1998, at the age of 70.

MLK's autopsy revealed that despite being aged just 39, his heart was in the condition of a 60-year-old man, which was attributed to the stress of his 13 years in the Civil Rights Movement.

~April 5~

"Portugal's Schindler"

On this day, April 5, 1883, Carlos de Almeida Fonseca Sampaio Garrido was born. Garrido (April 5, 1883 – April 1960) was a Portuguese diplomat credited with saving the lives of approximately 1,000 Jews in Nazi-occupied Hungary while serving as Portugal's ambassador in Budapest between July and December 1944.

~April 6~

"Time"

On this day, April 6, 1991, or so, I wrote this poem for my Dad and gave it to him for his birthday, April 7th. He didn't seem to like it much; maybe he thought I was calling him old?

Time
Spring has no meaning,
As Seasons progress concern grows,
In winter time falls like snow and covers the land,
Parks abound, they are white gardens.

~~~

"The Shot Heard 'Round Rwanda"

On this day, April 6, 1994, the aircraft carrying Rwandan President Juvénal Habyarimana and Burundian President Cyprien Ntaryamira was shot down. This is the nominal cause, or spark, of the Rwandan Genocide.

One million people were viciously murdered, mostly by machete, in only 3 months. UN General Romeo Dallaire, now a retired Canadian Senator, was in charge of UN forces. While small in number, Dallaire argued he could have stopped the genocide with his superior weapons and APCs. France, who was vested financially in the Hutu regime, blocked UN action for months until the genocide was essentially ended by the RPF invasion by Paul Kagame.

122

~April 7~

"Letter from Birmingham Jail"

On this day, April 7, 1963, Ministers John Thomas Porter, Nelson H. Smith, and A. D. King led a group of 2,000 marchers to protest the jailing of movement leaders in Birmingham. On April 12, 1963, King was roughly arrested with SCLC activists. King was given a newspaper from April 12th, which contained "A Call for Unity," a statement made by eight white Alabama clergymen against King and his methods. The letter provoked King, and he began to write a response from jail. The *Letter from Birmingham Jail*, also known *The Negro Is Your Brother*, is an open letter written on April 16, 1963, by Martin Luther King Jr.

The letter defends the strategy of nonviolent resistance to racism. It says that people have a moral responsibility to break unjust laws and to take direct action rather than waiting potentially forever for justice to come through the courts. The letter, written during the 1963 Birmingham campaign, was widely published and became an important text for the American Civil Rights Movement. Responding to being referred to as an 'outsider,' King wrote:

"Injustice anywhere is a threat to justice everywhere."

~~~

"The Rwandan Genocide"

On this day, April 7, 1994, Hutus began their massacre of Tutsis in Kigali, Rwanda.

~April 8~

"Shearith Israel"

On this day, April 8, 1730, Shearith Israel, the first synagogue in New York City, was dedicated. The Congregation Shearith Israel (Hebrew, "Remnant of Israel") – often called The Spanish and Portuguese Synagogue – is the oldest Jewish congregation in the United States.

The first group of Spanish and Portuguese Jews arrived in New Amsterdam in September 1654. After being initially rebuffed by anti-Semitic Governor Peter Stuyvesant, Jews were given official permission to settle in the colony in 1655. This marks the official founding of the Congregation Shearith Israel. Despite their permission to stay in New Amsterdam they continued to face discrimination and were not given permission to worship in a public synagogue for some time (throughout the Dutch period and even into the British), though they were allowed to dedicate a cemetery in 1656.

It was not until 1730 that the Congregation was able to build a synagogue of its own; it was built on Mill Street in lower Manhattan.

~April 9~

"Journey of Reconciliation"

On this day, April 9, 1947, the Journey of Reconciliation, the first interracial Freedom Ride began through the upper South in violation of Jim Crow laws. The riders wanted enforcement of the United States Supreme Court's 1946 Irene Morgan decision that banned racial segregation in interstate travel.

~~~

"Zog"

On this day, April 9, 1961, Zog I, King of the Albanians died in Suresnes, Paris, France. Born Ahmet Muhtar Zogolli, Zog (October 8, 1895 – April 9, 1961) was the autocratic leader of Albania from 1922 to 1939. At the end of the war, Albania's Jewish population was greater than it was prior to the war, making it the only country in Europe where the Jewish population increased during World War II.

Out of two thousand Jews in total, only five Albanian Jews perished at the hands of the Nazis (when were discovered by the Germans and subsequently deported to Pristina, Kosovo. Between February and March in 1939, King Zog I of Albania granted asylum to 300 Jewish refugees before being overthrown by the Italian fascists in April the same year. When the Italians requisitioned the Albanian puppet government to expel its Jewish refugees, the Albanian leaders valiantly refused, and, in the following years, 400 more Jewish refugees found sanctuary in Albania.

~April 10~

"The Good Friday Agreement"

On this day, April 10, 1998, the Good Friday Agreement was signed in Belfast, Northern Ireland. It is without a doubt, one of the most important days in the history of peace studies and post-conflict reconciliation.

~~~

"Matthew Perry"

On this day, April 10, 1794, Matthew Calbraith Perry (April 10, 1794 – March 4, 1858) was a Commodore of the United States Navy.

Perry served in several wars, most notably in the War of 1812 and the Mexican–American War (1846-48). He played a leading role in the opening of Japan to the West with the Convention of Kanagawa in 1854. Perry took an interest in the education of naval officers and assisted in the development of an apprentice system that helped establish the curriculum at the United States Naval Academy.

With the advent of the steam engine, he became a leading advocate of modernizing the US Navy and came to be considered "The Father of the Steam Navy."

~April 11~

"Idi Amin"

On this day, April 11, 1979, Ugandan dictator Idi Amin was deposed. Amin purged the Ugandan army of replaced President Apollo Milton Obote supporters, predominantly those from the Acholi and Lango ethnic groups. In July 1971, Lango and Acholi soldiers were massacred in the Jinja and Mbarara barracks, and, by early 1972, some 5,000 Acholi and Lango soldiers, and at least twice as many civilians, had disappeared.

The killings, motivated by ethnic, political, and financial factors, continued throughout Amin's eight-year reign. The exact number of people killed is unknown. The International Commission of Jurists estimated the death toll at no fewer than 80,000 and more likely around 300,000. Amnesty International puts the number killed at 500,000. Among the most prominent people killed were Benedicto Kiwanuka, a former prime minister and chief justice; Janani Luwum, the Anglican archbishop; Joseph Mubiru, the former governor of the central bank of Uganda; Frank Kalimuzo, the vice chancellor of Makerere University; Byron Kawadwa, a prominent playwright; and two of Amin's own cabinet ministers, Erinayo Wilson Oryema and Charles Oboth Ofumbi.

~April 12~

"Handel's *Messiah*"

On this day, April 13, 1742, Handel's *Messiah* is performed for the first time, conducted by the composer, at Mr. Neale's Great Musick Hall, Fishamble Street, Dublin, before an audience of 700. The performance was originally announced for April 12th but was deferred for a day "at the request of persons of Distinction." Handel had his own organ shipped to Ireland for the performances. Handel's decision to give a season of concerts in Dublin arose from an invitation from the Duke of Devonshire, then serving as Lord Lieutenant of Ireland.

~~~

"The Fort Pillow Massacre"

On this day, April 12, 1864, Confederate forces killed most of the African-American soldiers that surrendered at Fort Pillow, Tennessee. This event became known as The Fort Pillow Massacre. Though some historians discount the command responsibility for the massacre, it is worth noting that the commander of Confederate forces was Nathan Bedford Forrest who later served as the first Grand Wizard of the Ku Klux Klan.

~~~

"The Shanghai Massacre"

On this day, April 12, 1927, the Shanghai Massacre occurred. More than 300 Chinese communists were "purged," and more than 5000 remain "missing."

~~~

"Clara Barton"

On this day, April 12, 1912, Clarissa "Clara" Harlowe Barton (December 25, 1821 – April 12, 1912) died in Glen Echo, Maryland. Barton was a pioneering nurse who founded the American Red Cross on May 21, 1881. She was a hospital nurse in the American Civil War, a teacher, and patent clerk. Nursing education was not very formalized at that time, and Clara did not attend nursing school.

~~~

"Antal"

On this day, April 12, 2016, US Army Chaplain Christopher John Antal resigned his commission because of his conscientious objection to the United States' drone policy. In a letter addressed to Commander-in-Chief Barack Obama, Antal wrote, "The executive branch continues to claim the right to kill anyone, anywhere on Earth, at any time, for secret reasons, based on secret evidence, in a secret process, undertaken by unidentified officials. I refuse to support this policy of unaccountable killing."

~April 13~

"The Haganah Massacre"

On this day, April 13, 1948, a medical convoy, escorted by Haganah militia Hadassah Hospital on Mount Scopus was ambushed by Arab forces.

Seventy-Eight Jewish doctors, nurses, students, patients, faculty members and Haganah fighters, and one British soldier were killed in the attack. Dozens of unidentified bodies, burned beyond recognition, were buried in a mass grave in the Sanhedria Cemetery.

The convoy had military supplies as well as the medical supplies and workers but, after the massacre, an agreement was reached to separate the military convoys from the humanitarian convoys.

~April 14~

"The Destruction of the Temple"

On this day, April 14, 70, the future Emperor Titus surrounded Jerusalem with four Roman legions. The Siege of Jerusalem in the year 70 C.E. was the decisive event of the First Jewish–Roman War and culminated with the destruction of the Second Temple which had been occupied by its Jewish defenders in 66 C.E.

~~~

"Anne Sullivan"

On this day, April 14, 1866, Johanna Mansfield Sullivan Macy (April 14, 1866 – October 20, 1936), better known as Anne Sullivan, was born in Feeding Hills, Agawam, Massachusetts. Sullivan was an American teacher, best known for being the instructor and lifelong companion of Helen Keller.

~~~

"The Brazilian Schindler"

On this day, April 14, 1954, Luiz Martins de Souza Dantas died in Paris, France. Souza Dantas (February 17, 1876 – April 14, 1954) was a Brazilian diplomat who was awarded the Righteous Among the Nations by the Israeli Supreme Court. During the Holocaust, Souza Dantas helped Jews in France escape. It is estimated that he saved 80025 Jews as well as others including communists and homosexuals.

~April 15~

"Timur"

On this day, April 15, 1395, Timur defeated Tokhtamysh of the Golden Horde at the Battle of the Terek River. The Golden Horde capital city, Sarai, is razed to the ground and Timur installed a puppet ruler on the throne.

Timur is considered the last of the great nomadic conquerors of the Eurasian Steppe, and his empire set the stage for the rise of the more structured and lasting Gunpowder Empires in the 1500s and 1600s. He ruled over an empire that, in modern times, extends from southeastern Turkey, Syria, Iraq, and Iran, through Central Asia encompassing part of Kazakhstan, Afghanistan, Armenia, Azerbaijan, Georgia, Turkmenistan, Uzbekistan, Kyrgyzstan, Pakistan, and even approaches Kashgar in China. Scholars estimate that his military campaigns caused the deaths of 17 million people, amounting to about 5% of the world population.

~~~

"The Roerich Pact"

On this day, April 15, 1935, The Roerich Pact was signed in Washington, DC. The pact is an inter-American treaty on the Protection of Artistic and Scientific Institutions and Historic Monuments. Ultimately, the Pact was signed by 21 states in the Americas and was ratified by ten of them. The concept behind the Roerich Pact is the legal recognition that the defense of cultural objects is as, or more, important than military defense, and the protection of culture always has precedence over any military necessity. Conversely, the destruction of cultural artifacts is considered cultural genocide.

~~~

"George Washington in RI"

On this day, April 15, 1776, George Washington wrote to inform the President of Congress that he had left his headquarters at Cambridge, Massachusetts, earlier on April 4, 1776, heading for New York City.

On the morning of April 6, 1776, Washington stopped in Providence. He wrote to Nicholas Cooke, the Governor of Rhode Island governor, relaying his compliments to both Cooke and the "Gentlemen of Providence" accepted the invitation to be received by Governor Cooke.

During the three years of Cooke's tenure as governor, he had to constantly deal with issues stemming from the war with Britain. One of the most difficult situations was the British capture and occupation of Newport. The war took a heavy toll on Cooke, and in 1778 he refused re-election. Cooke lived for only four more years after his retirement, dying in Providence in November 1782. He is buried in the North Burial Ground in Providence.

~April 16~

"Those Darn Democrats"

On this day, April 16, 1890, Nathaniel Grigsby died and was interred at the Attica Cemetery in Attica, Kansas. Grigsby was a was a schoolmate and friend of Abraham Lincoln who was also an extended family member (his brother Aaron married Sarah Lincoln).

Grigsby blamed the Democratic party for his death and, indeed, the entire Civil War. Twenty years after Lincoln was assassinated, Grigsby dictated his own epitaph as he lay on his deathbed and asked one of his sons to ensure the inscription was carried out:

Through this inscription I wish to enter my dying protest against what is called the Democratic party I have watched it closely since the days of Jackson and know that all the misfortunes of our nation has come to it through this so called party therefore beware of this party of treason.

~~~

(See also January 20th)

~April 17~

"Martin Luther"

On this day, April 17, 1521, the Trial of Martin Luther began at the Diet of Worms. Initially intimidated, Luther asked for time to reflect before answering and is given a stay of one day.

~~~

"Independence"

On this day, April 17, 1949, the twenty-six southern Irish counties officially left the British Commonwealth. A 21-gun salute on O'Connell Bridge, Dublin, ushered in the Republic of Ireland.

It was the first time in 780 years (since the early Norman-English invasions of 1169) that the southern counties were free of British domination, including-at its worst- the Irish Penal Laws, which stripped Irish of their language, their religion, their right to property and their dignity.

~April 18~

"The Longest Game in History"

On this day, April 18, 1981, the PawSox played in and won the longest game in professional baseball history, a 33-inning affair against the Rochester Red Wings at McCoy Stadium. The game started on April 18, 1981. The game was suspended at 4:07 a.m. at the end of the 32nd inning.

~~~

"K-77"

On this day, April 18, 2007, Soviet submarine K-77, which was then being used as a museum, sank off Collier Point Park in Providence, Rhode Island. K-77 was a "Project 651" Juliett-class cruise missile submarine of the Soviet Navy. Her keel was laid down in the Krasnoye Sormovo shipyard in Gorky on January 31, 1963.

K-77 was launched on March 11, 1965, and commissioned on October 31, 1965, into the Northern Fleet. K-77 was also used as the set for the motion picture *K-19: The Widowmaker*, starring Harrison Ford and Liam Neeson. After the film wrapped up in 2002, the submarine was purchased by the USS Saratoga Museum Foundation in Rhode Island.

~April 19~

"OKC"

On this day, April 19, 1995, during the horror of the Oklahoma City Bombing, Firefighter Chris Fields was photographed carrying the infant Baylee Almon. Almon died as a result of the OKC Bombing; Fields resigned from the fire department.

~~~

"What a weird coincidence...."

On this day, April 19, 2014, David Ead died. Ead was the first witness to testify against former Providence Mayor Buddy Cianci and his Operation Plunder Dome trial co-defendants.

Ead was a Providence Police officer in the early 60's and was appointed in 1993 by Cianci to the Board of Tax Assessment Review. He became the board's vice chairman was one of the first city officials arrested in the Plunder Dome sweep. Deputy tax assessor Rosemary Glancy and Tax Board chairman Joseph Pannone were also implicated in 1999 in the federal investigation that a year later went all the way up to the mayor's office. In 1998, Ead was caught on video talking with the key prosecution informant about bribes that were made in exchange for property tax breaks.

On the day Ead testified against Cianci, Ead's vending machine business burned to the ground. What a weird coincidence...

~April 20~

"Bullenhuser Damm School"

On this day, April 20, 1945, twenty Jewish children used in medical experiments at Neuengamme were killed in the basement of the Bullenhuser Damm School.

~~~

On this day, April 20, 2013, Grace Keefe wrote *A Pug's Life*:

In January, the pugs all wait for the ball to drop,

February has them handing out hugs and licks, so much slobber you'll need a mop!

March has the pugs to dancing an Irish step,

April showers make puddles for the pugs to splash-in and get wet!

May brings May Flowers to run and play in,

And June brings a start of a long break, what a win!

July has fireworks to celebrate our country's birth,

In August, the pugs beat the heat with pool-time fun and mirth!

September brings a sad end to their almost three-month break,

For October, the pugs dress up for Halloween and eat all the candy they can take!

In November, the pugs gather round a big table and stuff themselves with the feast,

And December? Oh, don't forget Christmas where you should help the people with the least!

~April 21~

"The Rescue of Danish Jews"

On this day, April 21, 1903, Hans Hedtoft Hansen was born in Aarhus, Denmark.

Hedtoft (April 21, 1903 – January 29, 1955) was Prime Minister of Denmark from November 13, 1947, to October 30, 1950, as the leader of the Cabinet of Hans Hedtoft I and again from 30 September 1953 to 29 January 1955 as the leader of the Cabinet of Hans Hedtoft II.

Hedtoft was a Social Democrat and served as the first President of the Nordic Council in 1953. In 1939, Hedtoft became a party official but was forced by the Nazis to resign his posts in 1941 because he was too critical of the German occupation of Denmark.

In September 1943, he was instrumental in starting the rescue of the Danish Jews.

~April 22~

"Never say, "Never Again!"

On this day, April 22, 2017, I wrote this piece reflecting on the 101st Anniversary of the Armenian Genocide:

Please don't utter platitudes like "Never Again," while we watch it happen again and again...

April 24, 1915

November 9, 1938

April 17, 1975

April 6, 1992

April 7, 1994

February 26, 2003

and now December 15, 2013.

"Never Again" should mean NEVER AGAIN, no matter the race, ethnicity, religion, culture, or socio-economic status. Idris Elba's movie was titled "Sometimes in April" for a different reason, but as we can see from the history of genocide, sometimes in April, we fail ourselves as a human race...

~April 23~

"Clontarf"

On this day, April 23, 1014, the armies of Brian Bóruma mac Cennétig fought the armies of Leinster and Dublin, with Norsemen fighting on both sides, at Clontarf. The Battle of Clontarf, on Good Friday, was a bloody affair; Brian, his son Murchad, and Máel Mórda were among those killed. The *Annals of Ulster* include the Irish kings, Norse Gaels, Scotsmen, and Scandinavians who died that day.

Brian Boru (c. 941 – 23 April 1014) was an Irish king who had ended the domination of the High Kingship of Ireland by the Uí Néill. Building on the achievements of his father, Cennétig mac Lorcain, as well as his elder brother, Mathgamain, Brian established himself as King of Munster, then subjugated Leinster, and eventually became High King of Ireland.

~~~

"Lord Spencer"

On this day, April 23, 1675, Charles Spencer, 3rd Earl of Sunderland, was born in London, England, Kingdom of Great Britain. In 1714, Lord Spencer (April 23, 1675 – April 19, 1722) was appointed Lord Lieutenant of Ireland. Ultimately, Sunderland was implicated in the Atterbury Plot to restore the House of Stuart. He is an ancestor of Lady Diana Spencer, Princess of Wales, as well as her children and thus the heirs to the throne.

~~~

"Joe Mollicone"

On this day, April 23, 1993, Mollicone was convicted by a jury of 26 counts of embezzlement, bank fraud and conspiring to create false bank documents to deceive state regulators. The offenses took place from Jan. 1, 1986, until Nov. 8, 1990, when Mr. Mollicone fled the state after learning that he was the subject of a criminal investigation.

Mollicone, who was the president of Heritage Loan and Investment Company, was also ordered to pay $420,000 in fines and $12 million in restitution. Mollicone spent 18 months hiding in Salt Lake City under the name of John Fazzioli, a childhood friend who had died. In Utah, Mollicone lived for a time with Doris Heishman, who later had to file for bankruptcy because of credit card charges that Mollicone made in her name.

After Mollicone heard that his family lost their home to foreclosure and his wife, Joyce, had filed for bankruptcy, Mollicone surrendered in April 1992.

~April 24~

"Nothing happened here…"

On this day, April 24, 1915, apparently, nothing happened in the Ottoman Empire…

"The attempt to justify and rationalize the death of a whole nation, including women, children, the old and infirm, must itself be considered a crime against humanity."

Taner Akçam

A Shameful Act: The Armenian Genocide and the Question of Turkish Responsibility

~~~

"Easter Rising"

On this day, April 24, 1916, The Easter Rising, also known as the Éirí Amach na Cásca, began in Dublin, Ireland (Baile Átha Cliath, Eire). Members of the Irish Volunteers — led by schoolmaster and Irish language activist Patrick Pearse, joined by the smaller Irish Citizen Army of James Connolly, along with 200 members of Cumann na mBan — seized key locations in Dublin and proclaimed the Irish Republic independent of the United Kingdom.

A total of 3,430 men and 79 women were arrested, although most were subsequently released. In a series of courts martial, 90 people were sentenced to death. Fifteen of those (including all seven signatories of the Proclamation of 1916) were executed at Kilmainham Gaol by firing squad (among them the seriously wounded James Connolly who was shot while tied to a chair due to his shattered ankle).

~April 25~

"Battle of Almansa"

On this day, April 25 (April 14 O.S.), 1707, French-born Englishman James FitzJames, 1st Duke of Berwick, illegitimate son of King James II of England, and Irish mercenaries soundly defeated the combined forces of Portugal, England, and the Dutch Republic led by the French-born Huguenot in English service Henri de Massue, Earl of Galway. It has been described as probably the only Battle in history in which the English forces were commanded by a Frenchman, the French by an Englishman.

~~~

"George Mantello"

On this day, April 25, 1992, George Mantello died in Rome, Italy. Mantello (December 11, 1901 – April 25, 1992) was a diplomat working at the Salvadoran consulate in Geneva, Switzerland from 1942 to 1945; He saved thousands of Jews by providing them with fictive Salvadoran citizenship papers and publicizing the deportation of Hungarian Jews to the Auschwitz.

~~~

"Mo Cheeks"

On this day, April 25, 2003, 13-year-old Natalie Gilbert began to lose her composure singing the national anthem before the Portland Trailblazers – Dallas Mavericks game. Trailblazers coach Maurice Cheeks crossed the court to Gilbert, put his arm around her, encouraged her, and began singing along with her. Soon the entire area was singing along with the Gilbert and Cheeks.

144

~April 26~

"Oscar Wilde"

On this day, April 26, 1895, *Regina v. Wilde* began at the Old Bailey, Dublin, Ireland. Having lost *Wilde v. Queensbury*, Oscar Wilde was charged with homosexuality. Under cross examination, Charles Gill asked: What is "the love that dare not speak its name"? Wilde was at first hesitant, then spoke eloquently:

"The love that dare not speak its name" in this century is such a great affection of an elder for a younger man as there was between David and Jonathan, such as Plato made the very basis of his philosophy, and such as you find in the sonnets of Michelangelo and Shakespeare.

It is that deep spiritual affection that is as pure as it is perfect. It dictates and pervades great works of art, like those of Shakespeare and Michelangelo, and those two letters of mine, such as they are.

It is in this century misunderstood, so much misunderstood that it may be described as "the love that dare not speak its name," and on that account of it, I am placed where I am now.

It is beautiful, it is fine, it is the noblest form of affection. There is nothing unnatural about it. It is intellectual, and it repeatedly exists between an older and a younger man, when the older man has intellect, and the younger man has all the joy, hope, and glamour of life before him. That it should be so, the world does not understand. The world mocks at it and sometimes puts one in the pillory for it.

~April 26~

"Guernica"

On this day, April 26, 1937, Guernica (or Gernika in Basque) was bombed by German Luftwaffe during the Spanish Civil War. Pablo Picasso painted his famous *Guernica* painting commemorating the horrors of the bombing. René Iché made a violent sculpture, also known as *Guernica*. In 1988, *Gure Aitaren Etxea* by Basque sculptor Eduardo Chillida was unveiled in the city and, in 1990, *Large Figure in a Shelter*, by Henry Moore was erected beside *Gure Aitaren Etxea*.

~~~

"Sportsmanship"

On this day, April 26, 2008, Mallory Holtman and Liz Wallace college softball players for Central Washington, showed America what sportsmanship is all about. Down 2-1 to Central Washington, senior Sara Tucholsky hit the first home run of her career with two runners on base. But as Tucholsky turned to retag first base, she collapsed with a torn anterior cruciate ligament in her knee injury. Tucholsky crawled to firstbase but could not stand up. The first base umpire said she would be called out if her teammates tried to help her or, if a pinch-runner was called in, the homer would count as just a single.

Then, Mallory Holtman and Liz Wallace asked if there was a rule against the other team helping, picked up Tucholsky, and carried her around the bases Saturday so the three-run homer would count - an act that contributed to their own elimination from the playoffs. Western Oregon won 4-2 victory, ending Central Washington's chances of winning the conference and advancing to the playoffs.

~April 27~

"End of the Confederate Wars"

On this day, April 27, 1653, Philip O'Reilly and the last Irish forces of the Confederate's Ulster Army formally surrendered at Cloughoughter in County Cavan to the Cromwellian army and thus ended the Confederate Wars and completed the Cromwellian Conquest of Ireland. Cromwell's Conquest destroyed the native Irish Catholic land-owning classes and replaced them with colonists with a British identity. The bitterness caused by the Cromwellian settlement was a powerful source of Irish nationalism from the 17th century onwards.

~~~

"Persona Non-Grata"

On this day, April 27, 1987, the Reagan Administration declared Austrian President Kurt Waldheim *persona non-grata* and barred his entry to the United States. The US Justice Department alleged Waldheim had aided in the deportation and execution of thousands of Jews and others as a German Army officer during World War II. Ironically, he had also been the 4th Secretary-General of the United Nations and dealt with numerous international humanitarian crises. In his 1985 autobiography, he lied about his service in the Germany army. He was elected President of Austria in 1986, barred from the US in 1987, and he did not seek re-election in 1992. Two days after Waldheim death in 2007, the Austrian press published a posthumous apology for his "mistakes." An independent investigation found no evidence of any personal involvement in those crimes. Although Waldheim had stated that he was unaware of any crimes taking place, the committee cited evidence that Waldheim must have known about war crimes.

~April 28~

"Oskar Schindler"

On this day, April 28, 1908, Oskar Schindler was born in Moravia, Brno, Czechoslovakia. Schindler (April 28, 1908 – October 9, 1974) was a German industrialist and member of the Nazi Party who is credited with saving the lives of 1,200 Jews during the Holocaust by employing them in his enamelware and ammunitions factories, which were located in occupied Poland and the Protectorate of Bohemia and Moravia. His story was told in *Schindler's Ark* (1982). The subsequent *film Schindler's List* (1993) showed him as an opportunist initially motivated by profit, who then slowly came to show his extraordinary initiative, tenacity, and dedication to saving the lives of his Jewish employees.

~~~

"The End of WWII"

On this day, April 28, 1952, the *Treaty of San Francisco* came into force (after having been signed September 8, 1951). The treaty officially ended World War II (six years after combat!!), allocated compensation to Allied civilians and former prisoners of war who had suffered Japanese war crimes, ended the Allies' military occupation, and return sovereignty to Japan. It is the first notable treaty to make extensive use of the UN Charter and the Universal Declaration of Human Rights. By Article 11, Japan accepted the judgments of the International Military Tribunal for the Far East and of other Allied War Crimes Courts both within and outside Japan and agreed to carry out the sentences imposed thereby upon Japanese nationals imprisoned in Japan.

~April 29~

"Tojo Indicted"

On this day, April 29, 1946, the International Military Tribunal for the Far East convened and indicted former Prime Minister of Japan Hideki Tojo and 28 former Japanese leaders for war crimes. Seven were later given death sentences and executed; 16 received prison sentences. The chief prosecutor Joseph B. Keenan was from Pawtucket, RI, United States.

~~~

"Strategic Withdrawal"

On this day, April 29, 1975, the Fall of Saigon (or Liberation of Saigon) occurred when the People's Army of Vietnam and the National Liberation Front of South Vietnam (also known as the Việt Cộng) captured of Saigon, the capital of South Vietnam.

~~~

"Profound Respect"

On this day, April 29, 2015, Shinzo Abe became the first Prime Minister of Japan to address a joint session of the US Congress and offered his "profound respect" for US soldiers who died in WWII. On December 27, 2016, Prime Minister Shinzo Abe also became the first Prime Minister of Japan to visit Pearl Harbor and laid a wreath at the USS Arizona Memorial. (US President Barack Obama similarly became the first sitting US President to visit the Peace Memorial Park and Museum in Hiroshima, Japan. The US use of atomic weapons on Hiroshima and Nagasaki killed an estimated 220, 000 people combined.)

~April 30~

"Bishop Wolf"

On this day, April 30, 1947, Geralyn Wolf was born in West Chester, Pennsylvania. She became the twelfth diocesan bishop of the Diocese of Rhode Island on February 17, 1996. Before her election as bishop, Wolf was Dean of Christ Church Cathedral in the Diocese of Kentucky, the first female dean of a cathedral in the United States. She is the author of *Down and Out in Providence: Memoir of a Homeless Bishop* (2005). The book is a recollection of Wolf's experiences when she took a sabbatical and lived as a homeless woman named "Aly" on the streets.

~~~

"First Toy Commercial on Television"

On this day, April 30, 1952, the first toy commercial ever aired on television was for Hasbro's own Mr. Potato Head.

~~~

"Dan Berrigan"

On this day, April 30, 2016, Daniel Joseph Berrigan, S.J. died in the Bronx, New York City, New York, U.S. Berrigan (May 9, 1921 – April 30, 2016), was an American Jesuit priest, anti-war activist, and poet. (See also December 6th)

My people are few. They resemble the scattering trees of a storm-swept plain...There was a time when our people covered the land as the waves of a wind-ruffled sea cover its shell-paved floor, but that time long since passed away with the greatness of tribes that are now but a mournful memory.

Chief Seattle

The Chief Seattle's Speech

~May 1~

"Hasta Luego, Senior Hitler!"

On this day, May 1, 1945, a German newsreader officially announced that Adolf Hitler has "fallen at his command post in the Reich Chancellery fighting to the last breath against Bolshevism and for Germany" (The last known photo of Hitler is from the previous day, April 30). The Soviet flag was then raised over the Reich Chancellery, by order of Joseph Stalin.

~May 2~

"Wilhelm Hosenfeld"

On this day, May 2, 1895, Wilhelm Adalbert Hosenfeld (May 2, 1895 – August 13, 1952), originally a schoolteacher, was a German Army officer who by the end of the Second World War had risen to the rank of Hauptmann (Captain).

Hosenfeld helped to hide or rescue several Polish people, including Jews, in Nazi-occupied Poland and helped Polish-Jewish pianist and composer Władysław Szpilman to survive, hidden, in the ruins of Warsaw during the last months of 1944, an act which was portrayed in the 2002 film *The Pianist*. He was taken prisoner by the Red Army and died in Soviet captivity seven years later. In June 2009, Hosenfeld was posthumously recognized by Yad Vashem (Israel's official memorial to the victims of The Holocaust) as one of the Righteous Among the Nations.

~May 3~

"Anne Frank"

On this day, May 3, 1960, the Anne Frank House museum opened in Amsterdam, Netherlands. (See August 4th, August 6th, and December 3rd.)

~~~

"The Government of Ireland Act"

On this day, May 3, 1920, the British Parliament passed *The Government of Ireland Act* (1920) dividing Ireland into Northern Ireland and Southern Ireland.

The Act was intended to establish separate Home Rule institutions within two new subdivisions of Ireland: the six north-eastern counties were to form "Northern Ireland," while the larger part of the country was to form "Southern Ireland." Both areas of Ireland were to continue as a part of the United Kingdom of Great Britain and Ireland, and provision was made for their future reunification under common Home Rule institutions.

Home Rule never took effect in Southern Ireland, due to the Irish War of Independence, which resulted instead in the Anglo-Irish Treaty and the establishment in 1922 of the Irish Free State. However, the institutions set up under this Act for Northern Ireland continued to function until they were suspended by the British parliament in 1972 as a consequence of the Troubles.
The remaining provisions of the Act still in force in Northern Ireland were repealed under the terms of the 1998 Good Friday Agreement.

~May 4~

"The Republic of Rhode Island"

On this day, May 4, 1776, the Colony of Rhode Island declared independence from the United Kingdom of Great Britain. Rhode Island declared its independence a full two months before the rest of the English colonies in North America and, thus, was a self-declared independent country for two months.

~~~

"A Nobel Peace Prize in Nazi Germany?

On this day, May 4, 1938, Carl von Ossietzky died in Berlin, Nazi Germany. Von Ossietzky (October 3, 1889 – May 4, 1938) was a German pacifist and the recipient of the 1935 Nobel Peace Prize for his work in exposing the clandestine German re-armament. He was convicted of high treason and espionage in 1931 after publishing details of Germany's violation of the *Treaty of Versailles* by rebuilding an air force, the predecessor of the Luftwaffe, and training pilots in the Soviet Union. Ossietzky's 1935 Nobel Prize was not allowed to be mentioned in the German press, and a government decree forbade German citizens from accepting future Nobel Prizes. In May 1936, he was hospitalized because of tuberculosis, but under Gestapo surveillance. He later died in the Nordend hospital, while still in police custody, of tuberculosis and from the after-effects of the abuse he suffered in the concentration camps.

In 1990, his daughter, Rosalinde von Ossietzky-Palm, called for a resumption of proceedings, but, in 1992, the verdict was upheld by the Federal Court of Justice.

ARE YOU KIDDING ME?

~~~

"Walter Gadsden"

On this day, May 4, 1963, Bill Hudson's photograph of Parker High School student Walter Gadsden being attacked by dogs was published in *The New York Times*.

~~~

"Yitzhak-Arafat"

On this day, May 4, 1994, Israeli Prime Minister Yitzhak Rabin and PLO leader Yasser Arafat signed a peace accord, granting self-rule in the Gaza Strip and Jericho.

~May 5~

"Gino Bartali"

On this day, May 5, 2000, Gino Bartali died in Florence, Italy. Bartali (July 18, 1914 – May 5, 2000) was a world champion cyclist. Bartali used his fame to carry messages and documents to the Italian Resistance. Bartali cycled from Florence through Tuscany, Umbria, and Marche, sometimes traveling as far afield as Rome, all the while wearing the racing jersey emblazoned with his name. Neither the Fascist police nor the German troops wanted to risk upsetting the Italian people by arresting Bartali.

Giorgio Nissim, a Jewish accountant from Pisa, had helped Jewish Italians escape persecution. When Nissim died in 2000, his sons found from his diaries that Bartali had used his fame to help. Nissim and the Oblati Friars of Lucca forged documents and photographs of those they were helping, then Bartali would to leave Florence in the morning, pretending to train, ride to a convent in which the Jews were hiding, collect their photographs and ride back to Nissim. Bartali also used his position to learn about raids on safehouses. Bartali was eventually taken to Villa Triste in Florence. The SD and the Italian RSS official Mario Carità questioned Bartali, threatening his life. Bartali simply answered, "I do what I feel [in my heart]." Bartali continued working with the Assisi Underground. In 1943, he led Jewish refugees towards the Swiss Alps himself. He cycled, pulling a wagon with a secret compartment, telling patrols it was just part of his training. In December 2010, it also emerged that Bartali had hidden a Jewish family in his cellar and, by doing so, had saved their lives.

In 2013, Yad Vashem awarded Gino Bartali the honor Righteous Among the Nations. Bartali never spoke of his heroic deeds but, later in life, Bartali simply told his son Andrea that "One does these things and then that's that."

~May 6~

"The Last Stand"

On this day, May 6, 1527, the Last Stand battle occurred near St. Peter's Basilica close to the Campo Santo Teutonico. During the battle, 147 of the 189 Swiss Guards, including their commander, died fighting the troops of Holy Roman Emperor Charles V during the Sack of Rome. The delaying tactic allowed Pope Clement VII to escape through the Passetto di Borgo, escorted by the remaining 42 Swiss Guards.

~~~

"The Chinese Exclusion Act"

On this day, May 6, 1882, the United States Congress passed the *Chinese Exclusion Act*. It was one of the most significant restrictions on free immigration in US history, prohibiting all immigration of Chinese laborers. The act followed revisions made in 1880 to the US-China *Burlingame Treaty of 1868*, revisions that allowed the US to suspend Chinese immigration. The act was initially intended to last for 10 years but was renewed in 1892 and made permanent in 1902. The *Chinese Exclusion Act* was the first law implemented to prevent a specific ethnic group from immigrating to the United States. It was finally repealed by the *Magnuson Act* on December 17, 1943.

~~~

"Pope in a Mosque?"

On this day, May 6, 2001, Pope John Paul II became the first pope to enter a mosque during his trip to Syria. The trip was a pilgrimage in the footsteps of St. Paul. At Olmayyad Mosque, once a Roman temple as well as a Christian church, the pope urged Muslims and Christians to forgive each other for the past. He also appealed against religious fundamentalism of any kind. He is also the first pope to visit a Canterbury Cathedral (May 29, 1982) as well as the first pope to visit a synagogue (April 4, 1986).

~May 7~

"Ján Kubiš"

On this day, May 7, 2016, UN envoy Ján Kubiš said more than 50 mass graves have so far been found in parts of Iraq that were previously controlled by so-called Islamic State (IS). Ján Kubiš (born November 12, 1952), was a Slovak diplomat and was formerly Secretary-General of the Organisation for Security and Cooperation in Europe (OSCE).

"I condemn in the strongest possible terms the continued killings, kidnapping, rape and torture of Iraqis by ISIL (IS), which may constitute crimes against humanity, war crimes, and even genocide."

Ján Kubiš

UN's Special Representative and Head of the United Nations Assistance Mission in Afghanistan (UNAMA).

~May 8 ~

"V-E"

On this day, May 8, 1945, German forces unconditionally surrendered at 23:01 CET. At 2:41 Central European Time (CET) on May 7, 1945, German Oberkommando der Wehrmacht, Alfred Jodl signed the capitulation papers in Reimsfirst, Reims, France. The signing took place in a red brick schoolhouse, the Collège Moderne et Technique de Reims, that served as the Supreme Headquarters Allied Expeditionary Force. Jodl signed the unconditional surrender of Germany as a representative for German president Karl Dönitz. At Nuremberg, Jodl was tried, sentenced to death and hanged as a war criminal. Dönitz, on the other hand, was convicted of war crimes and sentenced to ten years' imprisonment; after his release, he lived quietly in a village near Hamburg until his death in 1980.

~~~

"Szczurowa Massacre"

On this day, May 8, 1956, local inhabitants of the village and members of local veterans' associations erected a memorial stone with an inscription at the site of the mass grave of the victims of the Szczurowa Massacre. On August 3, 1943, Nazis massacred was the murder of 93 Romani people, including children, women, and the elderly in Szczurowa. Between ten and twenty families of settled Romani had lived in Szczurowa for generations, alongside ethnic Poles with whom they had friendly relations and even mixed-marriages. This became the first memorial commemorating victims of the Romani Holocaust in the world. The memorial is cared for by local schoolchildren, and the memory of the tragedy is part of the local historical consciousness.

~May 9~

"The North Pole"

On this day, May 9, 1926, Admiral Richard E. Byrd and Floyd Bennett claim to have flown over the North Pole (later discovery of Byrd's diary appears to cast some doubt on the claim.)

~~~

"The Vast Wasteland"

On this day, May 9, 1926, Federal Communications Commission Chairman Newton N. Minow gave a speech to the convention of the National Association of Broadcasters entitled "Television and the Public Interest." In the speech, Minow referred to American commercial television programming as a "vast wasteland" and advocated for programming in the public interest. Minow sfamously said:

"When television is good, nothing — not the theater, not the magazines or newspapers — nothing is better. But when television is bad, nothing is worse. I invite each of you to sit down in front of your own television set when your station goes on the air and stay there, for a day, without a book, without a magazine, without a newspaper, without a profit and loss sheet or a rating book to distract you. Keep your eyes glued to that set until the station signs off. I can assure you that what you will observe is a vast wasteland. You will see a procession of game shows, formula comedies about totally unbelievable families, blood and thunder, mayhem, violence, sadism, murder, western bad men, western good men, private eyes, gangsters, more violence, and cartoons. And endlessly commercials — many screaming, cajoling, and offending."

~May 10~

"A Prinz of a Rabbi"

On this day, May 10, 1902, Joachim Prinz was born in the village of Bierdzany (near Oppeln), in the Prussian province of Silesia. As a young rabbi in Berlin, Prinz (May 10, 1902 – September 30, 1988) was forced to confront the rise of Nazism and eventually emigrated to the United States in 1937. Prinz was a German-American rabbi who was outspoken against Nazism and became a Zionist leader. He became vice-chairman of the World Jewish Congress, an active member of the World Zionist Organization and a participant in the 1963 Civil Rights March on Washington. Dr. Prinz devoted much of his life in the United States to the Civil Rights movement. He saw the plight of African American and other minority groups in the context of his own experience under Hitler.

From his early days in Newark, a city with a very large minority community, he spoke from his pulpit about the disgrace of discrimination. He joined the picket lines across America protesting racial prejudice from unequal employment to segregated schools, housing and all other areas of life.

While serving as President of the American Jewish Congress, he represented the Jewish community as an organizer of the August 28, 1963, March on Washington. He came to the podium immediately following a stirring spiritual sung by the gospel singer Mahalia Jackson and just before Martin Luther King, Jr. delivered his famous "I Have a Dream" speech. Dr. Prinz's address is remembered for its contention that, based on his experience as a rabbi in Nazi Germany after the rise of Hitler, in the face of discrimination, "the most urgent, the most disgraceful, the most shameful and the most tragic problem is silence."

~ ~ ~

"U know him 2?"

On this day, May 10, 1960, Paul David Hewson was born in Dublin, Ireland. His mother was Iris Hewson née Rankin, a member of the Church of Ireland, and his father was, Brendan Robert "Bob" Hewson, a Roman Catholic. This dual religious parentage gave Hewson a unique perspective on The Troubles. Hewson is known as an Irish singer-songwriter, musician, venture capitalist, businessman, and philanthropist.

Hewson has established himself as a passionate musician through his expressive vocal style and grandiose gestures and songwriting. His lyrics are known for their social and political themes, and for their religious imagery inspired by his Christian beliefs. During the early years, Hewson's lyrics contributed to the group's rebellious and spiritual tone. As the band matured, his lyrics became inspired more by personal experiences shared with the other members. Hewson and his band have received 22 Grammy Awards and has been inducted into the Rock and Roll Hall of Fame.

More importantly, Hewson is widely known for his activism for social justice causes. He is particularly active in campaigning for Africa, for which he co-founded DATA, EDUN, the ONE Campaign, and Product Red. In pursuit of these causes, he has participated in benefit concerts and met with influential politicians.

~ ~ ~

"Mandela"

On May 10, 1994, Nelson Mandela was inaugurated as South Africa's first sub-Saharan black president.

~May 11~

"The Arcade"

On this day, May 11, 1976, the Arcade in Providence, Rhode Island, and the Governor Henry Lippitt House (also in Providence), were designated as National Historic Landmarks. The Arcade is the first enclosed shopping mall in the U.S., built in 1828 and the Lippitt House is an 1865 Italianate villa-style house was built for Governor Henry Lippitt. Also designated that same day were the Bellevue Avenue Historic District in Newport, Rhode Island, and Ocean Drive in Newport, Rhode Island.

The Bellevue Avenue Historic District includes the Newport mansions of many exemplary of period styles, built here by summer vacationers in late 19th and early 20th centuries.

There are 45 National Historic Landmarks (NHLs) in Rhode Island. In addition, there are two National Park Service administered or affiliated areas of national historic importance in the state.

~~~

"The Pentagon Papers"

On this day, May 11, 1973, the charges against Daniel Ellsberg, for his involvement in releasing the Pentagon Papers to *The New York Times*, were dismissed.

~May 12~

"The Female Schindler"

On this day, May 12, 2008, Irena Sendlerowa (more commonly known as Irena Sendler) passed away of pneumonia at the age of 98 in Warsaw. Sendler was a Polish nurse, humanitarian and social worker who served in the Polish Underground in German-occupied Warsaw during World War II, and was head of the children's section of Żegota, the Polish Council to Aid Jews Irena has often been referred to as "the female Oskar Schindler" in her native Poland for her daring and ingenuity in saving the lives of more than 2,500 Jews (most of them children) in German-occupied Poland during World War II.

~ ~ ~

"Jimmy Carter"

On this day, May 12, 2002, former US President Jimmy Carter arrived in Cuba for a five-day visit with Fidel Castro. In 1982, Jimmy Carter established the Carter Center in Atlanta to advance human rights and alleviate human suffering. The Carter Center promotes democracy, mediates, and prevents conflicts, and monitors the electoral process in support of free and fair elections. It also works to improve global health through the control and eradication of diseases. A major accomplishment of the Carter Center has been the elimination of more than 99 percent of cases of Guinea worm disease. In 2002, President Carter received the Nobel Peace Prize for his work "to find peaceful solutions to international conflicts, to advance democracy and human rights, and to promote economic and social development" through The Carter Center.

~May 13~

"Blood, toil, tears, and sweat"

On this day, May 13, 1940, British Prime Minister Winston Churchill delivered his "Blood, toil, tears, and sweat" speech to the House of Commons of the Parliament of the United Kingdom:

We are in the preliminary stage of one of the greatest battles in history.... That we are in action at many points—in Norway and in Holland—, that we have to be prepared in the Mediterranean. That the air battle is continuous, and that many preparations have to be made here at home.

I would say to the House as I said to those who have joined this government: I have nothing to offer but blood, toil, tears and sweat. We have before us an ordeal of the most grievous kind. We have before us many, many long months of struggle and of suffering.

You ask, what is our policy? I will say: It is to wage war, by sea, land and air, with all our might and with all the strength that God can give us; to wage war against a monstrous tyranny, never surpassed in the dark and lamentable catalogue of human crime. That is our policy. You ask, what is our aim? I can answer in one word: Victory. Victory at all costs—Victory in spite of all terror—Victory, however long and hard the road may be, for without victory there is no survival.

~May 14~

"Second Fiddle Belligerents Get Away with Everything"

On this day, May 14, 1922, Franjo Tuđman was born in Veliko Trgovišće, Kingdom of Serbs, Croats, and Slovenes. Tuđman (May 14, 1922 – December 10, 1999) was a Croatian politician and historian. Following the country's independence from Yugoslavia, he became the first President of Croatia and served as president from 1990 until his death. He was the strongman leader of Croatian during the Balkan Wars and Bosnian Genocide.

~~~

"Israeli Independence"

On this day, May 14, 1948, Israel declared its independence and a provisional government is established. Immediately after the declaration, Israel was attacked by its neighboring Arab states, triggering what is now known as the first Arab–Israeli War.

Earlier, on November 29, 1947, the United Nations General Assembly recommended the adoption and implementation of the Partition Plan for Palestine. This UN plan had specified borders for new Arab and Jewish states and also specified that Jerusalem be administered by the UN. The end of the British Mandate for Palestine was set for midnight on May 14, 1948, and, immediately, the dual events of May 14th occurred.

This also began the Palestinian Diaspora.

~May 15~

"Bernard Herzog"

On this day, May 15, 1945, Bernard Herzog and others were liberated from the Japanese POW camp of Santo Tomas, Manila, Philippines.

~May 16~

"The Oregon Trail"

On this day, May 16, 1843, the first major wagon train heading for the Pacific Northwest set out on the Oregon Trail with one thousand pioneers from Elm Grove, Missouri.

~May 17~

"Vampires!"

On this day, May 17, 1892, George Brown was persuaded to give permission to exhume several bodies of his family members.

Friends and neighbors believed that one of the dead family members was a vampire (although they did not use that name) and had caused Edwin Brown's illness. Villagers, the local doctor, and a newspaper reporter exhumed the bodies on March 17, 1892.

The bodies of both Mary and Mary Olive exhibited the expected level of decomposition, so they were thought not to be the cause. However, the corpse of a daughter, Mercy, which had been in a freezer-like, above-ground vault, exhibited almost no decomposition. She still had blood in the heart and liver. This was taken as a sign that the young woman was undead and was, of course, the cause of young Edwin's condition. (Her lack of decomposition was more likely due to her body being stored in freezer-like conditions in an above-ground crypt during the two months following her death.) As superstition dictated, Mercy's heart was burned, and the ashes were mixed with water and given to the sick Edwin to drink, as an effort to resolve his illness and stop the influence of the undead. The young man died two months later. What remained of Mercy's body was buried in the cemetery of the Baptist Church in Exeter after being desecrated.

~~~

On this day, May 17, 1954, the United States Supreme Court issued a unanimous decision in *Brown v. Board of Education of Topeka, Kansas.* Earl Warren, Chief Justice of the U.S. Supreme Court, wrote:

> *"Segregation of white and colored children in public schools has a detrimental effect upon the colored children. The impact is greater when it has the sanction of the law, for the policy of separating the races is usually interpreted as denoting the inferiority of the Negro group...Any language in contrary to this finding is rejected. We conclude that in the field of public education the doctrine of 'separate but equal' has no place. Separate educational facilities are inherently unequal."*

172

~May 18~

"Woodmansee and Foreman

On this day, May 18, 1975, Michael Woodmansee murdered Jason Foreman. Woodmansee was a sixteen-year-old junior at South Kingstown High School when he murdered Jason Foreman, a five-year-old child who lived nearby. He was not convicted of the murder until 1983 after he confessed to the crime upon questioning about the attempted strangulation of another child. The family lived on Schaeffer Street in the village of Peace Dale, South Kingstown. Foreman, who was 5 years old, was stabbed to death and his body was disposed of in undetermined circumstances. South Kingstown Police Chief Vincent Vespia has maintained possession of Woodmansee's diary ever since the evidence was collected.

~May 19~

"The Pontic Genocide"

This day, May 19th is recognized in Greece as Greek Genocide Remembrance Day. The Greek Genocide, or Pontic Genocide, refers to the systematic ethnic cleansing of the Ottoman Greek population during World War I and its aftermath (1914–22).

~~~

"Josiah Barlett"

On this day, May 19, 1795, Josiah Bartlett was born in Amesbury, Massachusetts Bay Colony. Josiah Bartlett (December 2, 1729, NS [November 21, 1729, OS] – May 19, 1795) was an American physician, delegate to the Continental Congress, a signatory of the Declaration of Independence, Chief Justice of the New Hampshire Superior Court of Judicature, and Governor of the New Hampshire. He is most well-known as the ancestor of Martin Sheen's character, US President Bartlett.

~~~

"The British Schindler"

On this day, May 19, 1909, Nicholas George Winton (May 19, 1909 – July 1, 2015) was born in Wertheim, United Kingdom of Great Britain and Ireland. a British humanitarian who organized the rescue of 669 children from Czechoslovakia on the eve of the Second World War in an operation later known as the Czech Kindertransport. Winton found homes for the children and arranged for their safe passage to Britain. The world found out about his work over 40 years later, in 1988.

~~~

"Seiichi Nakahara and Yuri Kochiyama"

On this day, May 19, 1921, Seiichi Nakahara was born in San Pedro, California. After Japan bombed Pearl Harbor, FBI agents arrested Seiichi Nakahara, the father of Yuri Kochiyama, as a potential threat to national security. You know, because he was Japanese, right? While Nakahara was in prison, he was denied medical care so by the time he was released; he was too sick to speak; he died the day after his release on January 20, 1942.

Kochiyama became a human rights activist. She is notable as one of the few prominent non-black supporters of Black Nationalism. Influenced by Marxism, Maoism, and the thoughts of Malcolm X. Through her activism through the 1960s and into the mid-2000s—Yuri participated in the Black, Asian-American, and Third World movements for civil rights, human rights, Black liberation, political prisoners, ethnic studies, anti-war, and other social justice issues.

Kochiyama, along with several Japanese-American organizations on the East Coast and West Coast, advocated for reparations and a government apology for injustices toward Japanese-Americans during the internment. President Ronald Reagan signed the Civil Liberties Act in 1988 which, among other things, awarded $20,000 to each Japanese-American internment survivor.

Later, Kochiyama was active in opposing the profiling and bigotry toward Muslims and Middle Easterners, a phenomenon many view as similar to the experience of Japanese Americans during World War II. She died on June 1, 2014.

I wonder, what would Kochiyama think of the decision in
Trump v. Hawaii on June 26, 2018?

~May 20~

"The Day of Remembrance"

This day, May 20th is the Day of Remembrance. Formerly called the National Day of Hatred, which always falls on May 20th, is an annual event in Cambodia which commemorates the Cambodian Genocide of the Khmer Rouge regime that ruled the country between 1975 and 1979.

~~~

"Slow down!!!"

On this day, May 20, 1899, New York City taxi driver Jacob German was arrested for speeding while driving 12 miles per hour on Lexington Street. Good thing too; if small things aren't nipped in the bud, you never know how things might grow into bigger problems…

~~~

"East Timor"

On this day, May 20, 2002, East Timor became the first new sovereign state of the 21st-century. Earlier, on August 30, 1999, East Timor voted for independence from Indonesia in a referendum. East Timor was colonized by Portugal in the 16th century and was known as Portuguese Timor.

In 1975, East Timor was invaded and declared Indonesia's 27th province the following year. The Indonesian occupation of East Timor was characterized by a highly violent decades-long conflict between separatist groups and the Indonesian military.

~May 21~

"Gee, why do Chechnyans hate Russians so much?"

On this day, May 21, 1864, Russia declared an end to the Russo-Circassian War after the scorched earth campaign initiated in 1862 under General Yevdokimov. When the Circassian people refused to convert to Christianity from Islam, almost the entire population was forced into exile from their North Caucasus homeland.

More than 1.5 million Circassians were expelled — 90% of the total population at the time. Most of them perished en route, victims of disease, hunger, and exhaustion. The day is designated the Circassian Day of Mourning, and the event is known as The Circassian Genocide.

The Sochi Olympics were held on former Circassian land which caused an outcry from Circassian people as well as humans rights activists worldwide.

~May 22~

"What a radical idea…"

On this day, May 22, 1942, Richard Oakes was born in Akwesasne, New York. Oakes (May 22, 1942 – September 20, 1972) was a Mohawk Native American activist who promoted the fundamental idea that Native peoples have a right to sovereignty, justice, respect, and control over their own destinies. His legacy reflects the struggles of Native peoples and all people to maintain their land, identity, and lifeways.

~~~

"Betty Williams"

On this day, May 22, 1943, Betty Williams was born in Belfast, Northern Ireland. Williams is a peace activist who co-founded, the Women for Peace, which later became the Community for Peace People, dedicated a peaceful resolution of The Troubles in Northern Ireland. Maguire and Williams were awarded the 1976 Nobel Peace Prize.

~~~

"The Windmill"

On this day, May 22, 1973, the Windmill Cottage was listed on the National Register of Historic Places. Windmill Cottage is a former windmill at 144 Division Street in East Greenwich, Rhode Island. It was the home of George Washington Greene, a former American consul to Rome who met Henry Wadsworth Longfellow in Italy. The two became friends, and Longfellow later purchased the cottage from Greene. It is believed that the Windmill Cottage inspired Longfellow's poem, "The Windmill."

The Windmill

Behold! a giant am I!
Aloft here in my tower,
With my granite jaws I devour
The maize, and the wheat, and the rye,
And grind them into flour.

I look down over the farms;
In the fields of grain I see
The harvest that is to be,
And I fling to the air my arms,
For I know it is all for me.

I hear the sound of flails
Far off, from the threshing-floors
In barns, with their open doors,
And the wind, the wind in my sails,
Louder and louder roars.

I stand here in my place,
With my foot on the rock below,
And whichever way it may blow,
I meet it face to face,
As a brave man meets his foe.

And while we wrestle and strive,
My master, the miller, stands
And feeds me with his hands;
For he knows who makes him thrive,
Who makes him lord of lands.

On Sundays I take my rest;
Church-going bells begin
Their low, melodious din;
I cross my arms on my breast,
And all is peace within.

~May 23~

"William Drennan"

On this day, May 23, 1820, William Drennan died, and at his request, his coffin was carried -per his Last Will and Testament- by an equal number of Catholics and Protestants. Drennan (May 23, 1754 – February 5, 1820) was one of the chief architects of the Society of United Irishmen. He is also known as the first person to refer in print to Ireland as "The Emerald Isle" in his poem *When Erin first rose.*

~~~

"Sideburns Burnside"

On this day, May 23, 1824, Ambrose Everett Burnside was born in Liberty, Indiana. Burnside (May 23, 1824 – September 13, 1881) was an American soldier, inventor, industrialist, and politician from Rhode Island, serving as governor and a United States Senator. As a Union Army general in the American Civil War, he conducted successful campaigns in North Carolina and East Tennessee, as well as countering the raids of Confederate General John Hunt Morgan but suffered disastrous defeats at the Battle of Fredericksburg and Battle of the Crater. His distinctive style of facial hair became known as sideburns, derived from his last name. He was also the first president of the National Rifle Association.

~~~

"Final Solution for Himmler"

On this day, May 23, 1945, Heinrich Himmler, the head of the Schutzstaffel, committed suicide in prison, Lüneburg, Germany.

~May 24~

"United Irishmen"

On this day, May 24, 1798, the Irish Rebellion of 1798 led by the United Irishmen against British rule began. The multi-religious Society of United Irishmen was founded as a liberal political organization in eighteenth century Ireland that initially sought Parliamentary reform. Inspired by the American Revolution and allied with Revolutionary France. However, it evolved into a revolutionary republican organization. One of the results of the failed rebellion was the British decision to abolish the Irish Parliament through the Act of Union and take even more direct control of Ireland.

~~~

"Operation Solomon"

On this day, May 24, 1991, Israel conducted Operation Solomon, evacuating Ethiopian Jews to Israel. Non-stop flights of 35 Israeli aircraft, including Israeli Air Force C-130s and El Al Boeing 747s, transported 14,325 Ethiopian Jews to Israel in 36 hours. World Jewish organizations and Israel had been concerned about the well-being of the Ethiopian Jews, known as Beta Israel, residing in Ethiopia. Also, the Mengistu regime had made mass emigration difficult for Beta Israel and the regime's dwindling power presented an opportunity for those wanting to emigrate to Israel. In 1990, the Israeli government and Israeli Defense Forces, aware of Mengistu's worsening political situation, made covert plans to airlift the Jews to Israel. The American government was involved in the organization of the airlift. The decision of the Ethiopian government to allow all the Jews to leave the country at once was largely motivated by a letter from President George H. W. Bush.

~May 25~

"Deportation of Armenians"

On this day, May 25, 1915, Mehmed Talat, the Ottoman minister of the interior, announced that all Armenians living near the battlefield zones in eastern Anatolia (under Ottoman rule) would be deported to Syria and Mosul. Large-scale deportations began five days later after the decision was sanctioned by the Ottoman council of ministers.

~~~

"Liberation Day"

On this day, May 25, 2000, Israel withdrew its army from most of the Lebanese territory 22 years after its first invasion in 1978. The day is now recognized as Liberation Day of Lebanon.

~May 26~

"Mystic Massacre"

On this day, May 26, 1637, Major John Mason led a combined English and Mohegan/Narragansett force against the Pequot people. Mason's army set fire to a fortified Pequot village near the Mystic River. They shot any Pequots who tried to escape the wooden palisade fortress and killed 400-700 Pequots, consisting mostly of women and children. The only survivors were the warriors who had been with their sachem, Sassacus, in a raiding party outside the village. The event is known as the Mystic Massacre.

After the subsequent Fairfield Swamp Fight in July 1637, the English sold captured Pequot as slaves or servants and took their lands. The Pequot numbers were so diminished that they ceased to be a tribe in most senses. Many of the remaining Pequot were to be absorbed into the Mohegan and Narragansett tribes and were not allowed to refer to themselves as Pequot. In the later 20th century, Pequot descendants revived the tribe, achieving federal recognition and settlement of some land claims.

A statue of Major John Mason is on the Palisado Green in Windsor, Connecticut. The statue was originally placed at the intersection of Pequot Avenue and Clift Street in Mystic, Connecticut, near what was thought to be one of the original Pequot forts. The statue remained there for 103 years. After studying the sensitivity and appropriateness of the statue's location near the historic massacre of Pequot people, a commission chartered by Groton, Connecticut voted to have it relocated. In 1993, the State of Connecticut relocated the statue to its current setting.

~~~

"The Vote That Saved the Presidency"

On this day, May 26, 1868, US Senator Edmund G. Ross (R-KS) cast the deciding vote to not remove US President Andrew Johnson from office. Ross is one of eight senators featured in *Profiles in Courage* (1956) by then-US Senator John F. Kennedy and ghostwriter Theodore Sorensen.

~~~

"Best-Namkai-Meche, and Fletcher"

On this day, May 26, 2017, Ricky John Best, Taliesin Myrddin Namkai-Meche, and Micah Fletcher acted as the heroes we all strive to be. Best, Namkai-Meche, and Fletcher stood up for those in need, the two girls being verbally abused because of their religion and race. Best, Namkai-Meche, and Fletcher are the best of America. Macy, one of the girls verbally attacked stayed with Namkai-Meche while waiting for emergency responders. "I just kept telling him, 'You're not alone. We're here,'" Macy recalled. "'What you did was total kindness. You're such a beautiful man. I'm sorry the world is so cruel.'" Namkai-Meche last words before being taken away on a stretcher were "Tell everyone on this train I love them." From the hospital, Micah Fletcher wrote:

> I, am alive,
> I spat in the eye of hate and lived.
> This is what we must do for one another
> We must live for one another
> We must fight for one another
> We must die in the name of freedom if we have to.
> Luckily, it's not my turn today.

~May 27~

"Obama Visits Hiroshima"

On this day, May 28, 2016, Barack Obama became the first sitting US President to visit Hiroshima, Japan:

"Seventy-one years ago, on a bright cloudless morning, death fell from the sky and the world was changed... "Technological progress without an equivalent progress in human institutions can doom us," Mr. Obama said, adding that such technology "requires a moral revolution as well."

Barack Obama

May 27, 2016
Hiroshima Peace Memorial

~May 28~

"Apartheid Begins"

On this day, May 28, 1948, DF Malan was elected Prime Minister of South Africa. Malan was seen as a champion of Afrikaner nationalism, and his National Party government came to power on the program of apartheid and began its implementation.

~~~

"Two Mass Murderers Meet"

On this day, May 28, 1948, President Nicolae Ceausescu of Romania made an official visit to Cambodia and was welcomed by General Secretary of the Communist Party of Kampuchea, Pol Pot. The two heads of state have both been accused of genocide.

Ceausescu was later executed by a dubious Romanian court for the crime of "genocide" during the Timişoara Revolution. This crackdown did involve Hungarian minorities but also grew into a national revolution and crackdown of revolutionaries involving not just ethnic minorities but Romanians of all backgrounds. For his part, Pol Pot is widely considered responsible for the death of an estimated 1 to 3 million people (out of a population of slightly over 8 million) who died due to the policies of his four-year rule.

~May 29~

"Papal Visits"

On this day, May 29, 1982, Pope John Paul II became the first pontiff to visit Canterbury Cathedral. He is also the first pope to visit a mosque (May 6, 2001) as well as the first pope to visit a synagogue (April4, 1986).

~~~

"Hands Across Hawthorne"

On this day, May 29, 2011, "Hands Across Hawthorne" was a rally held at the Hawthorne Bridge in Portland, Oregon, on May 29, 2011, in response to an attack on a gay male couple one week earlier for holding hands while walking across the bridge. News of the attack spread throughout the Pacific Northwest and the United States. According to the couple and the Portland Police Bureau, a group of five men followed Brad Forkner and Christopher Rosevear along the bridge and then physically assaulted the couple.

~May 30~

"Take Down That Flag!"

On this day, May 30, 1941, Manolis Glezos and Apostolos Santas climbed on the Acropolis and tore down the swastika, which had been there since Nazi occupation. It inspired the Greeks and established them both as two international anti-Nazi heroes. The Nazi regime responded by sentencing both Glezos and Santas to death in absentia. Glezos was eventually arrested by the German occupation forces on March 24, 1942, and was subjected to imprisonment, torture, and he developed tuberculosis. After his release, he was arrested again on April 21, 1943, by the Italian occupation forces and spent three more months in jail. On February 7, 1944, he was arrested for a third time, this time by Greek Nazi collaborators. Glezos spent seven and a half months in jail until he finally escaped on September 21, 1944.

On March 3, 1948, during the Greek Civil War, he was put on trial for his political convictions and sentenced to death multiple times by the right-wing government. His death penalties were reduced to a life sentence in 1950. From jail, Glezos was elected to the Hellenic Parliament in 1951and, after his election, he went on a hunger strike demanding the release of his MPs that were imprisoned or exiled. He ended his hunger strike upon the release of the MPs and was released from prison on July 16, 1954.

On December 5, 1958, he was arrested again and convicted for espionage but was later released on December 15, 1962. Finally, on April 21, 1967, Glezos was arrested again. Glezos' political persecution, from the Second World War to the Greek Civil War and the Regime of the Colonels totals to 11 years and 4 months of imprisonment, and 4 years and 6 months of exile.

~May 31~

"The Italian Fraud"

On this day, May 31, 1909, Giovanni Palatucci was born. Palatucci (May 31, 1909 – February 10, 1945) an Italian police official who was long believed to have saved thousands of Jews in Fiume between 1939 and 1944 (current Rijeka in Croatia) from being deported to Nazi extermination camps. It is now believed that his heroism is likely a fraud. In 2013, a research panel of historians led by the Centro Primo Levi reviewed almost 700 documents and concluded that Palatucci had followed RSI, and German orders concerning the Jews and enabling the deportation of the majority of the 570 Jews living in Fiume and surrounding areas, 412 of whom were deported to Auschwitz, a higher percentage than in any Italian city.

~~~

"Prisoner of the Vatican"

On this day, May 31, 1857, Pope Pius XI was born as Ambrogio Damiano Achille Ratti. Pius XI (May 31, 1857 – February 10, 1939) reigned as Pope from February 6, 1922, to his death in 1939. He was the last "Prisoner of the Vatican" and thus also the first sovereign of Vatican City from its creation as an independent state on February 11, 1929.

"Seventy-one years ago, on a bright cloudless morning,
death fell from the sky and the world was changed...
"Technological progress without an equivalent progress
in human institutions can doom us," Mr. Obama said,
adding that such technology "requires a moral
revolution as well."

Barack Obama

May 27, 2016
Hiroshima Peace Memorial

~June 1~

"Preaching Truth"

On this day, June 1, 1843, Isabella Baumfree, a former slave, changed her name to Sojourner Truth and began to preach for the abolition of slavery.

~~~

"Eichmann Executed"

On this day, June 1, 1962, Adolf Eichmann was executed, his body was cremated at a secret location, and his ashes were scattered in the Mediterranean Sea outside of Israeli waters.

At 8 p.m. on May 31, Eichmann had been informed his appeal had been denied. He refused a last meal (preferring instead a bottle of wine) as well as the traditional black hood. Eichmann's execution was scheduled for midnight, but due to a slight delay, it happened a few minutes after midnight at a prison in Ramla, Israel. His last words were:

"Long live Germany. Long live Argentina. Long live Austria. These are the three countries with which I have been most connected and which I will not forget. I greet my wife, my family, and my friends. I am ready. We'll meet again soon, as is the fate of all men. I die believing in God."

~June 2~

"It's about time…"

On this day, June 2, 1924, U.S. President Calvin Coolidge signed the Indian Citizenship Act into law, granting citizenship to all Native Americans born within the territorial limits of the United States.

It was enacted partially in recognition of the thousands of Indians who served in the armed forces during World War I. The Fourteenth Amendment already defined as citizens any person born in the U.S., but only if "subject to the jurisdiction thereof." This latter clause excluded anyone who already had citizenship in a foreign power such as a tribal nation.

~~~

"Conscientious Objector"

On this day, June 2, 1969, Joseph Guy LaPointe Jr. died in Quảng Tín Province, Vietnam. LaPointe (July 2, 1948 – June 2, 1969) was a medic in the United States Army. Patrolling Hill 376 in Quảng Tín Province, his unit came under heavy fire from entrenched enemy forces and took several casualties. LaPointe, a conscientious objector, ran through heavy fire to reach two wounded men. He treated the soldiers and shielded them with his body, even after being twice wounded, until an enemy grenade killed all three men. LaPointe was posthumously awarded the Medal of Honor for his actions during the Vietnam War.

~June 3~

"Are you kidding me?"

On this day, June 3, 1940, Franz Rademacher proposed plans to make Madagascar the "Jewish homeland," an idea that had first been considered by 19th century journalist Theodor Herzl.

Rademacher, an official in the Nazi government of the Third Reich during World War II, sought to forcibly deport all of Europe's Jews to the island of Madagascar. He played office politics with Adolf Eichmann over organizational control of the plan, but as Germany's position in World War II changed the plan was dropped. In October 1941, Rademacher was responsible for mass deportations and executions of Serbian Jews. He died on March 17, 1973, while on trial in Germany for war crimes.

Theodor Herzl, for his part, was an Austro-Hungarian journalist, playwright, political activist, and writer. He was one of the fathers of modern political Zionism and grew to believe that antisemitism could not be defeated or cured, only avoided, and that the only way to avoid it was the establishment of a Jewish state. Herzl formed the World Zionist Organization and promoted Jewish migration to Madagascar, and later Palestine in an effort to form a Jewish state (Israel). The fact that his idea was twisted by Rademacher is a sad footnote in the history of Judaism and the Jewish people.

~June 4~

"We shall fight on the beaches…"

On this day, June 4, 1940, British Prime Minister Winston Churchill delivered to the House of Commons of the Parliament of the United Kingdom this speech:

Even though large tracts of Europe and many old and famous States have fallen or may fall into the grip of the Gestapo and all the odious apparatus of Nazi rule, we shall not flag or fail. We shall go on to the end. We shall fight in France, we shall fight on the seas and oceans, we shall fight with growing confidence and growing strength in the air, we shall defend our island, whatever the cost may be. We shall fight on the beaches, we shall fight on the landing grounds, we shall fight in the fields and in the streets, we shall fight in the hills; we shall never surrender, and if, which I do not for a moment believe, this island or a large part of it were subjugated and starving, then our Empire beyond the seas, armed and guarded by the British Fleet, would carry on the struggle, until, in God's good time, the New World, with all its power and might, steps forth to the rescue and the liberation of the old.

~~~

"41 Shots"

On this day, June 4, 2000, "American Skin" was released by Bruce Springsteen, inspired by the police shooting death of Amadou Diallo. Diallo was shot 41 times while standing in front of his home as he reached into his pocket to get his house keys.

~June 5~

"RFK"

On this day, June 5, 1968, presidential candidate Robert F. Kennedy was mortally wounded shortly after midnight PDT at the Ambassador Hotel in Los Angeles. Kneeling beside RFK in that iconic photograph was 17-year-old busboy Juan Romero, who was shaking Kennedy's hand when Sirhan Sirhan fired the shots.

~~~

"A Soon to be Dead Prime Minister"

On this day, June 5, 1984, the Prime Minister of India, Indira Gandhi, ordered an attack on the Harmandir Sahib, the holiest site of the Sikh religion. The Indian army, led by General Kuldip Singh Brar, brought infantry, artillery, and tanks into the Harmandir Sahib to end the Dharam Yudh Morcha led by Jarnail Singh Bhindranwale. Fierce fighting ensued between Sikhs and the army, with heavy casualties on both sides. The Harmandir Sahib complex, also known as the Golden Temple, suffered extensive damage as well, especially the holy Akal Takht. On October 31, 1984, Indira Gandhi's Sikh bodyguards killed her as revenge for the Operation Blue Star.

~~~

"Tank Man"

On this day, June 5, 1984, the morning after the Chinese military had suppressed the Tiananmen Square protests of 1989 by force, Tank Man stood in front of a column of tanks. As the lead tank maneuvered to pass by the man, he repeatedly shifted his position in order to obstruct the tank's attempted path around him. The incident was filmed and seen worldwide.

~June 6~

"The Great Seattle Fire"

On this day, June 6, 1889, at 2:39 p.m., a cabinetmaker named Jonathan Edward Back accidentally overturned and ignited a glue pot. An attempt to extinguish it with water spread the burning grease-based glue. The fire chief was out of town, and although the volunteer fire department responded, they made the mistake of trying to use too many hoses at once. With the subsequent drop in water pressure, none of the hoses were effective, and the Great Seattle Fire destroyed 31 blocks.

~~~

"Angel of Death"

On this day, June 6, 1985, the grave of "Wolfgang Gerhard" was opened in Embu, Brazil. The exhumed remains were later proven to be those of Josef Mengele, Auschwitz's "Angel of Death." Mengele is thought to have drowned while swimming in February of 1979.

~June 7~

"Homer Plessy"

On this day, June 7, 1892, Homer Plessy was arrested for refusing to leave his seat in the "whites-only" car of a train; he lost the resulting court case, *Plessy v. Ferguson.*

~~~

"The Mines at Messines"

On this day, June 7, 1917, the mines at Messines were fired at 3:10AM. The joint explosion ranks among the largest non-nuclear explosions of all time and was considered the loudest man-made noise in history. Reports suggested that the sound was heard in London and Dublin.

~~~

"James Byrd"

On this day, June 7, 1998, James Byrd died along the highway in Jasper, Texas, after being chained to the back of a pickup truck and dragged for three miles by White Supremacists Shawn Allen Berry, Lawrence Russell Brewer, and John William King. Earlier the three men had beat Byrd, urinated, and defecated on him. Forensic evidence suggests that Byrd attempted to keep his head up while being dragged; thus, Byrd was alive during the dragging. Byrd died about halfway along the route of his dragging after his right arm and head were severed when his body hit a culvert. Berry, Brewer, and King dumped the mutilated remains of the body in front of an African-American church on Huff Creek Road, then drove off to a barbecue. A motorist found Byrd's decapitated remains the following morning.

~June 8 ~

"Muhammad"

On this day, June 8, 632, the Prophet Muhammad, died in Medina and was succeeded by Abu Bakr, the first caliph of the Rashidun Caliphate. Others felt Muhammad designated Ali ibn Abi Talib as his successor and there has been violent conflict between Abu Bakr's Sunni followers and Ali's Shi'a followers ever since. Like the Catholic-Protestant wars of religion, this enmity seems to undermine the call for peace that all religions purport to preach.

~~~

"The *USS Liberty* Incident"

On this day, June 8, 1967, the *USS Liberty*, United States Navy technical research ship, was attacked by Israeli Air Force jet fighter aircraft and Israeli Navy motor torpedo boats during the Six-Day War. The combined air and sea attack killed 34 crew members (naval officers, seamen, two marines, and one civilian), wounded 171 crew members, and severely damaged the ship. At the time, the ship was in international waters north of the Sinai Peninsula, about 25.5 nautical miles northwest from the Egyptian city of Arish.

Israel apologized for the attack, saying that the *USS Liberty* had been attacked in error after being mistaken for an Egyptian ship. Both the Israeli and U.S. governments conducted inquiries and issued reports that concluded the attack was a mistake due to Israeli confusion about the ship's identity, though others, including survivors of the attack, have rejected these conclusions and maintain that the attack was deliberate.

~June 9~

"Have you no sense of decency, sir, at long last?"

On this day, June 9, 1954, Joseph Welch, special counsel for the United States Army, lashed out at Senator Joseph McCarthy during hearings on whether Communism has infiltrated the Army giving McCarthy the famous rebuke, "You've done enough. Have you no sense of decency, sir, at long last? Have you left no sense of decency?" McCarthyism ended at that moment.

~June 10~

"Lidice"

On this day, June 10, 1942, all 173 men from the village of Lidice were executed. Another 11 men who were not in the village at the time were later arrested and executed. Meanwhile, 184 women and 88 children were later deported to concentration camps; a few children considered racially suitable for Germanisation were handed over to SS families, and the rest were sent to the Chełmno extermination camp. One hundred and fifty-three women and 17 children ultimately survived and returned to Lidice.

All this was in mistaken retaliation for the assassination of SS-Obergruppenführer and General of Police Reinhard Heydrich, Acting Reichsprotektor of the Nazi Protectorate of Bohemian and Moravia. The village of Lidice, unlike the village of Lezaky which was also destroyed, and its people massacred, had nothing to do with the assassination plot.

Finally, Lidice was set on fire, and the remains of the buildings destroyed with explosives. Even those buried in the town cemetery were not spared. Their remains were dug up and destroyed.

~~~

"Patrick Magee"

On this day, June 10, 1986, Patrick Joseph Magee was found guilty of the Brighton Bombing, an attempt to assassinate the Prime Minister and her Cabinet. Magee (born 1951 in Belfast) was convicted of planting a bomb at the Grand Hotel during the Conservative Party Conference on October 12, 1984.

Magee was released from prison in 1999 under the terms of the Good Friday Agreement, having served 14 years (including the time before his sentencing).

Magee defended his role in the blast, but he has expressed remorse for the loss of innocent lives. One of the victims of the bombing was Sir Anthony Berry, whose daughter Jo Berry publicly met Magee in November 2000 in an effort at achieving reconciliation.

Harvey Thomas, a senior adviser to Thatcher who survived the bombing, forgave Magee in 1998. Thomas has since developed a friendship with Magee, including hosting him in his own home.

Norman Tebbit, whose wife was paralyzed in the Brighton bombing, has asserted that he could only forgive Magee if he went to the police and provided them with the names of anyone else who was responsible for the bombing.

~June 11~

"Thích Quảng Đức"

On this day, June 11, 1963, Buddhist monk Thích Quảng Đức burned himself alive with gasoline in a busy Saigon intersection to protest the lack of religious freedom in South Vietnam.

~June 12~

"Ronal Reagan"

On this day, June 12, 1987, Ronald Reagan spoke in front of the Brandenburg Gates and famously challenged the Soviet leader:

"Mr. Gorbachev, tear down this wall!"

~June 13~

"No Salute"

On this day, June 13, 1936, August Landmesser refused to give the Nazi salute. Landmesser was a worker at the Blohm & Voss shipyard in Hamburg, Germany, and was photographed not performing the Nazi salute at the launch of the *Horst Wessel*.

Landmesser had been a member of the Nazi Party but was expelled in 1935 when he became engaged to a Jewish woman, Irma Eckler. In July 1937, he was charged and found guilty of "dishonoring the race" under Nazi racial laws. He was later, arrested again and sentenced to the Börgermoor concentration camp.

Irma was arrested and imprisoned; she was transferred from prison to a series of concentration camps and is believed to have there. In February 1944, Landmesser was drafted into a penal battalion and was killed in action on October 17, 1944.

The Landmesser's children were initially put in an orphanage. Later, the eldest daughter, Ingrid, was permitted to live with her maternal grandmother while Irene went to the home of foster parents.

Two lives lost; two children raised parentless. Because August and Irma loved each other and because of prejudice. Just like Mildred Jeter and Richard Loving in the 1960s, and James Obergefell and John Arthur in the 2010s.

~June 14~

"Mutiny on the Bounty"

On this day, June 14, 1789, Captain William Bligh of the HMS Bounty, as well as 18 other mutiny survivors, reach Timor after a nearly 4,600 mile journey in an open boat.

~~~

"Under God"

On this day, June 14, 1954, U.S. President Dwight D. Eisenhower signed a bill into law that places the words "under God" into the United States Pledge of Allegiance.

How could two words become so divisive, so inverse as the original intention?

~June 15~

"What Could Have Been?"

On this day, June 15, 1888, Frederick III of Germany died, causing the year 1888 to be known as the Year of the Three Emperors.

Frederick's death is interesting because of Frederick III's known critique of German conservatism. British Prime Minister William Gladstone described him as the "Barbarossa of German liberalism."

As the Crown Prince, he often opposed the conservative Chancellor Otto von Bismarck, particularly in speaking out against Bismarck's policy of uniting Germany through force, and in urging that the power of the Chancellorship be curbed. Liberals in both Germany and his wife's native Britain hoped that as emperor, Frederick III would move to liberalize the German Empire.

The premature demise of Frederick III is considered a potential turning point in German history, and whether or not he would have made the Empire more liberal if he had lived longer is still debated.

~June 16~

"Ken Taylor"

On this day, June 16, 1981, U.S. President Ronald Reagan awarded the Congressional Gold Medal to Ken Taylor, Canada's former ambassador to Iran. Taylor was the first foreign citizen bestowed the honor.

Kenneth D. Taylor (October 5, 1934 – October 15, 2015) risked his life to help six Americans escape from Iran during the Iran hostage crisis by procuring Canadian passports for the Americans to deceive the Iranian Revolutionary Guard, posing as a Canadian film crew scouting locations. Before the escape, the six Americans also spent several weeks hiding in the homes of Taylor and another Canadian diplomat, John Sheardown.

~June 17~

"Jimmy Brock"

On this day, June 17, 1964, Jimmy Brock, owner of the Monson Motel in St. Augustine, Florida, poured acid in the hotel pool.   The pool was filled with African-Americans civil rights advocates who had staged a swim-in at the hotel to protest his refusal to rent rooms to African-Americans.

~~~

"Rodney King"

On this day, June 17, 2012, Rodney Glen King (April 2, 1965 – June 17, 2012) died. King was a taxi driver who became internationally known after a tape was released of him being beaten on March 3, 1991, by Los Angeles Police Department officers following a high-speed car chase. A witness, George Holliday, videotaped much of the beating from his balcony and sent the footage to local news station KTLA. The footage shows four officers surrounding King, several of them striking him repeatedly, while other officers stood by. Parts of the footage were aired around the world and raised public concern about police treatment of minorities in the United States.

208

~June 18~

"This was their finest hour"

On this day, June 18, 1940, British Prime Minister Winston Churchill delivered to the House of Commons of the Parliament of the United Kingdom this speech in the aftermath of French surrender to Germany on June 16, 1940:

....However matters may go in France or with the French Government or with another French Government, we in this island and in the British Empire will never lose our sense of comradeship with the French people. If we are now called upon to endure what they have suffered we shall emulate their courage, and if final victory rewards our toils they shall share the gains, aye. And freedom shall be restored to all. We abate nothing of our just demands—Czechs, Poles, Norwegians, Dutch, Belgians, all who have joined their causes to our own shall be restored.

What General Weygand has called the Battle of France is over ... the Battle of Britain is about to begin. Upon this battle depends the survival of Christian civilisation. Upon it depends our own British life, and the long continuity of our institutions and our Empire. The whole fury and might of the enemy must very soon be turned on us. Hitler knows that he will have to break us in this island or lose the war. If we can stand up to him, all Europe may be freed and the life of the world may move forward into broad, sunlit uplands.

But if we fail, then the whole world, including the United States, including all that we have known and cared for, will sink into the abyss of a new dark age made more sinister, and perhaps more protracted, by the lights of perverted science. Let us therefore brace ourselves to our duties, and so bear ourselves, that if the British Empire and its Commonwealth[e] last for a thousand years, men will still say, "This was their finest hour."

~~~

"Israel Dresner"

On this day, June 18, 1964, the largest mass arrest of rabbis in American history occurred at the Monson Motor Lodge in St. Augustine, Florida. It was a result of a protest organized by Martin Luther King, Jr.'s friend, Rabbi Israel Dresner of New Jersey.

~June 19~

"The Butcher of Bosnia"

On this day, June 19, 1945, Radovan Karadžić, was born in Petnijica, Montenegro. A self-identified Bosnian Serb, he was a practicing psychiatrist, the co-founder the Serb Democratic Party in Bosnia and Herzegovina, and the first President of Republika Srpska from 1992 to 1996. Both he and General Ratko Mladić are known as the "Butchers of Bosnia," and he was indicted by the ICTY for his actions during the Bosnian War. The indictment concluded there were reasonable grounds for believing he committed war crimes, including genocide against Bosniak and Croat civilians during the Bosnian War (1992–95). He was a fugitive from 1996 until July 21, 2008. He was arrested in Belgrade, brought before Belgrade's War Crimes Court, then extradited to the Netherlands when he was convicted of genocide in Srebrenica, war crimes and crimes against humanity. He was sentenced to 40 years in prison.

~~~

"You Filibustered what?"

On this day, June 19, 1964, the Civil Rights Act of 1964 was approved after surviving an 83-day filibuster in the United States Senate. One of the most opposed to the legislation, U.S. Senator Strom Thurmond of South Carolina, also had spoken for 24 hours and 18 minutes against the Civil Rights Act of 1957. That filibuster is the longest individual filibuster in history, according to U.S. Senate records. Thurmond began speaking at 8:54 p.m. on August 28, 1957, and continued until 9:12 p.m. of the following evening, reciting the Declaration of Independence, Bill of Rights, President George Washington's farewell address and other documents as well as the Washington DC telephone book.

~June 20~

"The Tennis Court Oath"

On this day, June 20, 1789, the members of the French Third Estate take the Tennis Court Oath. The Serment du Jeu de Paume stated that the newly self-declared National Assembly would "not to separate, and to reassemble wherever circumstances require, until the constitution of the kingdom is established." It is perhaps one of the bravest moments in French history. All told, 576 of the 577 members from the Third Estate took the collective oath; only Joseph Martin-Dauch, representing from Castelnaudar, did not take the Tennis Court Oath.

~~~

"Lizzie Borden"

On this day, June 20, 1893, Lizzie Borden was acquitted of the murders of her father and stepmother during her trial in Fall River, Massachusetts.

Lizzie Borden took an axe,
And gave her mother forty whacks;
When she saw what she had done,
She gave her father forty-one.

~June 21~

"Mississippi Burning"

On this day, June 21, 1964, three civil rights workers disappeared and are later found murdered. Andrew Goodman and Michael "Mickey" Schwerner from New York City, and James Chaney from Meridian, Mississippi, were working with the Freedom Summer campaign by attempting to register African Americans in Mississippi to vote. This registration effort was a part of contesting over 70 years of laws and practices that supported a systematic policy of disenfranchisement of potential black voters by several southern states that began in 1890.

The three men had traveled from Meridian, Mississippi, to the community of Longdale to talk with congregation members at a church that had been burned. The trio was thereafter arrested following a traffic stop outside Philadelphia, Mississippi, for speeding escorted to the local jail and held for a number of hours. As the three civil rights activists left town in their car, they were followed by law enforcement and others. Before leaving Neshoba County, their car was pulled over, and all three were abducted, driven to another location, and shot at close range. The three men's bodies were then transported to an earthen dam where they were buried

The murders are collectively known as the Mississippi Burning Murders and are remembered in the 1988 film *Mississippi Burning*.

~June 22~

"Perfect Game?"

On this day, June 22, 2010, MLB umpire Jim Joyce erroneously called a Cleveland Indians runner Jason Donald safe, costing Detroit Tiger Armando Galarraga a perfect game. The next day, Armando Galarraga took the line-up card out to Jim Joyce in a gesture to show his forgiveness.

~~~

"A Gay Vietnam Vet"

On this day, June 22, 1988, Leonard P. Matlovich died in West Hollywood, California. Matlovich (July 6, 1943 – June 22, 1988) was a recipient of the Purple Heart and the Bronze Star for his service in the Vietnam War. Matlovich was the first gay service member to purposely out himself to the military to fight the military ban on gays. His photograph appeared on the cover of *Time* on September 8, 1975, making him the first named, openly gay, person to appear on the cover of a U.S. newsmagazine. A Mormon, Matlovich was twice excommunicated by The Church of Jesus Christ of Latter-day Saints for homosexual acts. He was first excommunicated on October 7, 1975, in Norfolk, Virginia, and then again January 17, 1979. In 1986, Matlovich found out he had AIDS; he wrote his own epitaph and arranged to be buried at the Congressional Cemetery in Washington, D.C. His gravestone does not include his name, but says "A Gay Vietnam Veteran" and his epitaph states:

"When I was in the military, they gave me a medal for killing two men and a discharge for loving one."

~June 23~

"Martti Ahtisaari"

On this day, June 23, 1937, Martti Ahtisaari was born in Russia. Early in his life, his family immigrated to Finland. He served in the Finnish military and rose through the diplomatic ranks of Finland. He eventually served in the United Nations where he secured the independence of Namibia. After his international service, he returned to Finland and became the tenth president of Finland. While president, Ahtisaari was instrumental in the Kosovo peace process. He also guided the Finnish entry into the European Union, has encouraged full membership in NATO and has been a critic of the historical tendency of Finnlandization. All this from an immigrant, who rose up to lead the country of his choice, not the country of his birth. Ahtisaari was awarded the Nobel Peace Prize in 2008.

~~~

"Donald Hall"

On this day, June 23, 2018, Donald Hall died in Wilmot, New Hampshire. Hall was a teacher, an essayist, and an editor; Hall was also the past Poet Laurette of the United States of America. In 2002, Hall discussed death in an interview with NPR:

"I expect my immortality to cease about seven minutes after my funeral. I write as good as I can, but I've had some people tell me that they knew they were great and that they would live in literature forever. And my response is to pat them on the back and say, maybe you'll feel better tomorrow."

~June 24~

"Raphael Lemkin"

On this day, June 24, 1900, Raphael Lemkin was born in what is now Vawkavysk, Belarus. Lemkin was a lawyer of Jewish-Polish decent who coined the term "genocide" in his book *Axis Rule in Occupied Europe* (1944). The term stems from the Greek word "genos," which refers to a nation or tribe, and the Latin word "cide," which means killing. Prior to Lemkin's conceptualization, Winston Churchill described the act of genocide as a "crime without a name." Lemkin died in New York City on August 28, 1959.

~~~

"Ležáky"

On this day, June 24, 1942, 500 Schutzstaffel SS troops and policemen surrounded Ležáky, took away all the inhabitants and the village was reduced to rubble. All 33 villagers (both men and women) were shot, and 13 children were taken away into custody. In mid-December 1943, the débris of Ležáky was pulled down by 65 men from Nazi work camps. This was all in retaliation for the assassination of Reinhard Heydrich. In the investigation of the assassination, Gestapo agents found the radio transmitter in Ležáky which belonged to Alfréd Bartoš, the leader of the resistance group, "Silver A." Among the 13 children taken into custody, sisters Jarmila and Marie Šťulík were selected for the Aryanisation programme (both were later found and returned after the war). The remaining 11 children were sent to the Chełmno extermination camp and were gassed (together with one girl from Lidice) in the summer of 1942. Ležáky was not rebuilt after the war and, today, only memorials exist were the village once stood.

~June 25~

"Little Big Horn"

On this day, June 25, 1876, the Battle of the Little Bighorn was fought, ultimately leading to the death of Lieutenant Colonel George Armstrong Custer and the entire American combat forces (Comanche, Custer's horse ironically survived).

The battle pitted the combined forces of the Lakota, Northern Cheyenne, and Arapaho tribes, against the 7th Cavalry Regiment of the United States Army. Opposing the US commander were an array of prominent Native American leaders including Crazy Horse, Chief Gall, Sitting Bull, Lame White Man, and Two Moon.

The Battle of the Little Bighorn is considered by many to be the greatest Native American military success against the US Armed Forces. However, the battle is also believed by some to be the motivation for the US massacre of Native Americans at Wounded Knee by the reconstituted 7th Cavalry.

~~~

"The Mormon Extermination Order"

On this day, June 25, 1976, Missouri Governor Kit Bond issued an executive order rescinding the Extermination Order, formally apologizing to The Church of Jesus Christ of Latter-day Saints. The Extermination Order, also known Missouri Executive Order 44, was an executive order issued on October 27, 1838, by the territorial governor of Missouri, Lilburn Boggs.

~June 26~

"Our Himmler"

On this day, June 26, 1953, Lavrentiy Beria was arrested and held in an undisclosed location near Moscow. He was personally responsible for war crimes and crimes against humanity. His arrest, trial, and execution in a merely politically motivated show-trial was a loss to the international community and to his victims. Stalin even famously introduced him to U.S. President Franklin D. Roosevelt as "our Himmler." Beria was particularly responsible for the expansion of the Gulag labor camps and the Circassian Genocide as well as the Katyn massacre. Sadly, this is not all on his resume: Beria also oversaw the genocidal acts against and the forced internal displacement of the Chechens, the Ingush, the Crimean Tatars, the Pontic Greeks and the Volga Germans. In 2003, the Soviet archives were opened; Simon Sebag-Montefiore, a biographer of Stalin, concluded the information "reveals a sexual predator who used his power to indulge himself in obsessive depravity." Some women were randomly identified while Beria was trolling the streets in his limousine.

~~~

"Berliner"

On this day, June 26, 1963, U.S. President John F. Kennedy visited West Berlin. Speaking on the steps of Rathaus Schöneberg before an audience of 450,000, Kennedy declared:

"Ich bin ein Berliner"

~~~

"The Pope Asks for Forgiveness"

On this day, June 26, 2016, Pope Francis said Christians and the Roman Catholic Church should seek forgiveness from homosexuals for the way they had treated them. He also said the Church should ask forgiveness for the way it has treated women, for turning a blind eye to child labor and for "blessing so many weapons" in the past. (See also July 23rd.)

~June 27~

"Thomas Dorr"

On this day, June 27, 1844, Thomas Wilson Dorr was committed to solitary confinement at hard labor for life. Dorr had been tried for treason against Rhode Island in Newport, a conservative stronghold, before the Rhode Island Supreme Court; he was convicted and sentenced. Dorr (November 5, 1805 – December 27, 1854) was an American politician and reformer in Rhode Island, best known for leading the Dorr Rebellion, an effort to broaden the franchise in the state for white males and to change apportionment in the legislature for better representation of urban populations.

In her celebrated 1873 stump speech in Monroe County, New York, suffragist Susan B. Anthony mocked Rhode Island's history of limiting enfranchisement by saying:

"If we once establish the false principle that United States citizenship does not carry with it the right to vote in every state in this Union, there is no end to the petty freaks and cunning devices that will be resorted to exclude one and another class of citizens from suffrage. It will not always be men combining to disfranchise all women; native born men combining to abridge the rights of all naturalised citizens, as in Rhode Island."

~~~

"Jack Lemmon"

On this day, June 27, 2001, comedian and actor Jack Lemmon died in Los Angeles, California. His epitaph reads simply and humorously:

"In"

~June 28~

"Franz Ferdinand"

On this day, June 28, 1914, the heir presumptive to the Austro-Hungarian throne, Archduke Franz Ferdinand of Austria, and his wife Sophie, Duchess of Hohenberg, were assassinated in Sarajevo by Bosnia Serb nationalist Gavrilo Princip, the *casus belli* of World War I.

~~~

"Slobodan Milošević"

On this day, June 28, 2001, Slobodan Milošević was deported from Serbia to the ICTY. He was the first former Head of State put on trial by the international community for war crimes, though he was technically acquitted by his death during the trials. Regardless, it was an important precedent in international law. The later trial of Charles Taylor and the indictment of Omar al-Bashir are direct results of this precedent.

~June 29~

"The Pardoning of John Gordon"

On this day, June 29, 2011, Rhode Island Governor Lincoln Chafee pardoned John Gordon on June 29, 2011, following passage of legislation by the state's General Assembly urging such action. The legislation was sponsored in the House of Representatives by Peter F. Martin and in the Senate by Michael McCaffrey. Chafee signed the proclamation of pardon at the Old State House, where Gordon's trial had taken place more than 150 years before. John Gordon (died February 14, 1845) was the last person executed by Rhode Island. His conviction and execution have been ascribed by researchers to anti-Roman Catholic and anti-Irish immigrant bias. In September 2014, Enda Kenny, the Taoiseach of Ireland, visited the Rhode Island Irish Famine Memorial and in a speech praised Chafee for pardoning Gordon.

~June 30~

"The Night of Long Knives"

On this day, June 30, 1934, the Night of the Long Knives, Adolf Hitler's violent purge of his political rivals, occurred in Germany.

Operation Hummingbird or, in Germany, the Röhm Putsch, eliminated Gregor Strasser and his leftist Strasserist wing of the Nazi Party, as well as prominent German conservatives including former Chancellor Kurt von Schleicher and Gustav Ritter von Kahr (who had suppressed Hitler's Beer Hall Putsch in 1923). In addition, Hitler turned on his own supporters and eliminated the Brownshirts (SA) and its leader, Ernst Röhm, effectively replacing them with the Blackshirts (SS).

At least 85 people died during the purge, although the final death toll may have been in the hundreds, and more than a thousand perceived opponents were arrested. Most of the killings were carried out by the Schutzstaffel (SS) and the Gestapo (Geheime Staatspolizei), the regime's secret police.

~~~

"Peter Rometti"

On this day, June 30, 2007, Peter Rometti sang the National Anthem at Fenway Park in Boston, Massachusetts, during Disability Awareness Day. Rometti had autism, and halfway through, he started to struggle… stammering, laughing nervously, and losing some of the words. 38,000 Red Sox fans responded and carried Rometti through the remainder of the *Star-Spangled Banner*.

Two thousand years ago, the proudest boast was *civis romanus sum* ["I am a Roman citizen"]. Today, in the world of freedom, the proudest boast is "Ich bin ein Berliner!" ...All free men, wherever they may live, are citizens of Berlin, and therefore, as a free man, I take pride in the words "Ich bin ein Berliner!"

~JFK~

June 26, 1963

~July 1~

"Moctezuma II"

On this day, July 1, 1520, Moctezuma II died under disputed circumstances. Moctezuma appeared on the balcony of his palace, ordering rebel Aztecs army to disperse. Four leaders of the Aztec army met with Moctezuma to talk, while the others to cease their paused their attack.

The historian Bernal Díaz wrote: "Many of the Mexican Chieftains and Captains knew him well and at once ordered their people to be silent and not to discharge darts, stones or arrows, and four of them reached a spot where Montezuma could speak to them." The Aztecs told Moctezuma that another had been recognized as the new King of the Aztecs and had ordered them to attack until all of the Spanish were annihilated but expressed remorse at Moctezuma's captivity and stated that they intended to revere him even more if they could rescue him.

Regardless of the earlier orders to hold fire, however, the discussion between Moctezuma and the Aztec leaders was immediately followed by an outbreak of violence. Díaz continued: "They had hardly finished this speech when suddenly such a shower of stones and darts were discharged that (our men who were shielding him having neglected for a moment their duty, because they saw how the attack ceased while he spoke to them) he was hit by three stones, one on the head, another on the arm and another on the leg, and although they begged him to have the wounds dressed and to take food, and spoke kind words to him about it, he would not. Indeed, when we least expected it, they came to say that he was dead." Cortés similarly reported that Moctezuma was stabbed by his countrymen. On the other hand, the indigenous accounts claim that he was killed by the Spanish prior to their leaving the city.

~~~

"Nicholas Winton"

On this day, July 1, 2015, Sir Nicholas Winton died at Wexham Park Hospital, Slough, United Kingdom. Winton was a British humanitarian who organized the rescue of 669 children, most of them Jewish, from Czechoslovakia on the eve of the Second World War in an operation later known as the Czech *Kindertransport.*

~~~

"Clarence Thomas"

On this day, July 1, 1991, George H. W. Bush nominated Clarence Thomas to fill the seat of retiring Associate Justice Thurgood Marshall on the United States Supreme Court. Clarence Thomas (born June 23, 1948) grew up in Savannah, Georgia, and was educated at the College of the Holy Cross and at Yale Law School. In 1974, he was appointed an Assistant Attorney General in Missouri and subsequently practiced law there in the private sector. In 1979, he became a legislative assistant to Senator John Danforth (R-MO) and in 1981 was appointed Assistant Secretary for Civil Rights at the U.S. Department of Education. In 1982, President Ronald Reagan appointed Thomas Chairman of the Equal Employment Opportunity Commission. In 1990, President George H. W. Bush nominated Thomas for a seat on the United States Court of Appeals for the District of Columbia Circuit, until nominated to the Supreme Court. Thomas's confirmation hearings were bitter and intensely fought, centering on an accusation that he had sexually harassed attorney Anita Hill, a subordinate at the DoE and subsequently at the EEOC. The Democratic-controlled U.S. Senate ultimately confirmed Thomas by a vote of 52–48.

~July 2~

"Adam Bevell"

On this day, July 2, 2016, Bono invited Adam Bevell onto the stage to jam with U2 during their U2 360 tour concert in Nashville, Tennessee. Adam Bevell's brother-in-law had sketched out the small sign for him right there in the stadium and Adam held it over his head for the entire concert "BLIND GUITAR PLAYER. Bring me up." at the end of the concert Adam's wish was granted. The crowd hoisted him up on stage at the band's request, and Bono took his hand to lead him over to a guitar." The guitar was strapped onto him, and Adam chose to play his and his wife's wedding song, "All I Want Is You," while Bono sang along.

~~~

"Elie Wiesel"

On this day, July 2, 2016, Elie Wiesel אליעזר ויזל died in New York, New York. Wiesel (September 30, 1928 – July 2, 2016) was a writer, professor, and political activist. He was the author of 57 books, including *Night*, a work based on his experiences as a prisoner in the Auschwitz and Buchenwald concentration camps. Wiesel was involved with Jewish causes and helped establish the United States Holocaust Memorial Museum in Washington, D.C. In his political activities, he also campaigned for victims of oppression in places like South Africa, Nicaragua and Sudan. He was outspoken against the Darfur Genocide and silence surrounding the silence surrounding the Armenian and Darfur genocides. The *L.A. Times* called him "the most important Jew in America." In 1986, Wiesel was awarded the Nobel Peace Prize at which time the Norwegian Nobel Committee called him a "messenger to mankind."

~July 3~

"The Battle of Lower Falls"

On this day, July 3, 1970, the Falls Curfew, also called the Battle of the Falls (or Lower Falls) began in the Falls district of Belfast, Northern Ireland.

The operation began as a search for weapons in the staunchly Irish nationalist district. As the search ended, local youths attacked the British soldiers with stones, and petrol bombs and the soldiers responded with CS gas. This quickly developed into gun battles between British soldiers and the Official Irish Republican Army (as opposed to the Provisional Irish Republican Army).

After four hours of continuous clashes, the British commander sealed off the area—comprising 3,000 homes—and imposed a curfew which would last for 36 hours. Thousands of British troops moved into the curfew zone and carried out house-to-house searches for weapons while coming under intermittent attack from the IRA and rioters. The searches caused much destruction, and a large amount of CS gas was fired into the area. Many residents complained of suffering abuse at the hands of the soldiers.

On July 5th, the curfew was ended when thousands of women and children from Andersonstown marched into the curfew zone with food and groceries for the locals.

~July 4~

"The Luckiest Man"

On this day, July 4, 1939, Henry Louis Gehrig (born Heinrich Ludwig Gehrig) delivered what has been called "baseball's Gettysburg Address" to a sold-out crowd at Yankee Stadium:

For the past two weeks you've been reading about a bad break. (pause) Today I consider myself the luckiest man on the face of the earth. (cut) When you look around, wouldn't you consider it a privilege to associate yourself with such fine-looking men as are standing in uniform in this ballpark today? (cut) ... that I might have been given a bad break, but I've got an awful lot to live for. Thank you.

Gehrig (June 19, 1903 – June 2, 1941) died less than two years later in Riverdale, Bronx, New York City, New York, U.S.A.

~~~

"Born of the 4th of July"

On this day, July 4, 1946, Ronald Kovic was born in Ladysmith, Wisconsin. Kovic is an anti-war activist, writer, and veteran who was wounded paralyzed in the Vietnam War. He attended his first peace demonstration soon after the Kent State shootings in May 1970 and gave his first speech against the war at Levittown Memorial High School in Levittown, NY. By the end of the war, Kovic had become one of the best-known peace activists among the Vietnam veterans.

Kovic is best known as the author of the memoir *Born on the Fourth of July* in 1976, which was made into an Academy Award–winning film.

In March 2005, Kovic wrote:

"I wanted people to understand. I wanted to share with them as nakedly and openly and intimately as possible what I had gone through, what I had endured. I wanted them to know what it really meant to be in a war, to be shot and wounded, to be fighting for my life on the intensive care ward, not the myth we had grown up believing. I wanted people to know about the hospitals and the enema room, about why I had become opposed to the war, why I had grown more committed to peace and nonviolence. I had been beaten by the police and arrested twelve times for protesting the war, and I had spent many nights in jail in my wheelchair. I had been called a Communist and a traitor, simply for trying to tell the truth about what had happened in that war, but I refused to be intimidated...

The scar will always be there, a living reminder of that war, but it has also become something beautiful now, something of faith and hope and love. I have been given the opportunity to move through that dark night of the soul to a new shore, to gain an understanding, a knowledge, and entirely different vision. I now believe I have suffered for a reason and in many ways, I have found that reason in my commitment to peace and nonviolence.

My life has been a blessing in disguise, even with the pain and great difficulty that my physical disability continues to bring. It is a blessing to speak on behalf of peace, to be able to reach such a great number of people."

~July 5~

"Justice?"

On this day, July 5, 2010, Jorge Rafael Videla took full responsibility for his army's actions during his rule. "I accept the responsibility as the highest military authority during the internal war. My subordinates followed my orders," he told an Argentine court. Videla also sheltered many Nazi fugitives along with Juan Perón, Alfredo Stroessner of Paraguay and Hugo Banzer of Bolivia. He was under house arrest until October 10, 2008.

Jorge Rafael Videla was, a senior commander in the Argentine Army and President of Argentina from 1976 to 1981. He came to power in a coup d'état that deposed Isabel Martínez de Perón. Two years after the return of a representative democratic government in 1983, he was prosecuted in the Trial of the Juntas for large-scale human rights abuses and crimes against humanity that took place under his rule, including kidnappings or forced disappearance, widespread torture and extrajudicial murder of activists, and political opponents as well as their families at secret concentration camps. An estimated 13,000-30,000 political dissidents vanished during this period. Videla was also convicted of the theft of many babies born during the captivity of their mothers at the illegal detention centers and passing them on for illegal adoption by associates of the regime. In his defense, Videla maintains the female guerrilla detainees allowed themselves to fall pregnant in the belief they wouldn't be tortured or executed. Following a new trial, on December 22, 2010, Videla was sentenced to life in a civilian prison for the deaths of 31 prisoners following his coup. On July 5, 2012, Videla was sentenced to 50 years in prison for the systematic kidnapping of children during his tenure. The following year, Videla died in the Marcos Paz prison, Marcos Paz, Buenos Aires, Argentina, after suffering a fall in the shower.

~July 6~

"The Dalai Lama"

On this day, July 6, 1935, Lhamo Thondup was born in Taktser, Amdo, Tibet. In 1937, he was recognized as the tulku of the 13th Dalai Lama, formally recognized as the 14th Dalai Lama, and changed his name to Tenzin Gyatso. During the Tibetan Uprising of 1959, the Dalai Lama fled to India, where he still currently lives as a refugee. He has traveled the world and has spoken about the welfare of Tibetans, the environment, women's rights, non-violence, interfaith dialogue, Buddhism and science, cognitive neuroscience, health, and sexuality, along with various Mahayana and Vajrayana topics. The Dalai Lama received the Nobel Peace Prize in 1989.

~~~

"Jackie Robinson"

On this day, July 6, 1944, Second Lieutenant Jackie Robinson, who became the first African-American to play in Major League Baseball in the modern era, refused to move to the back of a bus and was court-martialed. (See also October 30th.)

~~~

"Louis Armstrong"

On this day, July 6, 1971, Louis Armstrong died in Corona, New York City, New York. While a well-known musician as he grew older, as a child, Armstrong worked for a Lithuanian-Jewish immigrant family, the Karnofskys, who had a junk-hauling business and gave him odd jobs. The family took him in and treated him like family; knowing he lived without a father, they fed and nurtured him. He later wrote a memoir of his relationship with the Karnofskys, *Louis Armstrong + the Jewish Family in New Orleans*. In it, he described his discovery that this family was also subject to discrimination by "other white folks" who felt that they were better than Jews: "I was only seven years old, but I could easily see the ungodly treatment that the White Folks were handing the poor Jewish family whom I worked for." For the rest of his life, Armstrong wore a Star of David pendant for the Farnofskys. The influence of Karnofsky is remembered in New Orleans by the Karnofsky Project, a nonprofit organization dedicated to accepting donated musical instruments to "put them into the hands of an eager child who could not otherwise take part in a wonderful learning experience."

~~~

"The Srebrenica Massacre"

On this day, July 6, 1995, General Ratko Mladić and Serbian forces began the attack on the Bosnian town of Srebrenica. The subsequent Srebrenica Massacre is one of the deadliest events of the Bosnian Genocide.

~July 7~

"Samantha Smith"

On this day, July 7, 1983, Samantha Reed Smith, a U.S. schoolgirl, flew to the Soviet Union at the invitation of Secretary General Yuri Andropov.

Smith (June 29, 1972 – August 25, 1985) was an American schoolgirl, peace activist and child actress from Manchester, Maine, who became famous in the Cold War Era between the United States and the Soviet Union. In 1982, Smith wrote a letter to the newly appointed CPSU General Secretary Yuri Andropov and received a personal reply with a personal invitation to visit the Soviet Union, which she accepted. Smith attracted extensive media attention in both countries as a "Goodwill Ambassador" and became known as "America's Youngest Ambassador."

~ July 8 ~

"The Grandest Instrument of Human Liberty Ever Constructed"

On this day, July 8, 1663, Charles II of England granted John Clarke a Royal Charter to Rhode Island. Though founded in 1636, the colonists of Rhode Island sought legal protection in the form of a royal charter after the chaos of the English Civil War (1642–1651), The Interregnum (1649-1660), The Restoration of 1660, and increasing centralization policies of Charles II.

The Royal Charter of Rhode Island, written by John Clarke and signed by Charles II, gave official recognition to the Colony of Rhode Island and the Providence Plantations. It codified the two tenets that marked the remarkableness of the RI experiment: the recognition that the Native Americans were the rightful owners of the land and the extensive protection for the freedom of religion. Educator and historian Thomas Bicknell described the charter as "the grandest instrument of human liberty ever constructed."

~~~

"Brother Álvaro"

On this day, July 8, 1942, Brother Álvaro Rodríguez Echeverria was born in San José de Costa Rica. After his studies, Brother Alvaro was sent to Mexico where he continued his university studies while helping in the Mexico novitiate. For the next 25 years of his life, he worked in Guatemala and Nicaragua during the tumultuous period of the 1970's and 1980's. He was a teacher, Director, Auxiliary Visitor and Visitor of the District of Central America, comprising Costa Rica, Guatemala, Honduras, Nicaragua, and Panama. He was the 26th Superior General of the Institute of the Brothers of the Christian Schools.

~July 9~

"U.S. Chief Justice Earl Warren"

On this day July 9, 1974, Earl Warren died in Washington, DC. Warren was an American jurist and politician, as well as the 14th Chief Justice of the United States. He is best known for the decisions of the so-called Warren Court, which outlawed segregation in public schools and transformed many areas of American law, especially regarding the rights of the accused, ending public school-sponsored prayers, and requiring one man—one vote rules of apportionment of election districts.

Warren made the Supreme Court a power center on a more equal basis with Congress and the Presidency, especially through four landmark decisions: *Brown v. Board of Education* (1954), *Gideon v. Wainwright* (1963), *Reynolds v. Sims* (1964), and *Miranda v. Arizona* (1966).

~July 10~

"12 Years a Slave"

On this day, July 10, 1807, Solomon Northup was born in Minerva, New York. Northup (July 10, 1807/1808 – c.1863) was an American abolitionist and the primary author of the memoir *Twelve Years a Slave*. A free-born African American from New York, he was the son of a freed slave and free woman of color. A farmer and professional violinist, Northup had been a landowner in Hebron, New York.

In 1841, he was offered a traveling musician's job and went to Washington, D.C. (where slavery was legal); there he was drugged, kidnapped, and sold as a slave. He was shipped to New Orleans, purchased by a planter, and held as a slave for 12 years in the Red River region of Louisiana, mostly in Avoyelles Parish.

He remained in slavery until he met a Canadian working on his plantation who helped get word to New York, where state law provided aid to free New York citizens kidnapped into slavery. Family and friends enlisted the aid of the Governor of New York, Washington Hunt, and Northup regained his freedom on January 3, 1853.

~~~

"The Man of a Thousand Voices"

On this day, July 10, 1989, Melvin Jerome Blanc died in Los Angeles, California. Blanc (May 30, 1908 – July 10, 1989) was an American voice actor, comedian, singer, radio personality, and recording artist of Russian-Jewish descent.

After beginning his career in radio, Blanc became even more well-known for his work in animation as the voices of Bugs Bunny, Daffy Duck, Porky Pig, Tweety Bird, Sylvester the Cat, Yosemite Sam, Foghorn Leghorn, Marvin the Martian, Pepé Le Pew, Speedy Gonzales, Wile E. Coyote, Road Runner, the Tasmanian Devil and many of the other characters from the Looney Tunes and Merrie Melodies theatrical cartoons during the Golden Age of American animation. He voiced all of the major male Warner Brother cartoon characters except for Elmer Fudd, whose voice was provided by Arthur Q. Bryan, but after Bryan's death, Blanc later voiced Fudd as well. His epitaph states:

"That's all folks!"

238

~July 11~

"Shoes on the Danube Bank"

On this day, July 11, 1898, Miklós Voglhut (also known as Miklós Vig) was born in Budapest, Hungary. He was a successful actor and comedian but had his greatest success as a cabaret singer. In 1924, he changed his surname to Vig because, as a Jewish-Hungarian, he was aware of increasing antisemitism. On December 19, 1944, Miklós Vig was murdered by members of the Hungarian fascist Arrow Cross Party.

The Execution of Miklós Vig, as well as the murder of so many other Jewish-Hungarians, is remembered in Shoes on the Danube Bank in Budapest, Hungary. Can Togay and Gyula Pauer created the memorial to honor the victims who were ordered to take off their shoes and were shot at the edge of the water so that their bodies fell into the river and were carried away by the Danube River.

~July 12~

"Malala"

On this day, July 12, 1997, Malala Yousafzai ملاله يوسفزئی ملاله يوسفزی was born in Mingora, Swat, Pakistan. Yousafzai (July 12, 1997) is a Pakistani activist for female education and the youngest-ever Nobel Prize laureate. She is known for human rights advocacy, especially the education of women in her native Swat Valley in Khyber Pakhtunkhwa, northwest Pakistan, where the local Taliban had at times banned girls from attending school. Her advocacy has since grown into an international movement.

~July 13~

"To Be King?"

On this day, July 13, 2000, Seretse Goitsebeng Maphiri Khama died in Gaborone, Botswana. Khama (July 1, 1921 – July 13, 1980) was the first President of Botswana, in office from 1966 to 1980. He was the son of Queen Tebogo and Sekgoma Khama II, the paramount chief of the Bamangwato people, and the grandson of Khama III, their king. The name "Seretse" means "the clay that binds." He was named this to celebrate the recent reconciliation of his father and grandfather; this reconciliation assured Seretse's own ascension to the throne with his aged father's death in 1925. At the age of 4, Seretse became kgosi (king), with his uncle Tshekedi Khama as his regent.

The international ramifications of his marriage were not, however, so easily resolved. Having banned interracial marriage under the apartheid system, South Africa's government opposed having an interracial couple ruling just across their northern border. As Bechuanaland was then a British protectorate (not a colony), the South African government immediately exerted pressure on the UK to have Khama removed from his chieftainship. Britain's Labour government, then heavily in debt from World War II, could not afford to lose cheap South African gold and uranium supplies.

The British government conducted an inquiry into Khama's fitness for the chieftainship. Although the investigation reported that he was eminently fit to rule the Bamangwato, "but for his unfortunate marriage," the government ordered that the report be suppressed (for thirty years).

Britain exiled Khama and his wife from Bechuanaland in 1951. Various groups protested against the government decision, holding it up as evidence of British racism. In Britain, there was wide anger at the decision and calls for the resignation of Lord Salisbury, the minister responsible. A deputation Bamangwato traveled to London to protest against the decision, but with no success. However, when ordered by the British High Commission to replace Khama, the people refused to comply.

In 1956, both Khama and his wife were allowed to return to Bechuanaland as private citizens, after he had renounced the tribal throne. Khama began an unsuccessful stint as a cattle rancher. He became involved in local politics, being elected to the tribal council in 1957 and in 1961, Khama founded the nationalist Bechuanaland Democratic Party. His exile gave him increased credibility with an independence-minded electorate, and the BDP swept aside its Socialist and Pan-Africanist rivals to dominate the 1965 elections. As Prime Minister of Bechuanaland, Khama continued to push for Botswana's independence. The 1965 Constitution created a new Botswana government, and on 30 September 30, 1966, Botswana gained its independence and Khama became President.

At the time of its independence in 1966, Botswana was the world's third-poorest country in the world. It had no infrastructure only 22 citizens were university graduates and only a 100 secondary school graduates. Khama set out on a vigorous economic program intended to transform the nation into an export-based economy, built around beef, copper, and diamonds.

Khama instituted strong measures against corruption, the bane of so many other newly independent African nations. Unlike other countries in Africa, his administration adopted market-friendly policies to foster economic development. Khama promised low and stable taxes to mining companies, liberalized trade, and increased personal freedoms. He upheld liberal democracy and non-racism. Between 1966 and 1980 Botswana had the fastest-growing economy in the world. By the mid-1970s, Botswana had a budget surplus. The government used these revenues to heavily invest in the expansion of infrastructure, health care, and the education system, resulting in further economic development.

~July 14~

"Serra"

On this day, July 14, 1771, the Mission San Antonio de Padua in modern California was established by the Franciscan friar Junípero Serra. Serra was beatified by Pope John Paul II on September 25, 1988, and Pope Francis expects to canonize him in September 2015 during his first visit to the United States. This was understandable controversial with some Native Americans who criticize Serra's treatment of their ancestors and associate him with the suppression of their culture.

Pope Francis, I have but one question for you, "Why?"

~~~

"Jane Goodall"

On this day, July 14, 1960, Jane Goodall arrives at the Gombe Stream Reserve in present-day Tanzania to begin her famous study of chimpanzees in the wild. Jane Morris Goodall (b. April 3, 1934), is a British primatologist, ethologist, anthropologist, and UN Messenger of Peace. Considered to be the world's foremost expert on chimpanzees, Goodall is best known for her over a 55-year study of social and family interactions of wild chimpanzees. She is the founder of the Jane Goodall Institute and the Roots & Shoots program, and she has worked extensively on conservation and animal welfare issues. She has served on the board of the Nonhuman Rights Project since its founding in 1996.

~July 15~

"It's the Inquisition!"

On this day, July 15, 1834, the Spanish Inquisition was officially disbanded after nearly 356 years. When Ferdinand VII of Spain died on September 29, 1833, Queen-consort Maria Christina became regent for their daughter Isabella II. However, Isabella's claim to the throne was disputed by her uncle, the Infante Carlos, Count of Molina, who claimed that his brother Ferdinand had unlawfully changed the succession law to permit females to inherit the crown. Carlos' attempt to seize power resulted in the Carlist Wars. Despite considerable support for Carlos from the Roman Catholic Church and conservative elements in Spain, Maria Christina successfully retained the throne for her daughter. The supporters of Maria Christina and her daughter favored a liberal constitution and progressive social policies. It was Maria Christina, in the name of her daughter Isabella II, that disbanded the horrific Spanish Inquisition.

Apparently, the Inquisition is more than a dance routine by Mel Brooks in his film, *The History of the World, Part I* (2001).

~July 16~

"Henryk Sławik"

On this day, July 16, 1894, Henryk Sławik was born in Szeroka, Jastrzębie-Zdrój, Poland. Sławik (July 16, 1894 – August 23, 1944) was a Polish politician, social worker, activist, and diplomat, who during World War II helped save over 30,000 Polish refugees, including 5,000 Polish Jews in Budapest, Hungary by giving them false Polish passports with Catholic designation. Sławik was arrested by the Germans on March 19, 1944. He was brutally tortured and executed with some of his fellow Polish activists at concentration camp Gusen on August 23, 1944, under the orders of the Reichsführer.

~~~

"Operation Spring Breeze"

On this day, July 16, 1942, the Nazi government of occupied France directed raid and mass arrest of Jews in Paris by the French police, code named Opération Vent Printanier. The roundup was one of several aimed at eradicating the Jewish population in France. According to records of the Préfecture de Police, 13,152 Jews were arrested, including more than 4,000 children. They were held at the Vélodrome d'Hiver in extremely crowded conditions, almost without water, food, and no sanitary facilities, as well as at the Drancy, Pithiviers, and Beaune-la-Rolande internment camps, then shipped in rail cattle cars to Auschwitz for their mass murder. French President Jacques Chirac apologized in 1995 for the complicit role that French policemen and civil servants served in the raid.

~July 17~

"The American Schindler"

On this day, July 17, 1903, Hiram "Harry" Bingham IV was born in Connecticut, United States of America. Bingham (July 17, 1903 – January 12, 1988) was an American diplomat and served as a Vice Consul in Marseilles, France, during World War II. Along with Varian Fry, Bingham helped over 2,500 Jews to flee from France as Nazi forces advanced.

~~~

"I can't breathe"

On this day, July 17, 2014, NYPD officers approached Eric Garner on suspicion of selling single cigarettes from packs without tax stamps. Garner told the officers that he was not selling cigarettes and was that he was tired of being harassed.

The officers attempted to arrest Garner. When officer Daniel Pantaleo tried to take Garner's wrist behind his back, Garner pulled his arms away. Pantaleo then put his arm around Garner's neck and took him down onto the ground. After Pantaleo removed his arm from Garner's neck, he pushed the side of Garner's face into the ground while four officers moved to restrain Garner, who repeated "I can't breathe" eleven times while lying face down on the sidewalk.

Eric Garner died in Staten Island, New York City after a New York City Police Department (NYPD) officer put him in a headlock for about 15 to 19 seconds while arresting him.

NYPD policy prohibits the use of chokeholds. While the officer denied choking Garner, the New York City Medical Examiner's Office report stated, "Cause of Death: Compression of the neck, compression of chest and prone positioning during physical restraint by police" and "Contributing Conditions: "Acute and chronic bronchial asthma; Obesity; Hypertensive cardiovascular disease."

248

~July 18~

"Gino"

On this day, July 18, 1914, Gino Bartali was born in Ponte a Ema, Italy. A World Champion cyclist, Bartali has been recognized as a "Righteous Among the Nations" for his efforts to save Jews in WWII. (See May 5th.)

~~~

"Mandela"

On this day, July 18, 1918, Nelson Rolihlahla Mandela was born in Mvezo, Cape Province, Union of South Africa.

Mandela (July 18, 1918 – December 5, 2013) was a South African anti-apartheid revolutionary. Although imprisoned for fighting apartheid, he was released and served as President of South Africa from 1994 to 1999.

He was the country's first Sub-Saharan black head of state and the first elected in a fully representative democratic election. His government focused on dismantling the legacy of apartheid by tackling institutionalized racism and fostering racial reconciliation; for example, former apartheid President F.W. de Klerk served as Mandela's Deputy President. Mandela made a significant contribution to peace in South Africa, seeking to forgive and work with the former political powerful white minority. Mandela became a global symbol of goodwill and how people can make a real contribution to peace.

~~~

"The Korbel Effect"

On this day, July 18, 1977, Josef Korbel died in Denver, Colorado, USA. Korbel (September 20, 1909 – July 18, 1977) was a Czech-American diplomat and political scientist of Jewish descent. He served as Czechoslovakia's ambassador to Yugoslavia, the chair of the United Nations Commission for India and Pakistan, and then as a professor of international politics at the University of Denver, where he founded the Josef Korbel School of International Studies. His daughter Madeleine Albright served as Secretary of State under President Bill Clinton, and he was the mentor of George W. Bush's Secretary of State, Condoleezza Rice. After his death, the University of Denver established the Josef Korbel Humanitarian Award in 2000. Since then, 28 people have received it.

~~~

"The Elders"

On this day, July 18, 2007, Nelson Mandela, Graça Machel, and Tutu convened The Elders, a group of world leaders to contribute their wisdom, kindness, leadership, and integrity to tackle some of the world's toughest problems. Mandela said, "This group can speak freely and boldly... to support courage where there is fear, foster agreement where there is conflict, and inspire hope where there is despair."

~July 19~

"The Portuguese Schindler"

On this day, July 19, 1885, Aristides de Sousa Mendes do Amaral e Abranches was born in Cabanas de Viriato, Viseu District, Portugal. Sousa Mendes (July 19, 1885 – April 3, 1954) was a Portuguese consul during World War II.

As the Portuguese consul-general in the French city of Bordeaux, he defied the orders of António de Oliveira Salazar's Estado Novo regime, issuing visas and passports to an undetermined number of refugees fleeing Nazi Germany, including Jews. For this, Sousa Mendes was punished by the Salazar regime with one year's suspension on half-pay, but afterwards, he kept on receiving his full consul salary until his death in 1954. Sousa Mendes was vindicated in 1988, more than a decade after the Carnation Revolution that toppled the Estado Novo.

For his efforts to save Jewish refugees, Sousa Mendes was recognized by Israel as one of the Righteous Among the Nations, the first diplomat to be so honored, in 1966.

~July 20~

"Claus von Staffenberg"

On this day, July 20, 1944, German Army Colonel Claus von Stauffenberg attempted to assassinate Adolf Hitler.

~~~

"Apollo 11"

On this day, July 20, 1969, Neil Armstrong and Buzz Aldrin landed the lunar module *Eagle* on the Moon at 20:18 UTC. Armstrong was the first human to step onto the lunar surface six hours after landing on July 21 at 02:56:15 UTC; Aldrin joined him about 20 minutes later. The two American astronauts spent about two and a quarter hours together outside the spacecraft and collected 47.5 pounds of lunar material to bring back to Earth. Michael Collins piloted the command module *Columbia* alone in lunar orbit while the Armstrong and Aldrin were on the Moon's surface. Armstrong and Aldrin spent a total of 21.5 hours on the lunar surface before rejoining *Columbia* in lunar orbit.

~July 21~

"Pirate Walter Kennedy"

On this day, July 21, 1721, Walter Kennedy was executed at Execution Dock, Wapping, England. Walter Kennedy (ca. 1695 - July 21, 1721) was an English pirate who served as a crew member under Howell Davis and Bartholomew Roberts. Kennedy was a mate on the sloop-of-war *Buck* when the crew, including Kennedy, mutinied. Later when Captain Roberts was on the *Buck*, Kennedy took command of Roberts' ship, *Royal Rover*, and proclaim himself captain. Under his leadership, the crew decided to give up piracy and to set sail for Ireland. Though his original destination was Ireland, Kennedy's poor navigation skills led them to land on the north-west coast of Scotland. The crew was suspected of piracy, Kennedy slipped away and reached Ireland. Having soon spent all his ill-gotten gains in Dublin, he went to Deptford and managed a brothel. When one of his prostitutes accused him of theft, Kenney was sent to Bridewell Prison, where he was denounced as a pirate by the mate of a ship he had taken. Kennedy was transferred to the Marshalsea prison and put on trial for piracy. Finally, Walter Kennedy was hanged at Execution Dock on July 21, 1721, amid a rather long-winded speech.

~~~

"Albert Lutuli"

On this day, July 21, 1967, Albert John Lutuli died in Stanger, KwaZulu-Natal, South Africa. Lutuli (c. 1898 – July 21, 1967), was a South African teacher, activist, and politician. He was awarded the 1960 Nobel Peace Prize for his role in the non-violent struggle against apartheid. He was the first African, and the first person from outside Europe and the Americas, to be awarded the Nobel Peace Prize.

~July 22~

"The Battle of Dornach"

On this day, July 22, 1499, the Battle of Dornach was the last armed conflict between the Swiss and any member state of the Holy Roman Empire; essentially the Battle of Dornach was the beginning of Swiss independence. The *Treaty of Basel* (September 22, 1499) formally concluded the war, revoking the imperial ban against the Swiss cantons, legalizing the alliance of the League of the Ten Jurisdictions with the Confederates and placing the Thurgau region under Swiss jurisdiction.

~~~

"A Bridge Too Far"

On this day, July 22, 1937, the Democratically-controlled United States Senate (Democrats 75-17 Republicans) voted down fellow Democrat Franklin D. Roosevelt's proposal to add more justices to the Supreme Court of the United States. The political maneuver by President Franklin Roosevelt is known as the attempted Court-Packing.

~July 23~

"Homosexual "Limitations" are not Discrimination"

On this day, July 23, 1992, a Vatican commission, led by the future Pope Benedict XVI (Cardinal Joseph Ratzinger), "established" that limiting certain rights of homosexual people and non-married couples are not equivalent to discrimination on the grounds of race or gender.

WHAT???????

~July 24~

"Remember Orr"

On this day, July 24, 1750, John Philpot Curran was born in Newmarket, County Cork. Curran (July 24, 1750 – October 14, 1817) was an Irish orator, politician, wit, lawyer, and judge.

He was a liberal Protestant whose politics were similar to Henry Grattan and opposed the Act of Union with Britain.

Curran defended several of the United Irishmen in prominent high treason cases in the 1790s. Among them was the Revd. William Jackson, Archibald Hamilton Rowan, Wolfe Tone, Napper Tandy, The Sheares Brothers, Lord Edward Fitzgerald, William Orr, and William Drennan. Making his cases more difficult was the fact that in Ireland, the government could rely upon one witness to secure a conviction, while in England the law required that the prosecution had to use two or more witnesses.

Perhaps Curran's most famous trial was the Trial of William Orr. The only evidence used against Orr was the unsupported evidence of Hugh Wheatly. Even the presiding judge, Yelverton, was said to have shed tears at the passing of the death sentence. Orr's friend, and United Irishmen poet, William Drennan wrote, of Orr's death:

Hapless land!
Heap of uncementing sand!
Crumbled by a foreign weight:
And, by worse, domestic hate.

The execution of William Orr is regarded by many as an example of "judicial murder" and the phrase "Remember Orr" was a United Irishmen rallying cry during the 1798 rebellion.

~July 25~

"The Crittenden–Johnson Resolution"

On this day, July 25, 1755, British Governor of Nova Scotia, Charles Lawrence, and the Nova Scotia Council ordered the deportation of the Acadians. The Expulsion of the Acadians, also known as the Great Upheaval, the Great Expulsion, the Great Deportation and Le Grand Dérangement, was the forced removal the Acadian people from the present day Canadian Maritime provinces of Nova Scotia, New Brunswick, Prince Edward Island— parts of an area also known as Acadia.

The Expulsion (1755–1764) occurred during the French and Indian War (the North American theatre of the Seven Years' War) and was part of the British military campaign against New France. The British first deported Acadians to the Thirteen Colonies, and after 1758 transported additional Acadians to Britain and France. An estimated 11,500 Acadians were deported (a census of 1764 indicates that 2,600 Acadians remained in the colony, presumably having eluded capture).

The 1713 Treaty of Utrecht which ceded Nova Scotia to Great Britain had allowed the Acadians to keep their lands. Over the next forty-five years, however, the Acadians refused to sign an unconditional oath of allegiance to Britain and some Acadians also supported supply lines to the French fortresses of Louisbourg and Fort Beauséjour. As a result, the British sought to eliminate any future military threat posed by the Acadians and to permanently cut the supply lines they provided to Louisbourg by removing them from the area. Without making distinctions between the Acadians who had been neutral and those who had resisted the occupation of Acadia, the British governor Charles Lawrence and the Nova Scotia Council ordered them to be deported to other British colonies, like the Thirteen Colonies.

During the second wave, they were deported to Britain and France, from where they migrated to Louisiana. Acadians fled initially to Francophone colonies such as Canada, the uncolonized northern part of Acadia, Isle Saint-Jean (present-day Prince Edward Island) and Isle Royale (present-day Cape Breton Island). During the second wave of the expulsion, these Acadians were either imprisoned or deported.

~~~

"The Crittenden–Johnson Resolution"

On this day, July 25, 1861, the United States Congress passed the Crittenden–Johnson Resolution, stating that the war was being fought to preserve the Union and not to end slavery.

~~~

"*SS Andrea Doria*"

On this day, June 25, 1956, the Italian ocean liner *SS Andrea Doria* collides with the *MS Stockholm* in heavy fog forty-five miles south of Nantucket Island and sinks the next day, killing 51.

~July 26~

"Desegregation"

On this day, July 26, 1948, U.S. President Harry S. Truman signed Executive Order 9981 which desegregated the Armed Forces of the United States.

~July 27~

"America"

On this day, July 27, 2004, future US President Barrack Obama gave the keynote speech at the 2004 Democratic Convention nominating US Senator John Kerry of Massachusetts and US Senator Johnathan Edwards of North Carolina. Obama declared:

"...There is not a liberal America and a conservative America — there is the United States of America. There is not a black America and a white America and Latino America and Asian America — there's the United States of America.
The pundits like to slice-and-dice our country into Red States and Blue States; Red States for Republicans, Blue States for Democrats. But I've got news for them, too: We worship an awesome God in the Blue States, and we don't like federal agents poking around in our libraries in the Red States. We coach Little League in the Blue States, and, yes, we've got some gay friends in the Red States. There are patriots who opposed the war in Iraq and there are patriots who supported the war in Iraq."

~~~

The original speech ended with the sentence, "We're not red states and blue states; we're all Americans, standing up together for the red, white, and blue" but Obama was instructed to drop the line from his speech so that Kerry could say "Maybe some just see us divided into those red states and blue states, but I see us as one America: red, white, and blue" in his own speech.

~July 28~

"A Day of Civil Rights and the Disregard of Civil Rights"

"The Fourteenth Amendment"

On this day, July 28, 1868, the 14th Amendment to the United States Constitution was certified, establishing African American citizenship, and guaranteeing due process of law.

~~~

"Haiti"

On this day, July 28, 1915, the United States began an extrajudicial 19-year occupation of the Republic of Haiti.

~~~

"The Silent Parade"

On this day, July 28, 1917, the Silent Parade took place in New York City to protest the murders and lynchings of African-Americans as well as other violence to African-Americans. (See also August 7th and August 17th)

~~~

"The Bonus Army"

On this day, July 28, 1932, U.S. President Herbert Hoover ordered the United States Army to forcibly evict the "Bonus Army" of World War I veterans gathered in Washington, D.C. It was the last action of the US Calvary using horses.

~July 29~

"Dag and Dad"

On this day, July 29, 1905, Dag Hammarskjöld was born in Jönköping, United Kingdoms of Sweden and Norway. Hammarskjöld (July 29, 1905 – September 18, 1961) was a Swedish diplomat, economist, and served as the second Secretary-General of the United Nations. Hammarskjöld is credited with saying: "I would rather live my life as though there is a God and die to find out that there isn't than to live my life as though there is no God and die to find out there is." In 1953, Hammarskjöld was interviewed by Edward R. Murrow. In this discussion, Hammarskjöld declared: "But the explanation of how man should live a life of active social service in full harmony with himself as a member of the community of spirit, I found in the writings of those great medieval mystics [Meister Eckhart and Jan van Ruysbroek] for whom 'self-surrender' had been the way to self-realization, and who in 'singleness of mind' and 'inwardness' had found strength to say yes to every demand which the needs of their neighbors made them face, and to say yes also to every fate life had in store for them when they followed the call of duty as they understood it." He was killed in an airplane crash en route to the Congo Crisis cease-fire negotiations. Hammarskjöld's only book, *Vägmärken* (or *Markings*), was published in 1963 and is a collection of his diary reflections from 1925 until the month before his death. Hammarskjöld was posthumously awarded the 1961 Nobel Peace Prize. US President John F. Kennedy called Hammarskjöld the greatest statesman of our century.

Included in honor of my father, Thomas J. Keefe, Jr.

~July 30~

"William Penn"

On this day, July 30, 1718, William Penn died in Ruscombe, Berkshire, England, Great Britain. Penn (October 14, 1644 – July 30, 1718) was an English real estate entrepreneur, philosopher, early Quaker, and founder of the Province of Pennsylvania. He was an early advocate of democracy and religious freedom, notable for his good relations and successful treaties with the Lenape Native Americans. Under his direction, the city of Philadelphia, The City of Brotherly Love, was planned and developed.

It was in Cork, Ireland, that Penn became attracted to Quakerism. Penn's interest soon had Penn arrested for attending Meetings, but rather than state that he was not a Quaker and thereby dodge any charges, he publicly declared himself a Friend. Just 22 years old, Penn pled his case and stated that since the Quakers had no political agenda, they should not be subject to laws that restricted minority religions. He was released from prison, but it was his wealthy father's intervention and his legal arguments.

Though freed, Penn demonstrated no remorse for his aggressive stance and vowed to keep fighting against the wrongs of the Church and the King. For its part, the Crown continued to confiscate Quaker property and put thousands of Quakers in jail. Penn's religious views effectively exiled him from English society; he was expelled from Christ Church, Oxford for being a Quaker, and was arrested several times. In 1670, Penn was arrested was accused of preaching to "more than five persons in addition to members of the family, for any religious purpose not according to the rules of the Church of England."

He was again released because of his father's influence, but Penn continued writing essays espousing religious tolerance and railing against discriminatory laws. Finally, after his father's death, Penn found himself in jail again for six months as he continued to agitate. Seeing conditions deteriorating, Penn decided to appeal directly to the King and the Duke for a mutually beneficial solution. Penn proposed the mass emigration of English Quakers.

In 1677, Penn and other prominent Quakers purchased the colonial province of West Jersey (half of the current state of New Jersey). That same year, two hundred Quaker settlers arrived and founded the town of Burlington, New Jersey. Quaker leader George Fox himself had made a journey to America to verify the potential of further expansion of the early Quaker settlements and, in 1682, East Jersey was also purchased by Quakers.

With the New Jersey foothold in place, Penn pressed his case to extend the Quaker region. Whether from personal sympathy or political expediency, King Charles II granted an extraordinarily generous charter which made Penn the world's largest private (non-royal) landowner. Penn became the sole proprietor of a huge tract of land west of New Jersey and north of Maryland (which belonged to Catholic leader, Lord Baltimore), and gained sovereign rule of the territory with all rights and privileges (except the power to declare war).

Having proved himself an influential scholar and theoretician, Penn set forth on his "Holy Experiment," to create the province of Pennsylvania.

~July 31~

"Raoul Wallenberg"

On this day, July 31, 1947, Raoul Gustaf Wallenberg died in Moscow, Russia (August 4, 1912 – July 31, 1947) was a Swedish architect, businessman, diplomat, and humanitarian who save tens of thousands of Jews in Nazi-occupied Hungary during the Holocaust from German Nazis and Hungarian. While serving as Sweden's special envoy in Budapest from July to December 1944, Wallenberg issued protective passports and sheltered Jews in buildings designated as Swedish territory. On January 17, 1945, during the Siege of Budapest by the Red Army, Wallenberg was detained on suspicion of espionage and disappeared. He was later reported to have died on July 17, 1947, while imprisoned by the KGB in the Lubyanka headquarters. In 1981, U.S. Congressman Tom Lantos, himself one of those saved by Wallenberg (see February 11th and March 27th), sponsored a bill making Wallenberg an Honorary Citizen of the United States. Wallenberg is also an honorary citizen of Canada, Hungary, Australia, and Israel. Israel has also designated Wallenberg as one of the Righteous Among the Nations.

~~~

"Chiune Sugihara"

On this day, July 31, 1986, Chiune Sugihara 杉原 千畝 (January 1, 1900 – July 31, 1986) died in Tokyo, Japan. Sugihara was a Japanese diplomat who served as Vice-Consul for the Empire of Japan in Lithuania. During World War II, he helped between 10,000 and 40,000 Jews leave the country by issuing transit visas so that they could travel to Japanese territory, risking his career and his family's lives. In 1985, Israel named him to the Righteous Among the Nations.

"Houston, Tranquility Base here. The *Eagle* has landed."

~~~

"That's one small step for [a] man, one giant leap for mankind."

~Neil Armstrong~

~August 1~

"It's about time…"

On August 1, 1993, President William J. Clinton sent a personal apology to each living survivor of the Japanese-American internment camps.

~~~

"Lawrence Cook

On August 1, 2004, Lawrence Cook died after a long illness and, considering his wife had died in 1999; it's likely that his epitaph is meant to make visitors laugh and not provide a play-by-play of his last moments on Earth:

Ma loves Pa,

Pa loves women,

Ma caught Pa with two in swimmin'

Here lies Pa.

~August 2~

"Shimon Peres"

On this day, August 2, 1923, Shimon Peres שמעון פרס was born in Wiszniew, Poland. Peres (August 2, 1923 – September 28, 2016) was a member of twelve Israeli cabinets spanning seven decades. Peres was a protégé of David Ben Gurion, Israel's founding father. Peres began his political career in the late 1940s, holding several diplomatic and military positions during and directly after the 1948 Arab–Israeli War. In 1956, he took part in the historic negotiations on the Protocol of Sèvres described by British Prime Minister Anthony Eden as the "highest form of statesmanship."

Peres was first elected to the Knesset in 1959 and, except for a three-month-long hiatus in early 2006, was in office continuously until 2007. On October 26, 1994, Shimon Peres, as Foreign Minister, coordinated the Israel–Jordan peace treaty. Later, Peres was a co-winner of the 1994 Nobel Peace Prize together with Yitzhak Rabin and Yasser Arafat for the Oslo Accords.

Peres was polyglot, speaking Polish, French, English, Russian, Yiddish, and Hebrew. In his private life, he was a poet and songwriter, writing stanzas during cabinet meetings, with some of his poems later being recorded as songs in albums.

In 2007, Peres became the 9th President of Israel and, when he retired in 2014, Peres was the world's oldest Head of State.
After suffering a stroke, Peres died on September 28, 2016, in Tel Aviv, Israel. He was considered the last link to Israel's founding generation.

~August 3~

"President Bartlett"

On this day, August 3, 1940, Ramón Antonio Gerardo Estévez was born in Dayton, Ohio, USA. The son of immigrants, Estévez adopted the stage name Martin Sheen to help him gain employment. Sheen credited the Marianists at the University of Dayton as a major influence on his public activism, as well as Archbishop Desmond Tutu. Sheen is known for his outspoken support of liberal political causes, such as opposition to United States military actions and a hazardous-waste incinerator in East Liverpool, Ohio. Sheen has resisted calls to run for office, saying:

"There's no way that I could be the president. You can't have a pacifist in the White House . . . I'm an actor. This is what I do for a living."

Sheen supported the 1965 farm worker movement with Cesar Chavez in Delano, California. He is a proponent of the consistent life ethic, which advocates against abortion, euthanasia, capital punishment and war. He articulated this view further in an interview with *The Progressive*: "I'm inclined to be against abortion of any life. But I am equally against the death penalty or war." He also stated on the same occasion: "I personally am opposed to abortion, but I will not judge anybody else's right in that regard because I am not a woman and I could never face the actual reality of it."

On May 16, 1995, Martin Sheen and Paul Watson from the non-profit environmental organization Sea Shepherd Conservation Society, were confronted by a number of Canadian sealers in a hotel on the Magdalen Islands over Sea Shepherd's history of attacks on sealing and whaling ships. Sheen negotiated with the sealers while Watson was escorted to the airport by police.

In 1998, Martin Sheen crossed the line at Ft Benning to protest the School of the Americas during the memorial funeral procession in which the names of the SOA victims were chanted, and the crowd responded, *"Presente."*

Human rights activist Craig Kielburger described Sheen as having "a rap sheet almost as long as his list of film credits." On April 1, 2007, Sheen was arrested, along with 38 other activists, for trespassing at the Nevada Test Site. In a speech at Oxford University in 2009, Sheen stated that he had been arrested 66 times for protesting and acts of civil disobedience. In 2010, Sheen spoke to 18,000 young student activists:

"While acting is what I do for a living, activism is what I do to stay alive."

In 2003, Sheen was recipient of the Marquette University Degree of Doctor of Letters, *honoris causa* for his work on social and Catholic issues and on May 3, 2015 Sheen received an honorary degree Doctor of Human Letters from the University of Dayton for his lifelong commitment to peace, social justice and human rights exemplifying the Catholic, Marianist university's missions.

~~~

"Jesse Owens"

On this day, August 3, 1936, Jesse Owens won the 100 meter dash, defeating Ralph Metcalfe in front of Adolf Hitler at the Berlin Olympics. Owens' victory greatly upset Hitler's Aryan "master race" propaganda.

~August 4~

"Anne Frank"

On this day, August 4, 1944, Jewish diarist Anne Frank, her family, and four others were captured after a tip from a Dutch informer led the Gestapo to a sealed-off area in an Amsterdam warehouse. (See May 3rd, August 6th, December 3rd.)

~~~

"Jesse Owens"

On this day, August 4, 1936, Jesse Owens won the long jump with a leap of 8.06 m (26 ft 5 in), 3¼ inches short of his own world record. He later credited this achievement to the technical advice that he received from Luz Long, the German competitor whom he defeated in from of Adolph Hitler during the 1936 Olympics.

~~~

"Mississippi Burning"

On this day, August 4, 1964, American civil rights workers Michael Schwerner, Andrew Goodman and James Chaney were found dead in Mississippi after disappearing on June 21st.

~August 5~

"Nelson Mandela"

On this day, August 5, 1962, Nelson Mandela was jailed in South Africa and would not be released until 1990.

272

~August 6~

"Hiroshima"

On this day, August 6, 1945, under direct orders by US President Harry S. Truman, the United States of America dropped an atomic bomb on Hiroshima, Japan. The one that killed 199,000 humans immediately, thousands more hibakusha from radiation sickness and cancer, and has also infected later generations with residual effects, such as anxiety and somatization.

There are many rationalizations: punish Japan for Pearl Harbor; "They started it first;" it saved American soldiers lives; it avoided a protracted invasion; it was a prescient warning to the Soviet Union; it prevented Japan from being divided as Korea and Germany were divided; it was a necessary evil, or no one knew how destructive it would be. But after August 6th's bombing of Hiroshima, we knew. And after the bombing of Nagasaki, everyone knew. Tsutomu Yamaguchi knew. He survived both Hiroshima and Nagasaki; and later died of stomach cancer on January 4, 2010, at the age of 93.

In August 1945, more than 22,000 non-Japanese died simply because the US government had a new toy to play with. Civilians and non-combatants died: women, children, the elderly, teachers, policemen, etc. In fact, eight of those non-combatants were even European prisoners-of-war (one British national, and seven Dutch nationals). And one American soldier, Joe Kieyoomia, was captured by the Japanese Imperial forces and only survived Hiroshima because the falling wall of his cell shielded his body from the blast. Ask the Korean conscripted prisoners about the decision to bomb Hiroshima and Nagasaki. Approximately 22,000 innocent Korean prisoners died in the atomic blasts in Hiroshima and Nagasaki.

In total, almost a quarter of a million Japanese civilians perished in the bombing of Hiroshima and Nagasaki. Would the US have used an atomic bomb on Germany? Would you have utterly destroyed the great cities of Berlin, Hamburg or Munich? After all, Munich was the seat of Hitler's early rise to power, perhaps "they deserved it too"? Yes, the Allies fire-bombed Dresden and did incalculable damage, but would the US have vaporized a German city of innocent women, children and the elderly? Most likely not. There seems to be an inherent bias in the decision to bomb Japan and not Germany. After all, the US interned Japanese-Americans, not German-Americans. In the 1940s, a plurality of Americans was of German ancestry, and most Americans were of European descent. Europeans are Christian Caucasians, just like the power brokers in Washington, DC, were in the 1940s.

US Civil War General Sherman said it best: "War is hell." War is, by definition, violent and people die. Innocent people die. But, usually, decisions are made to spare the cities, civilian populations, and art work (think Albrecht Gaiswinkler and the real-life Monument Men). When one racial/ethnic/religious group of people are targeted while, at the same time, the human, historical, architectural and artistic heritage of another demographic group is not, it should make people uncomfortable. Perhaps we shouldn't necessarily condemn the leaders of the past. After all, we are all products of the context and cultural biases of our time. (For example, people have also debated President Woodrow Wilson's reputation and place in history.) Sparing condemnation, however, does not mean necessarily mean exoneration or impunity. President Truman gave the authorization that killed hundreds of thousands of innocent human beings in an instant yet withheld that same bloodlust when it came to bombing European cities and population centers.

A few years later, the United Nations (which Truman helped usher into existence) created a new international law known as the UN Convention on the Prevention and Punishment of the Crime of Genocide. In this statute, genocide is defined as:
"…any of the following acts committed with intent to destroy, in whole or in part, a national, ethnical, racial or religious group, as such:

(a) Killing members of the group; (b) Causing serious bodily or mental harm to members of the group; (c) Deliberately inflicting on the group conditions of life calculated to bring about its physical destruction in whole or in part; (d) Imposing measures intended to prevent births within the group; (e) Forcibly transferring children of the group to another group" (Convention on the Prevention and Punishment of the Crime of Genocide, Article 2, 1948).

The term genocide has a legal definition and, it says, genocide is defined as killing either in whole or in part a national, ethnic, racial or religious group. Mr. Truman killed hundreds of thousands of people that all belonged to a national/ethnic/racial/religious group that was distinct, not just from the majority of Americans, but also distinct from the other belligerents in Europe who were treated much differently.

Much later, in 1964, a WWII veteran famously said that pornography was difficult to define, but, said LTJG Stewart, "I know it when I see it." That Lieutenant Junior Grade officer was Potter Stewart, and he went on to become an Associate Justice of the United States Supreme Court. While US President Harry S. Truman acted admirably in many ways, there is the elephant in the room and, as another expression would have it, your decision to bomb Hiroshima and Nagasaki has failed the Elephant Test.

~~~

"Yoko Moriwaki"

On this day, August 6, 1945, Yoko Moriwaki (森脇 瑤子 Moriwaki Yōko) wrote the last entry in her diary.

Yoko Moriwaki was a thirteen-year-old Japanese girl who lived in Hiroshima, Japan, during World War II. Her diary, a record of wartime Japan before the bombing of Hiroshima, was published in Japan in 1996. It was published by Harper Collins in English in 2013 as *Yoko's Diary*. Her brother, Koji Hosokawa, who survived the attack on Hiroshima, made her diary available for publication.

Moriwaki started keeping her diary as an assignment at her school, the Hiroshima Prefectural Girls' HS #1. In addition to chronicling her daily life, it kept a record of wartime Japan, covering topics from what classes she was taking to sightings of war planes flying overhead. The diary starts on April 6, 1945, shortly before she started school, and the last entry is from August 5, 1945, the day before the atomic bomb was dropped on Hiroshima.

Moriwaki has been compared to World War II diarist Anne Frank, known for her own record of being Jewish in Germany during World War II. (See May 3rd, August 4th, & December 3rd.)

~August 7~

"Ralph Johnson Bunche"

On this day, August 7, 1927, Ralph Johnson Bunche was born in Detroit, Michigan. Bunche (August 7, 1903, or 1904 – December 9, 1971) was an American political scientist, academic, and diplomat who received the 1950 Nobel Peace Prize for his late 1940's mediation in Israel. He was the first African-American to be so honored in the history of the prize. He was involved in the formation and administration of the United Nations. In 1963, he was awarded the Medal of Freedom by President John F. Kennedy.

For more than two decades, Bunche served as chair of the Department of Political Science at Howard University, where he also taught generations of students. He served as a member of the Board of Overseers of his alma mater, Harvard University (1960–1965), as a member of the board of the Institute of International Education, and as a trustee of Oberlin College, Lincoln University, and New Lincoln School.

In August 2008, the United States National Archives and Records Administration made public the fact that Ralph Bunche had joined the U.S. Office of Strategic Services – the precursor organization to the Central Intelligence Agency – during World War II.

~~~

"The Last Lynching"

On this day, August 7, 1930, Thomas Shipp and Abram Smith, were killed in Marion, Indiana. It is the last confirmed lynching of African-Americans in the northern United States. (See also July 28th and August 17th)

~August 8~

"Quit India"

On this day, August 8, 1942, in response to Mohandas Gandhi's call for swaraj or complete independence, the Quit India Movement was born against the British rule in India.

~August 9~

"But I don't wanna!"

On this day, August 9, 1965, Singapore was expelled from Malaysia and becomes the only country to date to gain independence unwillingly. An ironic example of peaceful -if not unwanted- self-determination.

~~~

"Abner Louima"

On this day, August 9, 1997, Albner Louima was assaulted, brutalized, and forcibly sodomized with a broken-off broom handle by officers of the New York City Police Department.

~~~

"Darren Wilson fatally shot Michael Brown, Jr."

On this day, August 9, 2014, Ferguson Police Officer Darren Wilson fatally shot Michael Brown, Jr., an 18-year-old black man, who was accused of strong-arm robbing a convenience store. Brown was accompanied by his friend Dorian Johnson who was 22. Wilson alleged that an altercation ensued when Brown attacked Wilson in his police vehicle for control of Wilson's gun until it was fired. Brown and Johnson then fled, with Wilson in pursuit of Brown. In the entire altercation, Wilson fired a total of twelve bullets; the last was probably the fatal shot. At the time of the shooting, Darren Dean Wilson was 6 ft 4 in (1.93 m) tall and weighed about 210 lbs and was armed with a SIG Sauer P229. On November 24, 2014, a grand jury decided not to indict Wilson.

~August 10~

"Maria Mandl"

On this day, August 10, 1948, Maria Mandl was arrested by the US Army. She was later handed over to Poland in November 1946, tried in the Auschwitz Trial (1947) and executed on January 24, 1948, at the age of 36.

Born in Münzkirchen, Upper Austria, then part of Austria-Hungary, she went on to become the most famous female SS guard. She controlled all the female Auschwitz camps and female subcamps including at Hindenburg, Lichtewerden, and Raisko.
She oversaw the inmate lists, sending an estimated half a million women and children to their deaths in the gas chambers at Auschwitz I and Auschwitz II. (See also January 10th and February 1st).

~~~

"What the FARC?"

On this day, August 10, 1951, Columbian President Juan Manuel Santos Calderón was born in Bogotá, Colombia. He was 2016 recipient of the Nobel Peace Prize for his landmark peace agreement between Columbian and the FARC rebels. The treaty, had it been ratified by the Columbian people, would have ended more than 50 years of civil war.

~August 11~

"Nuts!"

On this day, August 11, 1975, Anthony McAuliffe died at Walter Reed Medical Center, Washington, DC. McAuliffe (July 2, 1898 – August 11, 1975) was a US Army General who earned fame as the acting commander of the U.S. 101st Airborne Division troops defending Bastogne, Belgium, during the Battle of the Bulge in World War II.

~~~

"The August 11th Speech"

On this day, August 11, 1947, Muhammad Ali Jinnah, founding father of Pakistan, gave the August 11th Speech to the Pakistani Constituent Assembly. While Pakistan was created as a result of what could be described as Indian Muslim nationalism, Jinnah was once the leader of Hindu-Muslim Unity. When the Partition of India finally occurred, Jinnah, soon-to-be Governor-General of the Dominion of Pakistan, outlined his vision of Pakistan in an address to the Constituent Assembly. He spoke of an inclusive and impartial government, religious freedom, the rule of law and equality for all. During the 60th anniversary of Jinnah's speech in 2007, Pakistani religious minorities, including Christians, Hindus and Sikhs held a large rally to celebrate Jinnah's legacy at the Minar-e-Pakistan calling for the implementation of Jinnah's vision in letter and spirit.

~August 12~

"You better pray!"

On this day, August 12, 1676, "Praying Indian" John Alderman shot and killed Metacomet, the Wampanoag war chief. With the death of Metacomet, known as King Philip to the English, the Native American rebellion again English colonization quickly evaporated, thus ending King Philip's War.

~~~

"American 'democracy' in Hawaii"

On this day, August 12, 1898, the Hawaiian flag was lowered from 'Iolani Palace in an elaborate annexation ceremony and replaced with the flag of the United States, signifying the transfer of sovereignty from the Republic of Hawaii to the United States. Both the annexation as well as the earlier overthrow of the Hawaiian kingdom were decided without the Hawaiian people.

~~~

"Merv Griffin"

On this day, August 12, 1898, Mervyn Edward Griffin Jr. died of prostate cancer in Los Angeles, California. Griffin (July 6, 1925 – August 12, 2007) was the host of *The Merv Griffin Show* and creator of *Jeopardy!* and *Wheel of Fortune*. While Griffin had said his epitaph would be "Stay Tuned," but ultimately, Griffin instead chose this to be engraved on his gravestone:

"I will not be right back after this message"

~August 13~

"Nat Turner"

On this day, August 13, 1831, Nat Turner witnessed a solar eclipse which caused the sky to appear a blue-green color, which he envisioned as a black man's hand reaching over the sun. Eight days later he and 70 other slaves kill between 55-65 whites in Southampton County, Virginia. Turner was hanged on November 11, 1831.

~~~

"The Brownsville Affair"

On this day, August 13, 1906, the all black infantrymen of the U.S. Army's 25th Infantry Regiment were accused of killing a white bartender and wounding a white police officer in Brownsville, Texas. The incident is known as the Brownsville Affair. Although military commanders testified that the black soldiers had been in the barracks at Fort Brown all night, evidence was planted against them. Despite the exculpatory evidence, the United States Army Inspector General's investigation recommended dishonorable discharge.

Over the objections and pleas of Booker T. Washington, US President Theodore Roosevelt ordered the dishonorable discharge of 167 soldiers of the 25th Infantry Regiment, costing them pensions and preventing them from their pensions and serving in civil service jobs. A renewed investigation in the early 1970s exonerated the discharged black troops.

The Nixon Administration pardoned the soldiers posthumously and restored their records to show honorable discharges but did not provide retroactive compensation.

~August 14~

"V-J Day in Times Square"

On this day, August 14, 1945, George Mendonsa of Newport, Rhode Island, was photographed kissing Greta Zimmer Friedman. Friedman later said, "It wasn't my choice to be kissed," in a 2005 interview with the Library of Congress. "The guy just came over and grabbed!" she said, adding, "That man was very strong. I wasn't kissing him. He was kissing me." "I did not see him approaching, and before I know it I was in this tight grip," Friedman told CBS News in 2012. An interesting anecdote in light of the 2017-2018 MeToo movement.

The photograph, *V-J Day in Times Square* (also V-Day and The Kiss) was taken by Alfred Eisenst Unconditional Surrender is a series of sculptures by Seward Johnson known as *Unconditional Surrender.*

~~~

"Cuba"

On this day, August 14, 2015, US President Barack H. Obama re-opened the US Embassy in Havana, Cuba after 54 years of being closed after when Cuba–United States diplomatic relations were broken off.

~August 15~

"Czeslawa Kwoka"

On this day, August 15, 1928, Czeslawa Kwoka was born in Wólka Złojecka, Poland. Czeslawa was a Polish Catholic child who died in the Auschwitz concentration camp at the age of 14. She was one of the thousands of child victims of German World War II crimes and is among those memorialized in the Auschwitz-Birkenau State Museum indoor exhibit called Block no. 6: Exhibition: The Life of the Prisoners.

Photographs of Kwoka and others were taken by the "famous photographer of Auschwitz," Wilhelm Brasse, from 1940 to 1945, displayed in that Museum photographic memorial.

~~~

"Giorgio Perlasca"

On this day, August 15, 1992, Giorgio Perlasca died in Padua, Italy. Perlasca (January 31, 1910 – August 15, 1992) was an Italian who, with the collaboration of official diplomats, posed as the Spanish consul-general to Hungary in the winter of 1944, and saved 5218 Jews from deportation to Nazi Germany death camps in eastern Europe.

~August 16~

"The Camp David Accords"

On this day, August 16, 1913, Menachem Begin (d. 1992) was born in Belarus. He was the Prime Minister of Israel who signed the Camp David Accords leading to the 1979 Israel-Egypt Peace Treaty. He was awarded the and was the recipient of the Nobel Peace Prize with Egyptian President Anwar Sadat in 1978.

~~~

"The Stateless Kurds"

On this day, August 16, 1946, Masoud Barzani, the President of Iraqi Kurdistan, was born in Mahabad, Iran. Iraqi Kurdistan is an autonomous region within Iraq and the first recognized expression of Kurdish self-determination. Greater Kurdistan is comprised of lands within the national boundaries of Turkey, Syria, Iraq, and Iran.

~August 17~

"The Missing Colony"

On this day, August 17, 1585, the first group of colonists sent by Sir Walter Raleigh under the charge of Ralph Lane landed in the New World to create Roanoke Colony on Roanoke Island, off the coast of present-day North Carolina.

~~~

"Blame the Jew?"

On this day, August 17, 1915, after a 13-year-old girl was murdered in Marietta, Georgia, Jewish-American Leo Frank was accused and lynched in Marietta, Georgia. (See also July 28th, August 7th, and August 17th.)

~August 18~

"The First English-American Born in America"

On this day, August 18, 1587, Virginia Dare, granddaughter of Governor John White of the Colony of Roanoke, was born. Dare was the first English child born in the Americas, and her naming is one of the first uses of the term 'Virginia' as a name. (See January 3rd.)

~~~

"Boris Yeltsin"

On this day, August 18, 1991, Boris Yeltsin stood atop a tank in Moscow, Russia, to demand the release of Mikhail Gorbachev and the end of the attempted coup d'état. (See August 19th.)

~August 19~

"To Conquer Conquering Bear"

On this day, August 19, 1854, United States Army soldiers murdered Lakota Chief Conquering Bear.

~~~

"Under Arrest"

On this day, August 19, 1991, Soviet President Mikhail Gorbachev was placed under house arrest while on holiday in the town of Foros, Ukraine. One of the major issues at the heart of the August Coup was whether Russia would recognize the European and non-Russian parts of the Soviet Empire right to self-determination. (See August 18th.)

~August 20~

"So Much for Being a 'Lionhearted' King"

On this day, August 20, 1191, the Massacre of Ayyadieh occurred. It was perpetrated by Richard Coeur de Lion, better known as King Richard the Lionheart of England, during the Crusades to recover the Holy Land from the Saracens under the command of Saladin. It is best understood in the context of Richard's attempt to take the city of Acre.

On the fall of Acre, King Richard attempted to negotiate with Saladin offering a large number of captured prisoners in exchange for the True Cross (reputedly the actual cross upon which Jesus Christ had been crucified), together with a large ransom and a number of Christian captives taken by Saladin's men in earlier clashes with the crusaders.

Saladin stalled for time in the hope that an approaching Muslim army would allow him to retake control of the city. When Saladin refused a request from Richard to provide a list of names of important Christians held by the Saracens, King Richard took this as a delaying tactic and insisted that the ransom payment and prisoner exchange should occur within one month. When the deadline was not met the King became infuriated and planned an execution which took place on a small hill called Ayyadieh, a few miles from Acre. The killings were carried out in full view of the Muslim army and Saladin's own field headquarters. Around 3000 soldiers, and possibly some of the women and children that usually accompanied them, were executed.

~August 21~

"What's in a name?"

On this day, August 21, 2001, NATO sent a peace-keeping force to the former Yugoslav Republic of Macedonia. It is worth noting that Macedonia and Slovenia were the only two former Yugoslav republics not directly drawn into the Balkan Wars and the presence of NATO troops also helped maintain the peace between the Republic of Macadonia and Greece, who objected to Macedonia's name.

On June 12, 2018, Greek Prime Minister Alexis Tsipras and Macedonian Prime Minister Zoran Zaev reached an agreement in which the Republic of Macedonia could be renamed the "Republic of North Macedonia." Zaev has stated his intent to put the new name to a referendum before officially renaming the country.

~August 22~

"Nat Turner's Rebellion"

On this day, August 22, 1831, Nat Turner's slave rebellion began just after midnight in Southampton County, Virginia, leading to the deaths of about 60 European-Americans and approximately 250 African slaves.

~~~

"Dorothy Parker"

On this day, August 22, 1893, Dorothy Parker (née Rothschild) was born in Long Branch, New Jersey. Parker (August 22, 1893 – June 7, 1967) was an American poet, writer, critic, and satirist, best known for her wit, wisecracks, and her eye for 20th-century urban foibles. Before her death in 1967, Dorothy Parker, the Jazz Age writer and critic renowned for her caustic wit, suggested her own epitaph: "Excuse my dust." Dorothy Parker left instructions that she be cremated, but she left no instructions as to what was to be done with her ashes.

Years later, Parker's ashes were finally laid to rest in a garden behind the national headquarters of the NAACP in Baltimore, Maryland. Adjacent the NAACP headquarters building, a brick path threads underneath a few pine trees, ending with a circle of brick, meant to evoke the Round Table at the Algonquin Hotel where Parker used to lunch. In the ground, there is a plaque with an inscription that includes, you guessed it, the epitaph she herself once suggested: "Excuse my dust."

~August 23~

"Don't Give Up the Ship!"

On this day, August 23, 1785, Oliver Hazard Perry was born in South Kingstown, Rhode Island. Perry (August 23, 1785 – August 23, 1819) was an American naval commander. He was the son of United States Navy Captain Christopher Raymond Perry and Sarah Wallace Alexander, and the older brother of Commodore Matthew C. Perry. Perry served in the West Indies during the Quasi War of 1798–1800 against France, in the Mediterranean during the Barbary Wars of 1801–1815, and in the Caribbean fighting piracy and the slave trade but is most noted for his heroic role in the War of 1812 during the 1813 Battle of Lake Erie. During the war against Britain, Perry supervised the building of a fleet at Erie, Pennsylvania. He earned the title "Hero of Lake Erie" for leading American forces in a decisive naval victory at the Battle of Lake Erie, receiving a Congressional Gold Medal and the "Thanks of Congress." His leadership materially aided the successful outcomes of all nine Lake Erie military campaign victories, and the victory was a turning point in the battle for the west in the war. He is remembered for the words on his battle flag, "Don't Give Up the Ship" and his message to General William Henry Harrison which reads in part,

"We have met the enemy and they are ours..."

~August 24~

"Genocide"

On this day, August 24, 1900, Raphael Lemkin was born in Vawkavysk, Belarus. Lemkin was a Polish lawyer credited with coining the term "genocide" in his 1944 book *Axis Rule in Occupied Europe*. The term stems from the Greek word "genos," which refers to a nation or tribe, and the Latin word "cide," which means killing. Prior to Lemkin's conceptualization, Winston Churchill described the act of genocide as a "crime without a name."

~~~

"Visiting Mabo"

On August 24, 2015, Australian Prime Minister Tony Abbott became the first Australian leader to visit Eddie Mabo's grave on Murray Island and pay tribute to his legacy.

~August 25~

"Samantha Reed"

On this day, August 25, 1985, Samantha Reed Smith died at the age of 13 in the Bar Harbor Airlines Flight 1808 plane crash.

Smith (June 29, 1972 – August 25, 1985) was an American schoolgirl, peace activist, and child actress from Manchester, Maine, who became famous in the Cold War Era between the United States and the Soviet Union.

In 1982, Smith wrote a letter to the newly appointed CPSU General Secretary Yuri Andropov and received a personal reply with a personal invitation to visit the Soviet Union, which she accepted. Smith attracted extensive media attention in both countries as a "Goodwill Ambassador" and became known as "America's Youngest Ambassador" participating in peacemaking activities in Japan. She wrote a book about her visit to the Soviet Union and co-starred in the television series *Lime Street*, before her death in 1985.

~August 26~

"The Nineteenth Amendment"

On this day, August 26, 1920, the 19th Amendment to the United States Constitution took effect, giving women the right to vote. The Nineteenth Amendment is identical to the Fifteenth Amendment, except that the Nineteenth prohibits the denial of suffrage because of sex and the Fifteenth because of "race, color, or previous condition of servitude." Colloquially known as the "Anthony Amendment," it was first introduced in the US Senate by Republican Senator Aaron A. Sargent of California. Sargent, who had met and befriended Anthony on a train ride in 1872, was a dedicated women's suffrage advocate. He had frequently attempted to insert women's suffrage provisions into unrelated bills but did not formally introduce a Constitutional Amendment until January 1878. Stanton and other women testified before the Senate in support of the amendment. The proposal sat in a committee until it was considered by the full Senate and rejected in a 16 to 34 vote in 1887.

After President Wilson spoke out in favor of women's suffrage in his State of the Union, another proposal was brought before the House on January 10, 1918. Wilson spent the night before the vote making strong and widely published appeals to the House to pass the amendment. It was passed by the required two-thirds of the House, with only one vote to spare. The vote was then carried into the Senate. Wilson again made an appeal, but on September 30, 1918, the proposal fell two votes short of passage. On February 10, 1919, it was again voted upon and failed by only one vote.

Wilson then called a special session of the Congress, to force another vote on the issue. Finally, on May 21, 1919, it passed the House, 42 votes more than necessary being obtained. On June 4, 1919, it was brought before the Senate where it passed, 56 ayes and 25 nays.

Within a few days, Illinois, Wisconsin, and Michigan ratified the amendment, their legislatures being in session. Other states followed suit at a regular pace until the amendment had been ratified by 35 of the necessary 36 state legislatures.

Much of the opposition to the amendment came from Southern Democrats, a trend which remained consistent with Tennessee as the last state to pass the amendment, during a special session right before the ratification period was to expire.

On August 18, 1920, Tennessee narrowly approved the Nineteenth Amendment, with 50 of 99 members of the Tennessee House of Representatives voting yes. The 15th Amendment to the US Constitution was ratified.

~August 27~

"Abie Nathan"

On this day, August 27, 2008, Avraham "Abie" Nathan אברהם נתן "אייבי" died in Tel Aviv, Israel. Nathan (April 29, 1927 – August 27, 2008) was an Israeli humanitarian and peace activist. He founded the Voice of Peace radio station.

In 1966, Nathan flew his plane, which he named *Shalom 1* (Peace 1), to Egypt carrying a message of peace. He landed in Port Said where he was arrested. He asked to meet Egyptian President Gamal Abdel Nasser to deliver a petition calling for peace between Israel and Egypt. He was refused and deported back to Israel, where he was arrested again for leaving the country by an illegal route. In 1978, Nathan began his first hunger strike to protest against the construction of Israeli settlements. In the early 1980s, he began meeting officials from the Palestine Liberation Organization. These meetings were later outlawed by the Knesset and, so, Nathan went on another hunger strike for 40 days to protest against that law. He stopped his hunger strike after President Chaim Herzog intervened. Nathan continued to meet with PLO head Yasser Arafat, however, and in 1991 he was sentenced to 18 months in prison. Herzog reduced the sentence, and Nathan was released after serving less than 6 months.

When he died, Israeli President Shimon Peres said about him: "He was one of the most prominent and special people in the country... He is the man who dedicated his life for other people and for a better humanity."

~August 28~

"Emmett Till"

On this day, August 28, 1955, black teenager Emmett Till was brutally murdered in Mississippi, galvanizing the Civil Rights Movement.

~~~

"Strom Thurmond"

On this day, August 28, 1957, U.S. Senator Strom Thurmond began his filibuster of the Civil Rights Act of 1957; he stopped speaking 24 hours and 18 minutes later, the longest filibuster ever conducted by a single senator. Thurmond began speaking at 8:54 p.m. on Aug. 28 and continued until 9:12 p.m. the next day, reciting the Declaration of Independence, Bill of Rights, President George Washington's Farewell Address, and other documents as well as the District of Columbia telephone book.

~~~

"I Have a Dream"

On this day, August 28, 1963, Martin Luther King, Jr. gave his *I Have a Dream* speech in Washington, D.C. Widely hailed as a masterpiece of rhetoric, King's speech invokes pivotal documents in American history, including the Declaration of Independence, the Emancipation Proclamation, and the US Constitution. Early in his speech, King alludes to Abraham Lincoln's Gettysburg Address by saying "Five score years ago..."

In reference to the abolition of slavery articulated in the Emancipation Proclamation, King says: "It came as a joyous daybreak to end the long night of their captivity." Anaphora is used throughout the speech. Early in his speech, King urges his audience to seize the moment; "Now is the time" is repeated three times in the sixth paragraph. The most widely cited example of anaphora is found in the often-quoted phrase "I have a dream," which is repeated eight times as King paints a picture of an integrated and unified America for his audience. Other occasions include "One hundred years later," "We can never be satisfied," "With this faith," "Let freedom ring," and "free at last." King was the sixteenth out of eighteen people to speak that day, according to the official program.

> "I still have a dream, a dream deeply rooted in the American dream – one day this nation will rise up and live up to its creed, "We hold these truths to be self-evident: that all men are created equal." I have a dream..."
> Martin Luther King Jr. (1963)

Among the most quoted lines of the speech include "have a dream that my four little children will one day live in a nation where they will not be judged by the color of their skin, but by the content of their character. I have a dream today!"

~August 29~

"Solomon's Temple"

On this day, August 29, 587 BCE, Babylon's siege of Jerusalem ended with the destruction of Solomon's Temple.

~~~

"The First Reservation"

On this day, August 29, 1758, the first Native American reservation was established, at Indian Mills, New Jersey.

~~~

"Ishi"

On this day, August 29, 1911, Ishi, considered the last uncontacted Native American, emerged from the wilderness in California. He was the last member of the Yahi, a group of the Yana of the U.S. state of California.

Known as the "last wild Indian," Ishi lived most of his life completely outside modern culture. At approximately 50 years of age, in 1911, he emerged out of the undeveloped area of Butte County, California, and spent the last five years of his life as a research subject at the University of California, San Francisco.

On March 25, 1916, the man known as Ishi died.

~August 30~

On this day, August 30, 1999, East Timor voted for independence from Indonesia.

East Timor was colonized by Portugal in the 16th century and was known as Portuguese Timor until November 28, 1975, when the Revolutionary Front for an Independent East Timor (FRETILIN) declared the territory's independence. Nine days later, it was invaded and occupied by Indonesia and was declared Indonesia's 27th province the following year. The Indonesian occupation of East Timor was characterized by a highly violent decades-long conflict between separatist groups and the Indonesian military.

In 1999, following the United Nations-sponsored act of self-determination, Indonesia relinquished control of the territory. East Timor became the first new sovereign state of the 21st century on May 20, 2002.

~August 31~

"Princess Di[ed]"

On this day, August 31, 1997, Diana Spencer died at Pitié-Salpêtrière Hospital, Paris, France. Lady Diana's extensive charity work included campaigning for animal protection and her fight against the use of landmines. She was the patroness of numerous charities and organizations working with the homeless, youth, drug addicts, and the elderly.

Diana was the patron of HALO Trust, an organization that removes debris left behind by war, in particular landmines. In January 1997, Diana toured an Angolan minefield in a ballistic helmet, and flak jacket and the pictures were disseminated worldwide. HALO states that Diana's efforts resulted in raising international awareness about landmines and the subsequent sufferings caused by them. From August 7th to 10th 1997, just days before her death, she visited Bosnia and Herzegovina with Landmine Survivors Network. Her work on the landmines issue has been described as influential in the signing of the Ottawa Treaty, which created an international ban on the use of anti-personnel landmines.

General Heinrich Freiherr von Lüttwitz
to General Anthony McAulliffe

To the U.S.A. Commander of the encircled town of Bastogne.

The fortune of war is changing. This time the U.S.A. forces in and near Bastogne have been encircled by strong German armored units. More German armored units have crossed the river Our near Ortheuville, have taken Marche and reached St. Hubert by passing through Hompre-Sibret-Tillet. Libramont is in German hands.

There is only one possibility to save the encircled U.S.A. troops from total annihilation: that is the honorable surrender of the encircled town. In order to think it over a term of two hours will be granted beginning with the presentation of this note.

If this proposal should be rejected one German Artillery Corps and six heavy A. A. Battalions are ready to annihilate the U.S.A. troops in and near Bastogne. The order for firing will be given immediately after this two hours term.

All the serious civilian losses caused by this artillery fire would not correspond with the well-known American humanity.

The German Commander.

~~~

General Anthony McAulliffe
to General Heinrich Freiherr von Lüttwitz

To the German Commander.

NUTS!

The American Commander.

~September 1~

"Adi Granth"

On this day, September 1, 1604, Adi Granth, now known as Guru Granth Sahib, the holy scripture of Sikhs, was first installed at Harmandir Sahib.

~~~

"Roger Casement"

On this day, September 1, 1864, Roger David Casement was born in Sandycove, Dublin, Ireland. Casement (September 1, 1864 – August 3, 1916), formerly known as Sir Roger Casement CMG, was an Irish nationalist who worked for the British Foreign Office as a diplomat and later became a humanitarian activist, poet, and Easter Rising leader. Casement made efforts to gain German military aid for the Easter Rising of 1916 seeking to gain Irish independence. As a result, Sir Roger David Casement was arrested, charged with treason, convicted, stripped of his knighthood, and executed.

~~~

"The 'Master Race' without Morality"

On this day, September 1, 1939, Adolf Hitler signed an order to begin the systematic euthanasia of mentally ill and disabled people. This order ultimately included members of his own family. Aloisia V was Hitler's second cousin once removed; Aloisia was the great-grandchild of the sister of Hitler's paternal grandmother in the Schicklgruber family.

~September 2~

"Shoot to Kill"

On this day, September 2, 1841, Robert Clay Allison was born near Waynesboro, Tennessee. Allison (September 2, 1841 – July 3, 1887) was a veteran of the Confederate Army, a cattle rancher, cattle broker, and gunfighter in the American Old West. Allison had a reputation for violence, having survived several one-on-one knife and gunfights, as well as being implicated in a number of vigilante jail break-ins and lynchings. A drunken Allison once rode his horse through town nearly naked, wearing only his gunbelt. Clay Allison died when he was hauling a wagon load of supplies. When the load shifted, a sack of grain fell from the wagon and Allison fell from the wagon as he tried to catch it; a wagon wheel rolled over him, breaking his neck. Allison was buried the next day in Pecos Cemetery, Pecos, Texas. His epitaph reads:

"He never killed a man that did not need killing"

~~~

"Brownie"

On this day, September 2, 2005, in the midst of the Hurricane Katrina disaster, U.S. President George W. Bush infamously uttered about the FEMA Director:

"Brownie, you're doing a heck of a job"

~September 3~

"Bullying Kids?"

On this day, September 3, 2001, Protestant loyalists began picketing Holy Cross, a Catholic primary school for girls in Belfast. How tough and cool are those adults, huh? Picketing and protesting elementary school girls. For the next 11 weeks, riot police had to escort the schoolchildren and their parents through hundreds of protesters, some of whom hurled missiles and verbal abuse at the girls...

~September 4~

"Mother Teresa"

On this day, September 4, 2016, Anjezë Gonxhe Bojaxhiu was canonized by the Catholic Church. Anjezë Gonxhe Bojaxhiu, also known as Mother Teresa born in Skopje (now the capital of the Republic of Macedonia), then part of the Kosovo Vilayet of the Ottoman Empire. Mother Teresa (August 26, 1910 – September 5, 1997) was an Albanian-Indian Roman Catholic nun and missionary. After living in Macedonia for eighteen years, she moved to Ireland and then to India, where she lived for most of her life.

In 1950, Teresa founded the Missionaries of Charity, a Roman Catholic religious congregation which had over 4,500 sisters and was active in 133 countries in 2012. The congregation manages homes for people dying of HIV/AIDS, leprosy, and tuberculosis; soup kitchens; dispensaries and mobile clinics; children's- and family-counselling programs; orphanages, and schools. Members, who take vows of chastity, poverty, and obedience, also profess a fourth vow: to give "wholehearted free service to the poorest of the poor." Teresa received a number of honors, including the 1962 Ramon Magsaysay Peace Prize and the 1979 Nobel Peace Prize.

~September 5~

"Nap Lajoie"

On this day, September 5, 1874, Napoléon "Nap" Lajoie was born in Woonsocket, Rhode Island.

Lajoie was known as Larry Lajoie and "The Frenchman," was an American professional baseball second baseman and player-manager. He played in Major League Baseball (MLB) for the Philadelphia Phillies, Philadelphia Athletics (twice), and Cleveland Naps between 1896 and 1916. He managed the Naps from 1905 through 1909. Lajoie was signed to the National Leagues' (NL) Phillies in 1896. By the beginning of the twentieth century, however, the upstart American League (AL) was looking to rival the supremacy of the NL, and in 1901, Lajoie and dozens of former National League players joined the American League. National League clubs contested the legality of contracts signed by players who jumped to the other league but eventually, Lajoie was allowed to play for Connie Mack's Athletics. During the season, Lajoie set the all-time American League single-season mark for the highest batting average (.426). One year later, Lajoie went to the Cleveland Bronchos where he would play until the 1915 season when he returned to play for Mack and the Athletics. While with Cleveland, Lajoie's popularity led to locals electing to change the club's team name from Bronchos to Napoleons ("Naps" for short), which remained until after Lajoie departed Cleveland and the name was changed to Indians (the team's present-day name).

~September 6~

"Football Diplomacy"

On this day, September 6, 2008, Turkish President Abdullah Gül attended a football match in Armenia after an invitation by Armenian President Serzh Sargsyan, making him the first Turkish head of state to visit the country.

~September 7~

"The Destruction of the Temple"

On this day, September 7, 70 C.E., a Roman army under Titus occupied and plundered Jerusalem. The siege ended with the sacking of the city and the destruction of its famous Second Temple. The destruction of both the first and second temples is still mourned annually as the Jewish fast Tisha B'Av. The Arch of Titus, celebrating the Roman sack of Jerusalem and the Temple, still stands in Rome.

~September 8 ~

"San Miguel School"

On this day, September 8, 1993, Br. Lawrence Goyette, FSC, opened the San Miguel School in Providence, Rhode Island. The San Miguel School of Providence has become a model for 13 other San Miguel Schools across the United States.

~~~

"Helen Herczberg Gawara"

On this day, September 8, 2002, Helen Herczberg Gawara died in Madison, Dane County, Wisconsin. She had been born on February 12, 1920, in Warsaw, Mazowieckie, Poland.

Her epitaph reads:

She bore witness to the Holocaust
She is now set free

~September 9~

"Smyrna"

On this day, September 9, 1922, four days after the Turks regained control of Smyrna at the end of the Greco-Turkish War, the Great Fire of Smyrna resulted in the massacre of the Greek and Armenian populations. The death toll is estimated to range from 10,000 to 100,000.

~~~

"The Treznea Massacre"

On this day, September 9, 1940, the Treznea Massacre occurred. The Hungarian Army, supported by local Hungarians kill 93 Romanian civilians in Treznea, a village in Northern Transylvania, as part of attempts to ethnic cleansing. The massacre occurred within the context of, and in reaction to, the Second Vienna Award which transferred Northern Transylvania from Romania to Hungary.

~September 10~

"Neto"

On this day, September 10, 1979, António Agostinho Neto died in Moscow, Russia. He had led the Popular Movement for the Liberation of Angola (MPLA) in the war for independence (1961–1974) and served as the first President of Angola (1975–1979).

Neto left Angola to study medicine at universities in Coimbra and Lisbon. He combined his academic life with covert political activity. PIDE, the security police force of fascist Portuguese Prime Minister Salazar, arrested Neto had detained him for three months in 1951. He was arrested again in 1952 for joining the Portuguese Movement for Democratic Youth Unity. He was arrested again in 1955 and held until 1957. He eventually finished his medical studies. He returned to Angola in 1959, was arrested again in 1960. His patients and supporters organized a protest march for his release from Bengo to Catete but were stopped when Portuguese soldiers shot at them, killing 30 and wounding more than 200. This is known as the Massacre of Icolo e Bengo.

Neto escaped from prison and took leadership of the struggle against Portuguese colonial rule. When Angola gained their independence in 1975, he became President and held the position until his death in 1979.

~September 11~

"Expulsion"

On this day, September 11, 1609, Spain issued the first in a series of expulsion orders against Moriscos. The first expulsion order announced against the Moriscos of Valencia. Moriscos were former Muslims who converted or were coerced into converting to Christianity after Spain finally outlawed the open practice of Islam by its sizable Mudejar population in the early 16th century. For a visual impression, check out *Embarkation of Moriscos in Valencia* by Pere Oromig (1615).

~September 12~

"Pre-Nazi"

On this day, September 12, 1919, Adolf Hitler joined the German Workers' Party (later renamed the National Socialist Workers Party, or Nazi Party).

~~~

"Sudetenland"

On this day, September 12, 1938, Adolf Hitler, then leader of Germany, demanded autonomy and self-determination for the Germans of the Sudetenland region of Czechoslovakia which prompted the Sudetenland Crisis and Munich Conference.

~September 13~

"The American Schindler"

On this day, September 13, 1967, Varian Mackey Fry died in Reading, Connecticut. Fry (October 15, 1907 – September 13, 1967) was an American journalist. While working as a foreign correspondent for the American journal *The Living Age*, Fry visited Berlin in 1935 and personally witnessed Nazi abuse against Jews on more than one occasion, which turned him into an ardent anti-Nazi. He said in 1945, "I could not remain idle as long as I had any chances at all of saving even a few of its intended victims." Following his visit to Berlin, Fry wrote about the savage treatment of Jews by Hitler's regime in the New York Times in 1935. Fry began and ran a rescue network in Vichy France that helped approximately 2,000 to 4,000 anti-Nazi and Jewish refugees to escape Nazi Germany and the Holocaust. He is known as the "American Schindler."

~~~

"Tutu"

On this day, September 13, 1989, Desmond Tutu led the largest anti-Apartheid march ever in South Africa. More than 30,000 people, of all ages and races, marched from the South African Parliament to St. George's Cathedral.

The event, led by Mayor Gordon Oliver, Archbishop Tutu, Rev Frank Chikane, Moulana Farid Esack, Allan Boesak, and other religious leaders, was held in defiance of the State of Emergency which banned political protests and apartheid laws which enforced racial segregation.

~September 14~

"Ip Massacre"

On this day, September 14, 1940, the Ip Massacre took place in the early hours in Ip, Sălaj - a village in Northern Transylvania. The Hungarian Army was supported by a local vigilante group, and together they killed 158 Romanian civilians. The massacred within the context of the Second Vienna Award. Immediately after the occupation of the Transylvanian territory, they started a series of massacres against the Romanian civilian populace. On September 8, 1940, the Second Army entered the city of Zalău. The area most affected by Horthyist terror was Sălaj, where 477 Romanians were massacred.

~September 15~

"The Nuremberg Laws"

On this day, September 15, 1935, the Nuremberg Laws were issued at the annual NSDAP Reich Party Congress. The Nuremberg Laws were actually a set of two laws: the Reich Citizenship Law and the Law for the Protection of German Blood and Honor and became collectively known as the Nuremberg Laws. The Nuremberg Laws stripped German citizenship from German Jews and outlawed both marriage and sex between Jews and non-Jews. Unlike historical antisemitism, the Nuremberg Laws defined Jewishness by heredity (race) rather than by practice.

~~~

"Swastika"

On this day, September 15, 1935, Nazi Germany adopted the national flag bearing the swastika. The flag had already been adopted by the Nazi Party on August 7, 1920. In Hitler's *Mein Kampf*, he stated that the Nazi Party needed a new flag–one that flew as "a symbol of our own struggle.

~~~

"Oh, _now_ you like the government?"

On this day, September 15, 2005, Dick Durbin (D-IL) spoke on the floor of the US Senate about Hurricane Katrina funs and quoted former US Senator Bill Cohen (R-ME) who once said, "the government is the enemy until you need a friend" as well as US Senator Trent Lott who once said, "You are a fiscal conservative until you get hit by a natural disaster."

~September 16~

"Suzanne Mol"

On this day, September 16, 1936, Suzanne Mol, was born in Paris, France. During the German occupation of France, she was arrested and deported to Auschwitz with her parents. She died in the gas chamber, six weeks before her 6th birthday.

~September 17~

"Assassination of the Guy Who Helped You?

On this day, September 17, 1948, Folke Bernadotte, the Count of Wisborg, was assassinated by the Lehi (also known as the Stern gang). Bernadotte, a Swedish diplomat and nobleman, was appointed by the United Nations to mediate between the Arab nations. During World War II, he had negotiated the release of about 31,000 prisoners from German concentration camps, including 450 Danish Jews, from the Theresienstadt camp released on April 14, 1945.

~~~

"Camp David"

On this day, September 17, 1978, the Camp David Accords were signed by Israel and Egypt.

~September 18~

"Escape from Sobibór"

On this day, September 18, 1943, Jewish prisoners from Minsk were massacred at Sobibór. This massacre, combined with rumors that the camp would be shut down, led Polish-Jewish prisoners to organize an underground committee aimed at escape from the camp.

On October 14, 1943, Polish-Jewish prisoner Leon Feldhendler (Lajbl) and Soviet-Jewish POW Alexander Pechersky covertly killed eleven German SS officers, overpowered the camp guards, and seized the armory. Although their plan was to kill all the SS and walk out of the main gate of the camp, the killings were discovered, and the inmates ran for their lives under fire. About 300 out of the 600 Sonderkommando prisoners in the camp escaped into the forests. Most of them were recaptured by the search squads.

Sobibór was the site of one of two successful uprisings by Jewish Sonderkommando prisoners during Operation Reinhard. The revolt at Treblinka extermination camp on August 2, 1943, resulted in more than 100 escapees.

In 1987, CBS aired a British film titled, *Escape from Sobibor*, a fictional account of the uprising.

~September 19~

"You Volunteered for WHAT?"

On this day, September 19, 1940, Witold Pilecki voluntarily allowed himself to be captured and sent to Auschwitz in order to smuggle out information and start a resistance movement.

As the author of Witol''s Report, the first intelligence report on Auschwitz concentration camp, Pilecki enabled the Polish government-in-exile to convince the Allies that the Holocaust was taking place.

At Auschwitz, while working in various kommandos and surviving pneumonia, Pilecki organized an underground Union of Military Organizations (Związek Organizacji Wojskowej, ZOW). Many smaller underground organizations at Auschwitz eventually merged with ZOW. ZOW's tasks were to improve inmate morale, provide news from outside, distribute extra food and clothing to members, set up intelligence networks and train detachments to take over the camp in the event of liberation.

From October 1940, ZOW sent reports to Warsaw, and beginning in March 1941, Pilecki's reports were being forwarded via the Polish resistance to the British government in London. In 1942, Pilecki's resistance movement was also broadcasting details on the number of arrivals and deaths in the camp and the inmates' conditions using a radio transmitter that was built by camp inmates. The secret radio station, built over seven months using smuggled parts, was broadcasting from the camp until the autumn of 1942 when it was dismantled by Pilecki's men after concerns that the Germans might discover its location.

Pilecki decided to break out of the camp with the hope of convincing Home Army leaders personally that a rescue attempt was a valid option. When he was assigned to a night shift at a camp bakery outside the fence, he and two comrades overpowered a guard, cut the phone line and escaped on the night of 26/27 April 1943, taking with them documents stolen from the Germans.

When the Warsaw Uprising broke out on 1 August 1944, Pilecki fought as a simple private, without revealing his actual rank. Later, as many officers fell, he disclosed his true identity and accepted command. His forces held a fortified area called the "Great Bastion of Warsaw." It was one of the most outlying partisan redoubts and caused considerable difficulties for German supply lines. He held for two weeks in the face of constant attacks by German infantry and armor. On the capitulation of the uprising, Pilecki hid some weapons in a private apartment before being captured. He spent the rest of the war in German prisoner-of-war camps at Łambinowie and Murnau.

Pilecki returned to Poland in October 1945, where he proceeded to organize his intelligence network document Soviet atrocities against the Polish people. On 8 May 1947, he was arrested by the Soviet-puppet Polish Ministry of Public Security. Prior to trial, he was repeatedly tortured. On May 25, 1948, Pilecki was executed at the Mokotów Prison in Warsaw.

~September 20~

"The (SHAMEFUL) Walking Purchase"

On this day, September 20, 1737, the Walking Purchase was completed which forced the cession of 1.2 million acres of Lenape-Delaware tribal land to the Pennsylvania Colony.

While William Penn enjoyed a reputation for fair-dealing with the Lenape, his heirs John Penn and Thomas Penn, abandoned many of the elder Penn's practices. In 1737, they claimed a deed from 1686 by which the Lenape promised to sell a tract beginning at the junction of the Delaware River and Lehigh River and extending as far west as a man could walk in a day and a half. This document may have been an unsigned, unratified treaty, or even an outright forgery. Penns' agents began selling land in the Lehigh Valley to colonists while the Lenape still inhabited the area.

In *Delaware Nation v. Pennsylvania* (2004), the Delaware nation (one of three federally recognized Lenape tribes) claimed 314 acres (1.27 km2) of land included in the original purchase, but the US District Court granted the Commonwealth's motion to dismiss. It ruled that the case was nonjusticiable, although it acknowledged that Indian title appeared to have been extinguished by fraud. This ruling held through the United States courts of appeals. The US Supreme Court refused to hear the case.

~September 21~

"Battle of Prestonpans"

On this day, September 21, 1745, a Hanoverian army under the command of Sir John Cope is defeated, in ten minutes, by the Jacobite forces of Prince Charles Edward Stuart during the Battle of Prestonpans.

~~~

"The Hobbit"

On this day, September 21, 1937, J. R. R. Tolkien's *The Hobbit* was first published.

~~~

"Orlando Letelier"

On this day, September 21, 1976, Orlando Letelier was assassinated in Washington, D.C. He was a member of the Chilean socialist government of Salvador Allende, overthrown in 1973 by Augusto Pinochet.

~~~

"Sandra Day O'Connor"

On this day, September 21, 1981, Sandra Day O'Connor was unanimously approved by the U.S. Senate as the first female Supreme Court Associate Justice of the United States of America.

~September 22~

"RI's Tarzan"

On this day, September 22, 1914, Ellison Myers Brown, Sr., was born in Porter Hill, Rhode Island. Brown (September 22, 1914 – August 23, 1975), widely known as Tarzan Brown, and Deerfoot amongst his people, was a two-time winner of the Boston Marathon, in 1936 (2:33:40) and 1939 (2:28:51). A member and a direct descendant of the last acknowledged royal family of the Narragansett Indian tribe of Rhode Island, he also participated in the 1936 Summer Olympics in Berlin. He was scheduled to participate in the 1940 Summer Olympics in Tokyo, but these were canceled due to the outbreak of World War II. Tarzan Brown is still one of only two Native Americans to have won the Boston Marathon (the other being Thomas Longboat of the Onondaga Nation from Canada, in 1907) and the only Native American to have more than one victory in Boston. He was inducted into the American Indian Athletic Hall of Fame in 1973.

~~~

"Berlin Candy Bomber"

On this day, September 22, 1948, Gail Halvorsen officially started parachuting candy to children as part of the Berlin Air lift. Colonel Gail Seymour "Hal" Halvorsen (b. October 10, 1920) is a retired officer and command pilot in the US Air Force. He is best known as the "Berlin Candy Bomber" or "Uncle Wiggly Wings" who dropped candy to children during the Berlin airlift from 1948 to 1949. Gail Halvorsen, one of the many Airlift pilots, decided to use his off time to fly into Berlin and make movies with his hand-held camera. He arrived at Tempelhof on July 17th on a C-54s and walked over to a crowd of children who had gathered at the end of the runway to watch the aircraft.

He introduced himself, and they started to ask him questions about the aircraft and their flights. As a goodwill gesture, he handed out his only two sticks of Wrigley's Doublemint Gum and promised that, if they did not fight over them, the next time he returned he would drop off more. The children quickly divided up the pieces as best they could. Before he left them, a child asked him how they would know it was him flying over, and he replied, "I'll wiggle my wings."

The next day, on his approach to Berlin, he rocked the aircraft and dropped some chocolate bars attached to a handkerchief parachute to the children waiting below. Every day after that the number of children increased, and he made several more drops. Soon there was a stack of mail in Base Ops addressed to "Uncle Wiggly Wings," "The Chocolate Uncle" and "The Chocolate Flier."

While his commanding officer was upset when the story appeared in the news, the gesture was immediately expanded it into "Operation Little Vittles." Other pilots participated, and when news reached the US, children all over the country sent in their own candy to help out. Soon, the major manufacturers joined in.

In the end, over 23 tons of candy were dropped on Berlin, and the "operation" became a major propaganda success. The candy-dropping aircrafts were christened "raisin bombers" by the German children.

~September 23~

"Sigmund Freud"

On this day, September 23, 1939, Sigmund Freud, Austrian neurologist and psychiatrist (b. 1856) died in exile in Hampstead, London, United Kingdom.

In creating psychoanalysis, Freud developed therapeutic techniques such as the use of free association and discovered transference, establishing its central role in the analytic process. Freud's redefinition of sexuality to include its infantile forms led him to formulate the Oedipus complex as the central tenet of psychoanalytical theory. His analysis of dreams as wish-fulfillments provided him with models for the clinical analysis of symptom formation and the underlying mechanisms of repression. On this basis, Freud elaborated his theory of the unconscious and went on to develop a model of psychic structure comprising id, ego, and super-ego. Freud postulated the existence of libido, an energy with which mental processes and structures are invested and which generates erotic attachments, and a death drive, the source of compulsive repetition, hate, aggression and neurotic guilt

~~~

"Padre Pio"

On this day, September 23, 1968, Francesco Forgione, also known as Pio of Pietrelcina or Padre Pio, died in San Giovanni Rotondo, Foggia, Italy. Pio (b. 1887) was Italian priest and saint who became famous for exhibiting stigmata for most of his life, thereby generating much interest and controversy. He was both beatified (1999) and canonized (2002) by Pope John Paul II.

~September 24~

"The First National Monument"

On this day, September 24, 1906, U.S. President Theodore Roosevelt proclaimed Devils Tower in Wyoming as the nation's first National Monument.

~~~

"Little Rock"

On this day, September 24, 1957, President Eisenhower sent US soldiers to Little Rock, AR, to enforce desegregation.

~~~

"James Meredith"

On this day, September 24, 1962, the US Court of Appeals ordered Ole Miss to admit James Meredith. In 1961, inspired the day before by JFK, Meredith applied to the Ole Miss insisting on his civil rights to attend the state-funded university. It had still only admitted Caucasian students under the state's culture of racial segregation, regardless of *Brown v. Board of Education* (1954). Meredith wrote in his application that he wanted admission for his country, race, family, and himself. He said,

"Nobody handpicked me...I believed, and believe now, that I have a Divine Responsibility... I am familiar with the probable difficulties involved in such a move as I am undertaking and I am fully prepared to pursue it all the way to a degree from the University of Mississippi."

~September 25~

"Wangari Muta Maathai"

On this day, September 25, 2011, Wangari Muta Maathai died in Nairobi, Kenya. Maathai (April 1, 1940 – September 25, 2011) was a Kenyan environmental political activist and Nobel laureate. She was educated in the United States at Mount St. Scholastica (Benedictine College) and the University of Pittsburgh, as well as the University of Nairobi in Kenya. In 1977, Maathai founded the Green Belt Movement; an environmental non-governmental organization focused on the planting of trees, environmental conservation, and women's rights. In 1984, she was awarded the Right Livelihood Award, and in 2004, she became the first African woman to receive the Nobel Peace Prize for "her contribution to sustainable development, democracy, and peace."

In Honor of Denzil Franklyn

~September 26~

"Borgia Bull"

On this day, September 26, 1493, Pope Alexander VI issued the papal bull *Dudum siquidem* to the Catholic Monarchs, extending the grant of new lands that he made to them in *Inter caetera*. This decision, like the *Treaty of Tordesillas*, was made without the consent of the native people living in the two continents.

~~~

"Torquemada"

On this day, September 26, 1468, Juan de Torquemada, Spanish cardinal and the person most associated with the Spanish Inquisition died Ávila, Spain.

~September 27~

"The Jesuits"

On this day, September 27, 1540, Pope Paul III chartered the Society of Jesus.

~September 28~

"Ángel Sanz-Briz"

On this day, September 28, 1997, Ángel Sanz-Briz was born in Zaragoza, Italy. Sanz-Briz (September 28, 1910 – June 11, 1980) was a Spanish professional diplomat of Francoist Spain during World War II who saved the lives of some five thousand Hungarian Jews from Nazi persecution.

~~~

"Fengshan"

On this day, September 28, 1997, Fengshan (b. September 10, 1901) died in San Francisco, California. Fengshan was a Chinese diplomat in Vienna who risked his own life and career during World War II to save more than three thousand Jews.

~September 29~

The Redemption of Dachau?

Homeless Given Asylum in Garden Complex at Dachau
by Hannah Vaitsblit of *The Tablet*

Buildings that were part of a herb garden at the former Dachau concentration camp are now home to 50 homeless people seeking refuge in Germany, reported the AFP on Tuesday. The herb garden is not part of the concentration camp memorial. In a statement, Florian Hartmann, the mayor of Dachau, which is reportedly going through a housing shortage, acknowledged the historical irony of re-purposing the buildings as a homeless shelter but stressed the need to assist "the weakest members of society" by allowing the buildings to assume a "useful social role... The buildings with their historical burden can be used for a socially meaningful purpose."

In an email to *The Guardian*, Hartmann wrote: "The buildings in the herb garden are used to house people who can't afford a flat at market rates. They're the more vulnerable members of our society. In that way, the buildings with their historical burden can be used for a socially meaningful purpose."

According to the *International Business Times*, "the German government has said it expects 800,000 people to seek asylum in Germany this year, as Europe struggles to cope with a huge influx of people fleeing war and poverty in countries in the Middle East, Asia, and Africa." Hartmann, however, would not specify whether any of the persons given shelter at the former concentration camp are those fleeing from Syria or elsewhere.[2]

---

[2] http://www.tabletmag.com/scroll/193810/homeless-given-asylum-in-garden-complex-at-former-dachau-concentration-camp

~September 30~

"Isaac P. Rodman"

On this day, September 30, 1862, Isaac Peace Rodman mortally wounded at the Battle of Antietam. (August 18, 1822 – September 30, 1862) was a Rhode Island banker and politician, and a Union Army brigadier general in the American Civil War, mortally wounded at the Battle of Antietam.

His obelisk in the Perry Cemetery, surrounded by the South County Sand and Gravel complex simply states:

> His was the patriot's
> His was the soldier's pride,
> His country called him,
> And for her he died.

~~~

"I'm from the Government, and I'm here to help"

Ronald Reagan (R-CA)

August 12, 1986
Presidential Press Conference on Agriculture

~ ~ ~

"Government is the enemy until you need a friend"

William Cohen (R-ME)

The Cohen Rule
Former US Representative, US Senator, US Secretary of Defense

~October 1~

"Nuremburg"

On this day, October 1, 1946, the Nazi leaders were finally sentenced at the Nuremburg Trials. Most were sentenced to death by hanging with the significant exception of Albert Speer.

The tribunal was given the task of trying 23 of the most important political and military leaders of the Third Reich, though one of the defendants, Martin Bormann, was tried in absentia, while another, Robert Ley, committed suicide within a week of the trial's commencement. (Not included were Adolf Hitler, Heinrich Himmler, and Joseph Goebbels, all of whom had committed suicide in the spring of 1945, well before the indictment was signed.)

~~~

"The Best Ex-President Ever"

On this day, October 1, 1924, James Earl Carter, Jr. was born on October 1, 1924, at the Wise Sanitarium in Plains, Georgia. In 1982, he established the Carter Center in Atlanta to advance human rights and alleviate human suffering. The non-profit, nongovernmental Center promotes democracy, mediates, and prevents conflicts, and monitors the electoral process in support of free and fair elections. It also works to improve global health through the control and eradication of diseases such as Guinea worm disease, river blindness, malaria, trachoma, lymphatic filariasis, and schistosomiasis. In 2002, President Carter received the Nobel Peace Prize for his work "to find peaceful solutions to international conflicts, to advance democracy and human rights, and to promote economic and social development" through The Carter Center.

~October 2~

"West Nickel Mines School"

On this day, October 2, 2006, there was a school shooting at the West Nickel Mines School, an Amish one-room schoolhouse in the Old Order Amish community of Nickel Mines, Bart Township, Lancaster County, Pennsylvania. Charles Carl Roberts IV took hostages and shot eight out of ten girls (aged 6–13), killing five, before committing suicide in the schoolhouse.

On the day of the shooting, a grandfather of one of the murdered Amish girls was heard warning some young relatives not to hate the killer, saying, "We must not think evil of this man." Another Amish father noted, "He had a mother and a wife and a soul and now he's standing before a just God." Jack Meyer, a member of the Brethren community living near the Amish in Lancaster County, explained: "I don't think there's anybody here that wants to do anything but forgive and not only reach out to those who have suffered a loss in that way but to reach out to the family of the man who committed these acts."

Amish community members visited and comforted Roberts' widow, parents, and parents-in-law. The Amish have also set up a charitable fund for the family of the shooter. About 30 members of the Amish community attended Roberts' funeral, and Marie Roberts, the widow of the killer, was one of the few outsiders invited to the funeral of one of the victims. Marie Roberts wrote an open letter to her Amish neighbors thanking them for their forgiveness, grace, and mercy. She wrote, "Your love for our family has helped to provide the healing we so desperately need. Gifts you've given have touched our hearts in a way no words can describe. Your compassion has reached beyond our family, beyond our community, and is changing our world, and for this we sincerely thank you."

~October 3~

"George Bell"

On this day, October 3, 1958, George Kennedy Allen Bell (February 4, 1883 – October 3, 1958) was an Anglican theologian and a pioneer of the ecumenical movement. From 1932 to 1934 he was the president of "Life and Work" at the ecumenical council in Geneva and, at the Berlin conference in February 1933, Bell witnessed the Nazi takeover at first hand.

In April 1933, he publicly expressed the international church's worries over the beginnings of the Nazis' anti-Semitic campaign in Germany, and in September that year carried a resolution protesting against the "Aryan paragraph" and its acceptance by parts of the German Evangelical Church. In November 1933, Bell met Dietrich Bonhoeffer, and the two became close friends. Bonhoeffer often informed Bell of what was going on in Germany, then Bell made this information known to the public of Europe and America, for example through letters to The Times.

On June 1, 1934, Bell signed the Barmen Declaration, which proclaimed that Christian belief and National Socialism were incompatible and condemned pro-Nazi German Christianity as "false teaching" or heresy. During the war, Bell was involved in helping not only displaced persons and refugees who had fled the continent to England but also interned Germans and British conscientious objectors. During WWII, Bell repeatedly condemned the Allied practice of area bombing. As a member of the House of Lords, he was a consistent parliamentary critic of area bombing in the House of Commons.

Even as early as 1939, he stated that the church should not be allowed to become simply a spiritual help to the state, but instead should be an advocate of peaceful international relations and make a stand against expulsion, enslavement and the destruction of morality. It should not be allowed to abandon these principles, ever ready to criticize retaliatory attacks or the bombing of civil populations. He also urged the European churches to remain critical of their own countries' ways of waging war. In November 1939, he published an article stating that the Church in wartime should not hesitate:

> to condemn the infliction of reprisals, or the bombing of civilian populations, by the military forces of its own nation. It should set itself against the propaganda of lies and hatred. It should be ready to encourage the resumption of friendly relations with the enemy nation. It should set its face against any war of extermination or enslavement, and any measures directly aimed to destroy the morale of a population.

In 1941, in a letter to *The Times*, he called the bombing of unarmed women and children "barbarian" which would destroy the *just bello*, thus openly criticizing the Prime Minister's advocacy of such a bombing strategy. On February 14, 1943 - two years ahead of the Dresden raids - he urged the House of Lords to resist the War Cabinet's decision for area bombing, stating that it called into question all the humane and democratic values for which Britain had gone to war. In 1944, during the debate, he again demanded that Britain stop area bombing of German cities such as Hamburg and Berlin as a disproportionate and illegal "policy of annihilation" and a crime against humanity.

~October 4~

"A Cute Picnic Between Murderers"

On this day, October 4, 1940, German Führer Adolf Hitler and Italian Duce Benito Mussolini met at Brenner Pass to celebrate their Pact of Steel of May 22, 1939. They met at the Brenner Pass multiple times in their alliance (for example, they also met on March 18, 1940). At the October 4th meeting, Mussolini confirmed his decision to enter the war on the side of Germany.

~October 5~

"Václav Havel"

On this day, October 5, 1936, Václav Havel was born in Prague, Czechoslovakia (now the Czech Republic). Havel (October 1936 – 18 December 2011) was a Czech writer, philosopher, political dissident, and politician. From 1989 to 1992, he served as the last president of Czechoslovakia. He then served as the first President of the Czech Republic (1993–2003) after the Czech–Slovak split. Within Czech literature, he is known for his plays, essays, and memoirs. He presided over the peaceful Velvet Revolution and the continuous but equally peaceful Hyphen War.

~~~

"I Don't Get No Respect"

On this day, October 5, 2004, Rodney Dangerfield died in Westwood, Los Angeles, California. Dangerfield (November 22, 1921 - October 5, 2004) was born Jacob Cohen and became a comedian, actor, producer, and screenwriter. His was known for his self-deprecating humor and his catchphrase "I don't get no respect!" His gravestone bears the epitaph, borrowed from Mel Brooks' film *Spaceballs* (1987)"

"There goes the neighborhood"

~October 6~

"This Day in Hungary"

~~~

"The 13 Martyrs of Arad"

On this day, October 6, 1849, the 13 Martyrs of Arad were executed after the failed Hungarian war of independence. The "Aradi vértanúk" were the thirteen Hungarian rebel generals who were executed by the Austrian Empire on October 6, 1849, in the city of Arad, then part of the Kingdom of Hungary (now in Romania), after the Hungarian Revolution (1848–1849).

~~~

"Austro-Hungarian Bosnia"

On this day, October 6, 1908, Austria-Hungary annexed Bosnia-Herzegovina, sparking a diplomatic crisis.

~~~

"Árpád Göncz"

On this day, October 6, 2015, Árpád Göncz died in Budapest, Hungary. Göncz (February 10, 1922 – October 6, 2015) was an author, playwright, politician, and the 1st President of Hungary in the post-Cold War period. Göncz was a participant in the 1956 Hungarian Revolution and survived the Soviet crackdown, reportedly, because of the personal intervention of Prime Minister of India Jawaharlal Nehru on behalf of Göncz.

~October 7~

"Tutu"

On this day, October 7, 1931, Desmond Mpilo Tutu was born in Klerksdorp, Western Transvaal, South Africa. Tutu is a South African social rights activist and retired Anglican bishop who rose to worldwide fame during the 1980s as an opponent of apartheid. He was the first black Archbishop of Cape Town and bishop of the Church of the Province of Southern Africa (now the Anglican Church of Southern Africa.

In 1975, he moved to Soweto's well known Vilakazi Street, which is also the location of a house in which Nelson Mandela once lived. It is said to be one of the few streets in the world where two Nobel Prize winners have lived. In 1976, the protests in Soweto, also known as the Soweto riots, against the government's use of Afrikaans as the compulsory language of instruction in black schools became an uprising against apartheid. From then on Tutu supported an economic boycott of his country. He vigorously opposed the "constructive engagement" policy of the Reagan administration in the United States, which advocated "friendly persuasion." Tutu pressed the advantage and organized peaceful marches which brought 30,000 people onto the streets of Cape Town.

After the fall of apartheid, Tutu headed the Truth and Reconciliation Commission. He retired as Archbishop of Cape Town in 1996 and was made emeritus Archbishop of Cape Town, an honorary title that is unusual in the Anglican church. Since the demise of apartheid, Tutu has campaigned to fight HIV/AIDS, tuberculosis, poverty, racism, sexism, homophobia, and transphobia. He has received the Nobel Peace Prize, the Albert Schweitzer Prize, the Pacem in Terris Award, the Gandhi Peace Prize, and the Presidential Medal of Freedom.

~~~

"Matthew Shepard"

On this day, October 7, 1998, Matthew Shepard, a gay student at the University of Wyoming, was found tied to a fence after being savagely beaten by two young adults in Laramie, Wyoming.

His death was a significant turning point in how Americans understand the pre-existing social acceptance of homophobia. Following her son's murder, Judy Shepard became a prominent LGBT rights activist and established the Matthew Shepard Foundation. In addition, Judy Shepard stood up for life when she would not assist the State of Wyoming in seeking the death penalty for Matthew's murderers.

The murder of Matthew Shepard brought national and international attention to hate crime legislation at the state and federal levels. In October 2009, the United States Congress passed the Matthew Shepard and James Byrd Jr. Hate Crimes Prevention Act (commonly the "Matthew Shepard Act" or "Shepard/Byrd Act"), and on October 28, 2009, President Barack Obama signed the legislation into law. Shepard's death inspired notable films, novels, plays, songs, and other works.

~October 8 ~

"Piomingo Day"

On this day, October 8, 2008, the Chickasaw Tribe replaced Columbus Day with Piomingo Day, named after Chickasaw war chief and diplomat: "Piomingo established a friendship with George Washington and the new federal government, and paved the way for cooperative living. President Washington had believed that the republic would not only honor Indian boundaries but protect them."

~October 9~

"Oskar Schindler"

On this day, October 9, 1974, Oskar Schindler (April 28, 1908 – October 9, 1974) was a German industrialist, spy, and member of the Nazi Party who is credited with saving the lives of 1,200 Jews during the Holocaust by employing them in his enamelware and ammunitions factories, which were located in occupied Poland and the Protectorate of Bohemia and Moravia. He is the subject of the 1982 novel *Schindler's Ark*, and the subsequent 1993 film *Schindler's List*, which reflected his life as an opportunist initially motivated by profit but who came to show extraordinary initiative, tenacity, and dedication to saving the lives of his Jewish employees.

~~~

"Jody Williams"

On this day, October 9, 1950, Jody Williams was born in Rutland, Vermont, United States. Williams is an American political activist known around the world for her work in banning anti-personnel landmines, her defense of human rights (especially those of women), and her efforts to promote new understandings of security in today's world. She was awarded the Nobel Peace Prize in 1997 for her work toward the banning and clearing of anti-personnel mines.

~October 10~

"Frank Keaney"

On this day, October 10, 1967, Frank William "Menty" Keaney died. Keaney (June 5, 1886 – October 10, 1967) was a college men's basketball coach known as the architect of modern 'run-and-shoot' basketball and the inventor of the fast break.

Keaney coached at the University of Rhode Island from 1920 to 1948. In his 28 years at Rhode Island, Keaney's basketball Rams won 8 conference championships and had only one losing season. In 1939, Keaney's Rams became the first college team to score more than 50 points per game, and in 1943 the team had an average of more than two points per minute (80.7 points per game), which led to the Rams being dubbed "The Firehouse Gang." During his tenure, the URI team had four NIT appearances. After retiring from coaching collegiate basketball, Keaney was offered the position of head coach of the Boston Celtics, but Keaney's doctor refused to let him take the job. As a result, Keaney remained at URI as the Athletic Director until 1959. Keaney's career record with the men's basketball team was 401-124 (.764).

The university named the Frank W. Keaney Gymnasium-Armory in his honor in 1953 and Keaney was inducted into the Basketball Hall of Fame in 1960.

~October 11~

"Thích Nhất Hạnh"

On this day, October 11, 1926, Thích Nhất Hạnh was born in Huế, Thừa Thiên-Huế Province, Vietnam. He is a Vietnamese Buddhist monk and peace activist and coined the term "Engaged Buddhism" in his book Vietnam: Lotus in a Sea of Fire. Thích Nhất Hạnh founded Lá Bối Press, the Vạn Hanh Buddhist University in Saigon, and the School of Youth for Social Service (SYSS), a neutral corps of Buddhist peaceworkers who went into rural areas to establish schools, build healthcare clinics and help rebuild villages. In 1967, Nobel laureate Martin Luther King, Jr. nominated Nhất Hạnh for the Nobel Peace Prize, but no award was granted that year due to the Vietnam Conflict and Cold War tensions.

~~~

"Craig Price"

On this day, October 11, 1973, Craig Chandler Price was born in Warwick, Rhode Island. Price, also known as the Warwick Slasher, is an American serial killer who committed his crimes in Warwick, Rhode Island. He was arrested in 1989 for four murders committed in his neighborhood: A woman and her two daughters that year, and the murder of another woman two years prior. While in prison, he allegedly assaulted a correctional officer and, though he was due to be released, had his sentence extended past his 21st birthday.

~October 12~

"Columbus"

On this day, October 12, 1492, Christopher Columbus's expedition made landfall in the Caribbean, specifically in The Bahamas. Under the auspices of the Catholic Monarchs of Spain, he completed four voyages across the Atlantic Ocean. Those voyages and his efforts to establish permanent settlements on the island of Hispaniola initiated the Spanish colonization of the New World. The native Taino people of the Hispaniola were systematically enslaved via the encomienda system implemented by Columbus, which resembled a feudal system in Medieval Europe. The combined effects of Columbus' forced labor regime, war, and slaughter resulted in the near-total eradication of 98% of the native Taino of Hispaniola. Bartolome De las Casas (1971) records that when he first came to Hispaniola in 1508,

"There were 60,000 people living on this island, including the Indians; so that from 1494 to 1508, over three million people had perished from war, slavery, and the mines. Who in future generations will believe this? I myself writing it as a knowledgeable eyewitness can hardly believe it...."

~~~

"Matthew Shepherd"

On this day, October 12, 1998, Matthew Shepherd died six days later after he had suffered severe head injuries at the hands of Aaron McKinney and Russell Henderson. McKinney and Henderson assaulted Shepherd for being gay.

~October 13~

"Marc H. Tanenbaum"

On this day, October 13, 1925, Rabbi Marc H. Tanenbaum was born in Baltimore, Maryland, USA. Rabbi Tanenbaum (October 13, 1925 – July 3, 1992) was a human rights and social justice activist who was known for building bridges with other faith communities to advance mutual understanding and cooperation and to eliminate entrenched stereotypes, particularly those rooted in religious teachings. He was an advocate during the Second Vatican Council (1962–1965) on behalf of what eventually emerged as Nostra aetate, a landmark document which overturned a long tradition of hostility toward Jews and Judaism, including the charge that the Jews were responsible for the death of Jesus—and affirmed the Jewish roots of Christianity. Nostra aetate established a new policy of outreach in dialogue to Jews and set Catholic-Jewish relations on a new course. Tanenbaum was dubbed "the human rights rabbi" for his work on behalf of Vietnamese boat people and Cambodian refugees. He helped organize humanitarian relief for victims of the Nigerian Civil War. In 1993, after Rabbi Tanenbaum's death, his wife Georgette Bennett launched the Rabbi Marc H. Tanenbaum Foundation, which operates today as the Tanenbaum Center for Interreligious Understanding.

The 2015 recipient of the Tanenbaum Center Peacemaker Award was Maria Ida (Deng) L. Giguiento. Giguiento is the Training Coordinator for the Peace and Reconciliation Program of Catholic Relief Services Philippines. A grassroots peacebuilder from the Philippines, Deng has dedicated nearly two decades to use the conflict transformation paradigm in working with partners in Mindanao and in post-independent Timor Leste. She has trained men and women from Caritas International partners to local military officials.

~October 14~

"The Liberator"

On this day, October 14, 1843, the British arrested Irish nationalist Daniel O'Connell for conspiracy to commit crimes, sentenced him to a year's imprisonment and fined him £2,000. His crime? Having already achieved Catholic Emancipation, O'Connell was campaigning for the repeal of the Act of Union, which in 1801 had merged the Parliaments of the Kingdom of Great Britain and the Kingdom of Ireland to form the United Kingdom of Great Britain and Ireland. To campaign for Repeal, O'Connell had set up the Repeal Association. He had argued for the re-creation of an independent Kingdom of Ireland to govern itself, with Queen Victoria as the Queen of Ireland. For that, he was arrested, tried, convicted, fined, and jailed.

O'Connell's philosophy and career have inspired leaders all over the world, including Mahatma Gandhi (1869–1948) and Martin Luther King (1929–1968). He was told by William Makepeace Thackeray (1811–1863) "you have done more for your nation than any man since Washington ever did." William Gladstone (1809–1898) described him as "the greatest popular leader the world has ever seen." Honoré de Balzac (1799–1850) wrote that "Napoleon and O'Connell were the only great men the 19th century had ever seen." Jean-Henri Merle d'Aubigné (1794–1872) wrote that "the only man like Luther, in the power he wielded was O'Connell." William Grenville (1759–1834) wrote that "history will speak of him as one of the most remarkable men that ever lived." O'Connell met, befriended, and became a great inspiration to Frederick Douglass (1818–1895) a former American slave who became a highly influential leader of the abolitionist movement, social reformer, orator, writer, and statesman.

~October 15~

"The Dreyfus Affair"

On this day, October 15, 1894, Alfred Dreyfus was arrested for spying which led to the Dreyfus Affair.

Dreyfus was a French artillery officer of Jewish background whose trial and conviction in 1894 on charges of treason became one of the tensest political dramas in modern French history. Known today as the Dreyfus Affair, the incident eventually ended with Dreyfus' complete exoneration.

~~~~~

"The Arrow Cross Party"

On this day, October 15, 1944, the Arrow Cross Party took power in Hungary. The Nyilaskeresztes Párt – Hungarista Mozgalom (Arrow Cross Party-Hungarist Movement) was a Hungarist party led by Ferenc Szálasi, which led a government in Hungary known as the Government of National Unity from October 15, 1944, to October 28, 1945. During its short rule, ten to fifteen thousand civilians (many of whom were Jews) were murdered outright, and 80,000 people were deported from Hungary to various camps in Austria. After the war, Szálasi and other Arrow Cross leaders were tried as war criminals by Hungarian courts.

In 2006, Sebastian Gorka, a former editor at Breitbart News and an advisor of US President Donald Trump, defend a Hungarian militia that has resurrected the Arrow Cross Party flag. Gorka was also photographed and interviewed at Trump's inauguration wearing the uniform and medal of Vitézi Rend, a Hungarian order of merit closely associated with Nazi Germany.

~October 16~

"Hungarian Hypocrisy"

On this day, October 16, 2015, Hungary finished construction of the Hungarian Border Barrier.

The fence was ordered by Prime Minister Orbán of Hungary's neo-Nyilaskeresztes Párt known as Fidesz. The people of Arpan, who had followed the White Stag till finding a home in the Carpathian Basin, have chosen to turn their backs on fellow migrates.   Forgetting their history, the Hungarian leadership also ignores their country's great heroine St.   Elizabeth of Hungary who fed the poor in the face of overwhelming disdain by her husband. In WWII, the Hungarian people watched the deport thousands and thousands of Jewish-Hungarian civilians to be killed, then watched the Soviets build the Iron Curtain to fence in Hungarians like animals. The Hungarian people rebelled in 1956 and asked why the world did not intervene to help, and now the Hungarian people return the favor and refuse to help other civilians in need.

Perhaps the West should redraw its own fences and leave Hungary outside of the EU and NATO, at the hands of Putin's new Russian Empire again.

Ironically, it had been a braver Hungarian Government that caused the Fall of the Berlin Wall when the Hungarian Government opened its border with Austria, thus ending the Cold War.

~~~

"Karol Wojtyla"

On this day, October 16, 1978, Karol Wojtyla was elected Pope John Paul II after the October 1978 Papal Conclave, the first non-Italian pontiff since 1523.

- On May 29, 1982, Pope John Paul II became the first pope to visit a Canterbury Cathedral

- On April 4, 1986, he became the first pope to visit a synagogue.

- On March 13, 2000, Blessed Pope John Paul II defied warnings from some theologians that the unprecedented apology would undermine the church's authority and asked God to forgive the persecution of the Jews: "We are deeply saddened by the behavior of those who in the course of history have caused these children of yours to suffer, and asking your forgiveness we wish to commit ourselves to genuine brotherhood."

- On May 6, 2001, Pope John Paul II became the first pope to enter a mosque during his trip to Syria. The trip was a pilgrimage in the footsteps of St. Paul. At Olmayyad Mosque, once a Roman temple as well as a Christian church, the Pope urged Muslims and Christians to forgive each other for the past. He also appealed against religious fundamentalism of any kind.

~October 17~

"Albert Einstein"

On this day, October 17, 1933, Albert Einstein fled Nazi Germany and moved to the United States. In 1939, a group of Hungarian scientists that included émigré physicist Leó Szilárd attempted to alert Washington to ongoing Nazi atomic bomb research. The group's warnings were discounted. Einstein and Szilárd, along with other refugees such as Edward Teller and Eugene Wigner, "regarded it as their responsibility to alert Americans to the possibility that German scientists might win the race to build an atomic bomb, and to warn that Hitler would be more than willing to resort to such a weapon."

To make certain the U.S. was aware of the danger, in July 1939, a few months before the beginning of World War II in Europe, Szilárd and Wigner visited Einstein to explain the possibility of atomic bombs, which Einstein, a pacifist, said he had never considered. On August 2, 1939, Albert Einstein and Leo Szilard wrote a letter to Franklin D. Roosevelt, urging him to begin the Manhattan Project to develop a nuclear weapon.

Later, Einstein changed his position on nuclear weapons.

Einstein was a passionate, committed antiracist and joined (NAACP) in Princeton, where he campaigned for the civil rights of African Americans. He considered racism America's "worst disease... handed down from one generation to the next." As part of his involvement, he corresponded with civil rights activist W. E. B. Du Bois. In 1951, Einstein offered to be a character witness for a trial against Du Bois, causing the judge to then dismiss the case.

~October 18~

"The Europa Plan"

On this day, October 18, 1944, Gisi Fleischmann died in the Auschwitz concentration camp in Oświęcim, Poland. Fleischmann (1894 – October 18, 1944) was a Zionist activist and co-leader of the Bratislava Working Group with Rabbi Michael Ber Weissmandl. The Working Group, a Holocaust era Jewish rescue group, bribed German and Slovakian officials and paid negotiated ransom to the Germans to delay the mass deportation of Slovakian Jews was delayed for two years, from 1942 to 1944.

Fleischmann played an important role in the ambitious Europa Plan which would have seen large numbers of European Jews rescued from the Nazi and Fascist murderers. An agreement was negotiated with the Nazis in late 1942 to stop the transportation of European Jews to concentration camps. However, the Nazis demanded one to two million dollars ransom or 10% down payment. Gisi Fleischmann met several times in Hungary with Jewish leaders and also attempted to enlist support from Sally Mayer, the Swiss representative of the Joint Distribution Committee, and Hechalutz representatives in order to raise the ransom money. Reportedly Sally Mayer was unwilling to provide the down-payment since currency transfer to Nazis was illegal. Others have said that Heinrich Himmler intervened in August 1943. In either case, the Europa Plan failed.

~October 19~

"TB"

On this day, October 19, 1943, Albert Schatz first isolated Streptomycin. Schatz (February 2, 1920 – January 17, 2005) was a Ph.D. student in the laboratory at Rutgers University, and his discovery of Streptomycin let to the first antibiotic remedy for tuberculosis.

~~~

"Alija Izetbegović"

On this day, October 19, 2003, Alija Izetbegović died in Sarajevo, Bosnia and Herzegovina. Izetbegović (August 8, 1925 – October 19, 2003) was a Bosnian politician, activist, lawyer, author, and philosopher who in 1992 became the first President of the newly-independent Republic of Bosnia and Herzegovina. He served in this role until 1996, when he became a member of the Presidency of Bosnia and Herzegovina, serving until 2000. He was also the author of several books, most notably *Islam Between East and West* and the *Islamic Declaration*.

~October 20~

"The Johnny Bright Incident"

On this day, October 20, 1951, the Johnny Bright incident occurred in Stillwater, Oklahoma. Johnny Bright, an African-American player, was violently assaulted on-field by Wilbanks Smith, a Caucasian-American, during an American college football game. Bright's injury also highlighted the racial tensions of the times and assumed notoriety when it was captured in what was later to become both a widely disseminated and eventually Pulitzer Prize winning photo sequence.

~October 21~

"Alfred Nobel"

On this day, October 21, 1833, Alfred Bernhard Nobel was born in Stockholm, Sweden, Kingdom of Sweden–Norway. Nobel (October 21, 1833 – December 10, 1896) was a Swedish chemist, engineer, inventor, businessman, and philanthropist.

Known for inventing dynamite, Nobel also redirected Bofors from its previous role as primarily an iron and steel producer to a major manufacturer of cannon and other armaments. After reading a premature obituary which condemned him for profiting from the sales of arms, he bequeathed his fortune to institute the Nobel Prizes.

~October 22~

"The Oracle at Daphne"

On this day, October 22, 362, The temple of Apollo at Daphne, outside Antioch, was destroyed by a mysterious fire.

~October 23~

"Seven Days of Freedom"

On this day, October 23, 1956, there was a spontaneous nationwide revolt against the government of the Hungarian People's Republic and its Soviet-imposed policies, lasting from October 23 until November 10, 1956. The revolt was ultimately crushed by the Soviet forces but was immortalized in Noel Barber's *Seven Days of Freedom*. Over 2,500 Hungarians and 700 Soviet troops were killed in the conflict, and 200,000 Hungarians fled as refugees.

During the anti-Soviet revolution in 1956, Imre Nagy became Chairman of the Council of Ministers of the People's Republic of Hungary. Nagy moved toward a multiparty political system. On November 1st, Nagy announced Hungary's withdrawal from the Warsaw Pact and appealed through the UN for the great powers, such as the United States and the United Kingdom, to recognize Hungary's status as a neutral state.

When the revolution was crushed by the Soviet invasion of Hungary, Nagy, with a few others, was given sanctuary in the Yugoslav Embassy. On November 22nd, in spite of a written safe conduct of free passage by János Kádár, Nagy was arrested by the Soviet forces as he was leaving the Yugoslav Embassy. Later, Nagy was secretly tried for treason, found guilty, sentenced to death, and executed by hanging.

Mass arrests and denunciations continued for months thereafter.

~October 24~

"Leave the kids alone!!"

On this day, October 24, 2002, Rhode Island Superior Court Judge Stephen Fortunato issued his decision in *Gorman v. St. Raphael's Academy*, 01-4821 (2002), C. A. NO. PC 2001-4821 (Sup. Ct. R.I. 2002), paraphrasing Pink Floyd, at least so far as hair styles are concerned: "Leave the kids alone!"

~October 25~

"Sadako Sasaki"

On this day, October 25, 1955, Sadako Sasaki died at the Red Cross Hospital in Hiroshima, Japan. She was 12 years old. Sasaki was a Japanese girl who was two years old when an American atomic bomb was dropped on Hiroshima on August 6, 1945, near her home next to the Misasa Bridge. Sadako became one of the most widely known *hibakushas* — a Japanese term meaning "bomb-affected person." She is remembered for the story of the one thousand origami cranes she folded before her death and is to this day a symbol of the innocent victims of nuclear warfare.

After her death, Sadako's friends and schoolmates published a collection of letters to raise funds to build a memorial to her and all of the children who had died from the effects of the atomic bomb. In 1958, a statue of Sadako holding a golden crane was unveiled in the Hiroshima Peace Memorial Park. Part of the memorial was donated by Hideki (né Ogawa) Yukawa, a Japanese theoretical physicist, and the first Japanese Nobel laureate. At the foot of the statue is a plaque that reads:

"This is our cry. This is our prayer. Peace in the world."

~October 26~

"Godwin's Law and Godwin's Inverse"

On this day, October 26, 1956, Michael Wayne "Mike" Godwin was born. Godwin is an American attorney and author. He was the first staff counsel of the Electronic Frontier Foundation (EFF), and he created the Internet adage "Godwin's Law" similar to *Reductio ad Hitlerum*.

German-American philosopher Leo Strauss (September 20, 1899 – October 18, 1973) coined the term *Reductio ad Hitlerum* as well as *argumentum ad Hitlerum* is a similar term. This phrase was coined by in 1951. According to Strauss, *Reductio ad Hitlerum* is a humorous observation where someone compares an opponent's views with those that would be held by Hitler or the Nazi Party.

Godwin's Law is an Internet adage asserting that "As an online discussion grows longer, the probability of a comparison involving Nazis or Hitler approaches 1." That is, if an online discussion (regardless of topic or scope) goes on long enough, sooner or later someone will compare someone or something to Hitler or Nazism.

In 2018, Tom Keefe suggested the Godwin's Inverse; that is, a false declaration of victimization designed to immune the speaker from responsibility. It goes like this, "Can you believe it? THEY'RE calling "me/us/Trump" Nazis! Nazis killed millions of people; I can't believe THEY'RE insulting the memory of the Holocaust victims."

It's a logical conceit to protect the speaker and anything he or she might say, from criticism. The conversation then becomes about the accusation (inferred or otherwise) and not about the content of the offensive language in the first place.

~October 27~

"Paul Grüninger"

On this day, October 27, 1891, Paul Grüninger was born in St. Gallen, Switzerland. Grüninger (October 27, 1891 - February 22, 1972) was a Swiss police commander in St. Gallen, and football player. He was recognized as one of the Righteous Among the Nations by the Yad Vashem Holocaust memorial foundation in 1971. Following the Austrian Anschluss, Grüninger saved about 3,600 Jewish refugees by backdating their visas and falsifying other documents to indicate that they had entered Switzerland at a time when legal entry of refugees was still possible. He was dismissed from the police force, convicted of official misconduct, and fined 300 Swiss francs. He received no pension and died in poverty in 1972.

~~~

"The Mormon Extermination Order"

On this day, October 27, 1838, Missouri governor Lilburn Boggs issued the Extermination Order, which ordered all Mormons to leave the state or be exterminated.

~~~

"Allen Schindler"

On this day, October 27, 1992, United States Navy radioman Allen R. Schindler, Jr. was brutally murdered by shipmate Terry M. Helvey for being gay, precipitating first military, then national, debate about gays in the military that resulted in the United States "Don't ask, don't tell" military policy.

~October 28~

"The Polio Vaccine"

On this day, October 28, 1914, Jonas Edward Salk was born in New York, New York. Salk (October 28, 1914 – June 23, 1995) was an American medical researcher and virologist who discovered and developed one of the first successful polio vaccines. Jonas Salk invented the polio vaccine in 1953 but never patented it. He believed that, like the sun, a vaccine for polio belonged to the people.

~October 29~

"The Return"

On this day, October 29, 539 BCE, Cyrus the Great (founder of Persian Empire) entered the capital of Babylon and allowed the Jewish people to return to their land, thus ending the Babylonian Exile.

~~~

"Loving v. Virginia"

On this day, October 29, 1933, Richard Perry Loving was born in Central Point, Virginia. Loving (October 29, 1933 – June 29, 1975) and his wife Mildred successfully fought racial marital laws.

~~~

"Ellen Johnson"

On this day, October 29, 1938, Ellen Johnson Sirleaf was Monrovia, Liberia. She is the first elected female head of state in the history of Africa. Her election as the 24th President of Liberia followed the transitional government and peace agreement ending the country's second civil war and the rule of the warlord, Charles Taylor.

~~~

"Truth and Reconciliation"

On this day, October 29, 1998, Archbishop Desmond Tutu and the Truth and Reconciliation Commission of South Africa presented its report, which condemns both sides for committing atrocities.

~October 30~

"John Adams"

On this day, October 30, 1735, John Adams was born in Braintree, Province of Massachusetts Bay, British America (now Quincy, Massachusetts). Adams (October 30, 1735 – July 4, 1826) was an American lawyer and the second President of the United States under the third government, the Constitution of the United States government. Adams is essential to the continuation of the American Experiment. His acceptance of the results of the Election of 1800 is noted for the peaceful transition of power to a political rival and rival political party.

~~~

"Hannah Robinson Rock"

On this day, October 30, 1773, Hannah Robinson died in Narragansett, Rhode Island.

Hannah Robinson was born in 1746 and was the daughter of Rowland Robinson Jr., a prominent member of the community of Narragansett's planter society. Hannah fell in love with Peter Simon, a teacher of French and dancing classes at a young woman's school in Newport. Her father disapproved of the relationship between Simon and Robinson, deeming him "unsuitable," although the two kept their relationship in secret. Most of the family supported the relationship, giving Simon a teaching job in a member's home. One night, Rowland Robinson found Simon hiding in the lilac bushes under Hannah's window. Robinson then was banned from ever seeing him again, nor letting her leave the house in Boston Neck.

Robinson had a stubborn streak and, during a trip to a ball in North Kingstown, the couple, with the help of Robinson's mother Anstis Gardiner, escaped the family. Simon and Robinson moved to Providence, and she soon gave birth to nine children, although they were stricken with poverty. When Simon realized that Robinson would not get one shilling of her family's wealth, he began to have affairs and soon abandoned her completely. Robinson held on a few more years in Providence, and her father suggested that if Hannah would just tell who helped her escape, he would allow her back into the family. Hannah agreed and Rowland rode up to Providence and brought Hannah home.

Along the ride home to Boston Neck, Hannah Robinson requested her father to pull over at the site of James McSparran's farm, which overlooked the Narragansett Bay and Boston Neck. Here, she requested her father let her sit on the cube-shaped rocks and look over her homeland. It became known as Hannah Robinson Rock. Hannah Robinson shortly thereafter from natural causes at the age 27.

~~~

"Jackie Robinson"

On this day, October 30, 1945, Jackie Robinson of the Kansas City Monarchs signed a contract for the Brooklyn Dodgers, thus breaking the baseball color barrier. (See also July 6th.)

~October 31~

"95 Theses"

On this day, October 31, 1517, Martin Luther posted his 95 Theses on the door of the Castle Church in Wittenberg.

In the intervening 500 years, how many people have been killed for belonging to this Christian sect, or that sect? How many humans have died for religious intolerance of all kinds?

It is not power that corrupts but fear.

Aung San Suu Kyi

(Perhaps Aung San Suu Kyi should reread her own past wisdom)

~~~

For the dead and the living,
we must bear witness.

Elie Wiesel

~November 1~

"Carlos Saavedra Lamas"

On this day, November 1, 1878, Carlos Saavedra Lamas was born in Buenos Aires, Argentina. Saavedra Lamas (November 1, 1878 – May 5, 1959) was an Argentine academic and politician, and in 1936, the first Latin American Nobel Peace Prize recipient.

~November 2~

"Preparing for the Great Swamp"

On this day, November 2, 1675, Plimouth [sic] Colony Governor Josiah Winslow organized a colonial militia against the neutral Narragansett during King Philip's War. His assault culminated on December 16, 1675, when he led the attack on the Narragansett's winter camp at the Great Swamp. A combined force of Plymouth, Massachusetts, and Connecticut militia numbering about 1000 men (including about 150 Pequots and Mohican Indian allies) attacked, burned the fort and destroyed most of the tribe's winter stores. More than 300 Narragansets were slaughtered escaping the burning fort and in fierce fighting.

~~~

"Steve Sciullo, Steve Perretta, and Byron Leftwich"

On this day, November 2, 2002, Steve Sciullo and Steve Perretta carried Byron Leftwich down the field on multiple series as he rallied his team to a 17-point comeback against Akron University. Leftwich had broken the left tibia, returned to the game, taking his Marshal Herd down the field using only one leg and throwing from the shotgun position.

~November 3~

"Tadatoshi Akiba"

On this day, November 3, 1942, Tadatoshi Akiba 秋葉忠利 was born in Arakawa, Tokyo.

Akiba is a Japanese mathematician and served as the mayor of the city of Hiroshima, Japan from 1999 to 2011. As mayor, he had been a visible peace activist. He was active in the Mayors for Peace organization, serving as the president of their World Conference. In the 2020 Vision Campaign launched in 2003, which aims to eliminate nuclear weapons, he earned the Mayors for Peace "World Citizenship Award" from the Nuclear Age Peace Foundation in 2004.

In 2006, Akiba was awarded the "Sean McBride" Award from the International Peace Bureau and, in 2007, he was awarded the Nuclear-Free Future Award from the Franz-Moll Foundation.

~November 4~

"Joseph Rotblat"

On this day, November 4, 1908, Joseph Rotblat was born in Warsaw, Poland. Rotblat (November 4, 1908 – August 31, 2005) was a Polish physicist, a self-described "Pole with a British passport."

Rotblat worked on the Manhattan Project during World War II but left the Los Alamos Laboratory after the war with Germany ended. His work on nuclear fallout was a major contribution toward the ratification of the 1963 Partial Nuclear Test Ban Treaty. A signatory of the 1955 Russell–Einstein Manifesto, he was secretary-general of the Pugwash Conferences on Science and World Affairs from their founding until 1973. With the Pugwash Conferences, Rotblat shared the 1995 Nobel Peace Prize" for efforts to diminish the part played by nuclear arms in international affairs and, in the longer run, to eliminate such arms.

~~~

"Resolution 61"

On this day, November 4, 1948, the United Nations Security Council passed Resolution 61. Resolution 61 reiterated Resolution 54 that ordered a ceasefire in the Arab-Israeli War, advocated for the demilitarization of Jerusalem, and -in the case of Resolution 61 specifically- ordered a withdrawal of forces to the battlelines of October 14, 1948. Both resolutions were agreed to by the United States, France, China (ROC), Great Britain. The Resolution has never been honored by the belligerent parties.

~November 5~

"The Fifth of November"

On this day, November 5, 1805, Guy Fawkes tried to blow-up the British Houses of Parliament in what is known as the Gunpowder Plot.

~~~

"The Dorr Rebellion"

On this day, November 5, 1805, Thomas Wilson Dorr was born in Providence, Rhode Island. Dorr (November 5, 1805 – December 27, 1854) was an American politician and reformer in Rhode Island. He led the Dorr Rebellion to expand the enfranchisement of voters and to address the gerrymandered legislative districts. Dorr was tried for treason against Rhode Island at Newport, a conservative stronghold, before the Rhode Island Supreme Court; he was convicted and sentenced to solitary confinement at hard labor for life.

~~~

"Pedro Arrupe"

On this day, November 5, 1991, Pedro Arrupe, S.J. was born in Bilbao, Spain. Arrupe (November 14, 1907 – February 5, 1991) was a Basque Jesuit priest. Stationed as novice master outside Hiroshima in 1946, he used his medical background as a first responder to the atomic bombing of Hiroshima. Arrupe also served as the twenty-eighth Superior General of the Society of Jesus (1965–83) and led the Jesuits in the implementation of the Second Vatican Council, especially with regard to a faith that does justice and the preferential option for the poor.

~November 6~

"Mohandas Gandhi"

On this day, November 6, 1913, Mohandas Gandhi was arrested while leading a march of Indian miners in South Africa.

"The things that will destroy us are: politics without principle; pleasure without conscience; wealth without work; knowledge without character; business without morality; science without humanity; and worship without sacrifice."

~Gandhi~

~~~

"Burning Draft Cards"

On this day, November 6, 1965, Thomas C. Cornell, Marc Paul Edelman, and Roy Lisker burned their draft cards at a public rally organized by the Committee for Non-Violent Action in Union Square, New York City. Edelman, Cornell, and Lisker were arrested, convicted, and sentenced to six months.

~November 7~

"Irony?"

On this day, November 7, 1941, Soviet hospital ship *Armenia* was sunk by German planes while evacuating refugees and wounded military and staff of several Crimean hospitals. It is estimated that over 5,000 people died in the sinking. The irony that the ship was named after the Forgotten Genocide is poignant.

~November 8 ~

"Br. Miguel"

On this day, November 7, 1854, Francisco Luis Febres-Cordero y Muñoz was born in Cuenca, Azuay, Ecuador.

Brother Miguel (November 7, 1854 – February 9, 1910) was an Ecuadorian Roman Catholic religious brother. He became a professed member of the Brothers of the Christian Schools, colloquially known as the La Salle Brothers. He held the position of a school teacher in Quito for over three decades where he became known as a gentle and dedicated individual. He published his own school textbooks, including one for the teaching of Spanish, as well as odes and discourses on teaching methods.

The government adopted some of his textbooks that were circulated across all schools. He also did research and authored books on literature and linguistics, which earned him membership in the Ecuadorian Academy of Letters in 1892, followed by the Academies of Spain, France, and Venezuela. Pope Paul VI beatified him on October 30, 1977, and Pope John Paul II canonized him almost a decade later on October 21, 1984, as the first Ecuadorian saint. He remains a national hero in his native land, and his tomb has become a site of pilgrimage.

~November 8 ~

"Dorothy Day"

On this day, November 8, 1897, Dorothy Day was born in Bath Beach, New York City, NY. Day (November 8, 1897 – November 29, 1980) was an American journalist, social activist, and Catholic convert.

"As we come to know the seriousness of the situation, the war, the racism, the poverty in our world, we come to realize that things will not be changed simply by words or demonstrations. Rather, it's a question of living one's life in a drastically different way."

~Dorothy Day~

~November 9~

"Napper Tandy"

On this day, November 9, 1791, Napper Tandy convened the first meeting of Dublin's United Irishmen.

James Napper Tandy (February 16, 1739 – August 24, 1803) was a member of the United Irishmen. Coming to the attention of the British, Tandy fled to the United States in 1795. In February 1798, he went to Paris where he joined Wolfe Tone in planning the Rebellion of 1798. For his part, Tandy sailed from Dunkirk with a small force of men and a considerable quantity of arms and ammunition for distribution in Ireland. He arrived at the isle of Arranmore, off the coast of County Donegal, on September 16, 1798. He took possession of the village of Rutland, where he hoisted an Irish flag and issued a proclamation; however, Tandy realized the futility of the enterprise when he learned of the defeat of Humbert's French expedition. Tandy returned to France, but the counter-Revolutionary Directory turned him over to the British.

Tandy was put on trial and acquitted, but remained in prison in Lifford Jail, County Donegal, until April 1801 when he was tried for the crime of landing on Rutland Island. He pleaded guilty and was sentenced to death, but he was reprieved and allowed to go…

You guessed it! Tandy returned to France where he died in Bordeaux on August 24, 1803.

~~~

"Kristallnacht"

On this day, November 9, 1938, Kristallnacht began in Nazi Germany. The Night of Broken Glass is considered, by some scholars, to mark the beginning of the Holocaust.

~~~

"Roger LaPorte"

On this day, November 9, 1965, Roger Allen LaPorte set himself on fire in front of the United Nations building. LaPorte (July 16, 1943 – November 10, 1965) was a Catholic Worker Movement member protesting against the Vietnam War. When asked why he had burned himself, LaPorte calmly replied, "I'm a Catholic Worker. I'm against war, all wars. I did this as a religious action...all the hatred of the world." He died of his wounds on November 10, 1965.

~~~

"Last Laugh?"

On this day, November 9, 1989, Mary Dolencie died in Yarmouth Port, Massachusetts. She upset her neighbors slightly by the epitaph she had engraved on her headstone:

"May eternal damnation be upon those in Whaling Port who, without knowing me, have maliciously vilified me. May the curse of God be upon them and theirs."

~ ~ ~

"9/11"

On this day, November 9, 1989, East Germany opened the Berlin Wall, allowing travel from East to West Berlin. The Wall was opened because Hungarian officials had opened the border between Hungary and Austria. East Germans could then circumvent the Wall by going through Hungary into Austria, and then into West Germany, effectively ended the purpose of the Berlin Wall. The following day, celebrating Germans began to tear the wall down. One of the ugliest and most infamous symbols of the Cold War was soon reduced to rubble that was quickly snatched up by souvenir hunters.

On November 9, 1989, East German official Günter Schabowski held an ambiguous press conference about travel through the Berlin Wall, and thousands of East Germans went to the wall seeking access to West Germany.

Harald Jäger (b. April 27, 1943) Jäger (born April 27, 1943) was East German Stasi lieutenant colonel in command of the the Bornholmer Straße border crossing of the Berlin Wall. Jäger heard Günter Schabowski speech and called his superiors and other border crossing officers along the Wall. After realizing that keeping the gate closed could imperil the lives of people in the crowd and his own officers, Jäger yielded to the masses and opened the Wall sometime between 10:45pm and 11:30pm.

[Heinz Schäfer claimed that he had opened his crossing at Waltersdorf in the south part of Berlin a few hours earlier.]

~November 10~

"Seven Days of Freedom"

On this day, November 10, 1956, the spontaneous nationwide revolt against the government of the Hungarian People's Republic and its Soviet-imposed policies, was crushed by the Soviet forces. It had begun on October 23 and lasted until November 10, 1956. It was immortalized in Noel Barber's *Seven Days of Freedom.*

Over 2,500 Hungarians and 700 Soviet troops were killed in the conflict, and 200,000 Hungarians fled as refugees. Mass arrests and denunciations continued for months thereafter.

~~~

"Confederate War Crimes"

On this day, November 10, 1865, Heinrich Hartmann Wirz (b. November 25, 1823) was executed for war crimes, including conspiracy and murder. Henry Wirz was a Swiss-born Confederate officer in the American Civil War. He was the commander of Camp Sumter, the Confederate prisoner-of-war camp near Andersonville, Georgia. Around 45,000 prisoners were incarcerated during the camp's 14-month existence, of whom close to 13,000 (28%) died from disease, dysentery, and malnutrition.

~November 11~

"Freddie Gray"

On this day, November 11, 2017, Officer Caesar Goodson was found not guilty of 21 administrative charges of violating department policies during Freddie Gray's arrest.

Goodson, who is African-American, drove the police van carrying Gray after he was arrested. Many of the administrative charges had related to Goodson's failure to ensure Gray was safe or ensure he received medical attention.

On April 12, 2015, Freddie Carlos Gray, Jr., a 25-year-old African-American man, was arrested by the Baltimore Police Department for possessing what the police alleged was an illegal switchblade under Baltimore law. While being transported in a police van, Gray fell into a coma and was taken to a trauma center. Gray died on April 19, 2015; his death was ascribed to injuries to his spinal cord. Gray, 25, was not restrained in a seat belt and died of a neck injury. His death triggered rioting and protests and led to court-ordered reforms of the police department.

~November 12~

"I Don't Remember Termos' Story Covered on Fox News?"

On this day, November 12, 2015, Adel Termos died in Beirut, Lebanon. Upon seeing a suicide bomber in a crowded Beirut market, Termos heroically tackled the bomber before he could enter a crowded Mosque. In addition to saving several lives that day, Termos sent a very powerful message that humanity will not back down in the face of violence.

~~~

"The Tartar Genocide"

On this day, November 12, 2015, the Parliament of Ukraine adopted a resolution recognizing the deportation of the Crimean Tatars a genocide and declared May 18 as a Day of Remembrance for the victims of Crimean Tatar genocide.

The forcible deportation of the Crimean Tatars from Crimea was ordered by Joseph Stalin as a form of collective punishment for alleged collaboration with the Nazi occupation regime in Taurida Subdistrict during 1942–1943. The state-organized removal is known as the Sürgünlik in Crimean Tatar. A total of more than 230,000 people were deported, mostly to the Uzbek Soviet Socialist Republic. This deportation included the entire ethnic Crimean Tatar population, at the time about a fifth of the total population of the Crimean Peninsula, as well as smaller numbers of ethnic Greeks and Bulgarians. In a clear case of ethnic cleansing, a large number of deportees (more than 100,000 according to a 1960s survey by Crimean Tatar activists) died from starvation or disease as a direct result of deportation.

~November 13~

"St. Brice's Day Massacre"

On this day, November 13, 1002, the English king Æthelred II ordered the killing of all Danes in England, known today as the St. Brice's Day Massacre.

~~~

"Montgomery Bus Boycott"

On this day, November 13, 1956, the Supreme Court of the United States declared Alabama laws requiring segregated buses illegal, thus ending the Montgomery Bus Boycott. On that day, while Martin Luther King, Jr., was in the courthouse being tried on the legality of the boycott's carpools, a reporter notified him that the U.S. Supreme Court had just affirmed the District Court's decision on Browder v. Gayle. King addressed a mass meeting at Holt Street Baptist Church the next evening, saying that the decision was "a reaffirmation of the principle that separate facilities are inherently unequal, and that the old Plessy Doctrine of separate but equal is no longer valid, either sociologically or legally."

Later, on December 17, 1956, the Supreme Court rejected appeals to reconsider their decision and three days later the order for integrated buses was delivered. On December 20, 1956, King and the Montgomery Improvement Association voted to end the 381-day Montgomery bus boycott. In a statement that day, King said: "The year-old protest against city buses is officially called off, and the Negro citizens of Montgomery are urged to return to the busses tomorrow morning on a non-segregated basis."

The Montgomery buses were integrated the following day.

~November 14~

"Ruby Bridges"

This day, November 14, 1960, was the day which Judge J. Skelly Wright had ordered to be the first day of integrated schools in New Orleans. The event was famously commemorated by Norman Rockwell in the painting, "The Problem We All Live With," published in *Look* magazine on January 14, 1964.

As Bridges described it, "Driving up I could see the crowd, but living in New Orleans, I actually thought it was Mardi Gras. There was a large crowd of people outside of the school. They were throwing things and shouting, and that sort of goes on in New Orleans at Mardi Gras."

Former United States Deputy Marshal Charles Burks later recalled, "She showed a lot of courage. She never cried. She didn't whimper. She just marched along like a little soldier, and we're all very proud of her."

U.S. Marshals escorted Bridges to and from school. As soon as Bridges entered the school, European-American parents pulled their own children out; all the teachers except for one refused to teach while a "black child" was enrolled. Barbara Henry, from Boston, Massachusetts, taught Ruby Bridges alone for over a year as if she were teaching a whole class.

~November 15~

"Himmler and the Roma"

On this day, November 15, 1943, German SS leader Heinrich Himmler ordered that Gypsies are to be put "on the same level as Jews and placed in concentration camps."

The correct term for "Gypsies" is Roma and the Roma were one of the main seven groups targeted by the Nazis (the others being Jews, Pole, homosexuals, mentally handicapped, physically handicapped, and Communists). Roma prisoners at Nazi concentration camps were forced to wear an inverted brown triangle. Today they continue to be persecuted, because like the Jews before the creation of the modern Israeli state, they are a stateless people. Slurs and propaganda continue to be used against them, specifically the line that 'all gypsies are thieves.' This discrimination was part of the storyline for Disney's *Hunchback of Notre Dame*. Modern discrimination has recently raised its head in Italy where it is debated whether Roma children are entitled to education and services. The Roma died at the highest rate per capita as a result of the German Genocide, yet they still have no state, nor political protection.

The Romani Holocaust, also known as the Porajmos, Pharrajimos ("Cutting up," "Fragmentation," "Destruction"), or Samudaripen killed an estimated 1.5 million people. In 1982, West Germany formally recognized that genocide had been committed against the Romani and, in 2011, the Polish Government passed a resolution for the official recognition of August 2 as a day of commemoration of the genocide.

~~~

On this day, November 15, 1985, the Anglo-Irish Agreement was signed at Hillsborough Castle by British Prime Minister Margaret Thatcher and Irish Taoiseach Garret FitzGerald.

"I had come to the conclusion that I must now give priority to heading off the growth of support for the IRA in Northern Ireland by seeking a new understanding with the British Government, even at the expense of my cherished, but for the time being at least clearly unachievable, objective of seeking a solution through negotiations with the Unionists."

Garret FitzGerald in his autobiography
All in a Life (FitzGerald, 1991)

~~~

"I started from the need for greater security, which was imperative. If this meant making limited political concession to the South, much as I disliked this kind of bargaining, I had to contemplate it."

Margaret Thatcher in her autobiography
The Downing Street Years (Thatcher, 1993)

~November 16~

"Burn her!"

On this day, November 16, 1688, "Goody" Ann Glover was hanged in Boston, Massachusetts, as a witch. Glover was an exiled Irish Catholic widow and is considered the last woman burned as a witch in Boston, though the Salem witch trials in nearby Salem, Massachusetts, occurred mainly in 1688.

~~~

"The El Salvador Jesuit Martyrs"

On this day, November 16, 1989, an El Salvadoran death squad murdered six Jesuit priests and two others at Jose Simeon Canas University. The massacre was carried out by members of the Atlacatl Battalion, an elite unit of the Salvadoran Army, created at the U.S. Army's School of the Americas, then located in Panama. In negotiations for a peaceful solution to the conflict, Father Ellacuria had played a pivotal role. Many of the armed forces identified the Jesuit priests with the rebels, because of their special concern for those Salvadorians who were poorest and thus most affected by the war. The Pastoral Centre of José Simeón Cañas Central American University (UCA) in San Salvador was considered a "refuge of subversives" by the Army; Colonel Juan Orlando Zepeda, Vice-Minister for Defence, had publicly accused UCA of being the center of operations for FMLN terrorists. Colonel Inocente Montano, Vice-Minister for Public Security, stated publicly that the Jesuits were "fully identified with subversive movements." Thus, the murders can be considered a form of ideological genocide.

The victims of the November 16, 1989, death squad massacred were:

Ignacio Ellacuría, S.J.

Ignacio Martín-Baró, S.J.

Segundo Montes, S.J.

Juan Ramón Moreno, S.J.

Joaquín López y López, S.J.

Amando López, S.J.

Elba Ramos

Celina Ramos (16 years old, daughter of Elba Ramos)

~November 17~

"H. H. Holmes"

On this day, November 17, 1894, H. H. Holmes, one of the first modern serial killers, was arrested in Boston, Massachusetts.

~~~

"The Blasket Islands"

On this day, November 17, 1953, the remaining human inhabitants of the Blasket Islands, Kerry, Ireland, are evacuated to the mainland. (See also December 12th.)

~~~

"I am not a crook"

On this day, November 17, 1973, while in Orlando, Florida, U.S. President Richard Nixon told 400 Associated Press managing editors "I am not a crook."

~~~

"The Star Wars Holiday Special"

On this day, November 17, 1978, the *Star Wars Holiday Special* airs on CBS, receiving negative reception from critics, fans, and even Star Wars creator George Lucas.

~November 18~

"Mr. X"

On this day, November 18, 1978, Jerry Bibb Balisok did not die in the Jonestown Massacre. Balisok (September 8, 1955 – April 18, 2013) was an American professional wrestler known as Mr. X. After being indicted for thirteen counts of check forgery, Balisok skipped bail, faked his own death, and convincing law enforcement officials that he had died in the 1978 Jonestown Massacre.

Majorie E. Balisok, Balisok's mother, believed her son had died in the Jonestown Massacre and commissioned this engraving on his gravestone in Oakland, California:

Murdered in Guyana Nov 13, 1978
Buried in Oakland Cal.
DAMN THE STATE DEPT.

However, Balisok was living freely under the fake identity Ricky Allen Wetta. In 1989, Balisok was arrested for attempted murder of Emmett Thompson, Jr., in King County, Washington. During the fingerprinting process, it became clear that Ricky Allen Wetta was actually Jerry Balisok.

Upon his release from prison, Balisok moved to Seattle, Washington. In 2006, Balisok legally changed his name to Harrison Rains Hanover and (how in the world?) began working as funds manager for JPierce Investments. Shockingly (NOT!), he was implicated in a scheme to defraud First Security Bank of Washington in 2009. What a guy, right?

~November 19~

"Gettysburg Address"

On this day, November 19, 1863, Abraham Lincoln dedicated the National Cemetery at Gettysburg by saying:

"Four score and seven years ago our fathers brought forth on this continent, a new nation, conceived in Liberty, and dedicated to the proposition that all men are created equal.

Now we are engaged in a great civil war, testing whether that nation, or any nation so conceived and so dedicated, can long endure. We are met on a great battle-field of that war. We have come to dedicate a portion of that field, as a final resting place for those who here gave their lives that that nation might live. It is altogether fitting and proper that we should do this.

But, in a larger sense, we can not dedicate—we can not consecrate—we can not hallow—this ground. The brave men, living and dead, who struggled here, have consecrated it, far above our poor power to add or detract. The world will little note, nor long remember what we say here, but it can never forget what they did here. It is for us the living, rather, to be dedicated here to the unfinished work which they who fought here have thus far so nobly advanced. It is rather for us to be here dedicated to the great task remaining before us—that from these honored dead we take increased devotion to that cause for which they gave the last full measure of devotion—that we here highly resolve that these dead shall not have died in vain—that this nation, under God, shall have a new birth of freedom—and that government of the people, by the people, for the people, shall not perish from the earth."

~November 20~

"Nuremberg"

On this day, November 20, 1945, the Nuremburg Trials began against Nazi war criminals at the Palace of Justice and continued from November 20, 1945, and October 1, 1946, in Nuremberg, Germany. The Tribunal was given the task of trying 24 of the most important political and military leaders of the Third Reich. Adolf Hitler, Heinrich Himmler, and Joseph Goebbels (all of whom had committed suicide in the spring of 1945) were not included in the Nuremburg Trials. Martin Bormann was tried *in absentia*, and Robert Ley committed suicide. The indictments were for 1) participation in a common plan or conspiracy for the accomplishment of a crime against peace, 2) planning, initiating and waging wars of aggression and other crimes against peace, 3) war crimes, and 4) crimes against humanity.

One was medically unfit to stand trial. Three were acquitted. Seven were given prison terms from terms of ten years to life. Twelve were convicted and sentenced to death were hanged. One committed suicide during the trial.

The death sentences were carried out on October 16, 1946. The executioner was John C. Woods. Woods had hanged 34 U.S. soldiers during the war, botching several of them. The executions took place by hanging in the gymnasium of the court building. Evidence suggests that some of the condemned men died agonizingly slowly, struggling for 14 to 28 minutes before finally choking to death. Although the rumor has long persisted that the bodies were taken to Dachau and burned there, the bodies were incinerated in a crematorium in Munich, and the ashes scattered over the Isar River.

~~~

"Nigeria's John Adams?"

On this day, November 20, 1957, Goodluck Ebele Azikiwe Jonathan was born in what is now Bayelsa State. Gookluck is a former President of Nigeria, having served from 2010 to 2015. He served as Vice-President of Nigeria from 2007 to 2010 and as Governor of Bayelsa State from 2005 to 2007. He ran for re-election in 2015 and lost the presidential election. Upon losing to Muhammadu Buhari, he conceded defeat and became the first sitting Nigerian president to do so.

~November 21~

"Rebecca Latimer Felton"

On this day, November 21, 1922, Rebecca Latimer Felton of Georgia takes the oath of office, becoming the first female United States Senator. (See also December 8th).

In 1922, Governor Thomas W. Hardwick was a candidate for the next general election to the Senate, when Senator Thomas E. Watson died prematurely. Seeking an appointee who would not be a competitor in the coming special election to fill the vacant seat and a way to secure the vote of the new women voters alienated by his opposition to the 19th Amendment, Hardwick appointed Felton. She was sworn in on November 21, 1922 and served just 24 hours as the oldest freshman U.S. Senator to date.

Felton was a prominent society woman; an advocate of prison reform, women's suffrage, and educational modernization, but also one of the few prominent women who spoke in favor of lynching. Felton and her husband owned slaves before the Civil War, and she was the last member of either house of Congress to have been a slave owner. Felton claimed that the more money that Georgia spent on Black education, the more crimes Blacks committed. For the 1893 World's Columbian Exhibition, she "proposed a southern exhibit 'illustrating the slave period,' with a cabin and 'real colored folks making mats, shuck collars, and baskets—a woman to spin and card cotton—and another to play banjo and show the actual life of [the] slave—not the Uncle Tom sort.'"

The first woman elected, not appointed, to the Senate was Hattie Caraway from Arkansas in 1932. Fifteen of the women who have served in the US Senate were appointed; seven of those were appointed to succeed their deceased husbands.

~November 22~

"The Assassination of JFK"

On this day, November 22, 1963, John F. Kennedy, was assassinated in Dealey Plaza, Dallas, Texas. Irrespective of any discussion of the actual assassination, it is unclear whether a Northerner like Kennedy would have been able to push the Civil Rights Act of 1964 through the US Congress as effectively as Lyndon Baines Johnson, who was Southern and expert legislator, was able to guide the legislation.

~~~

"The Orange Revolution"

On this day, November 22, 2004, the Orange Revolution began in Ukraine. The revolution was the result of fraudulent presidential elections between assassination survivor Viktor Yushchenko and Viktor Yanukovych, Yanukovych had been declared the winner, but as a result of the protests, the Supreme Court ordered a new election, which was closely monitored by international organizations; Yushchenko was declared the winner. The election was as much an expression of Ukrainian-Russian ethnic conflict within Ukraine as it was a debate on the role of Ukraine in Europe.

~~~

"Jewish-Armenian Understanding"

On this day, November 22, 2005, the Ashkenazi Chief Rabbi of Israel Yona Metzger visited the Memorial of Armenian Genocide in Yerevan, Armenia, and said: "no other nation can understand the pain of the Armenians better than Jews."

~November 23~

"The Good Nazi"

On this day, November 23, 1882, John Heinrich Detlev Rabe was born. Rabe was a German businessman and Nazi Party member. He is best known for his efforts to stop the atrocities of the Japanese army during the Nanking Occupation and his work to help the Chinese civilians during the event. He used his official capacity as Germany's representative and as senior chief of the European–American establishment in Nanjing, to protect Chinese civilians.

As the Japanese army approached the Chinese capital of Nanking (now Nanjing) and initiated bombing raids on the city, all but 22 foreigners fled the city. On November 22, 1937, as the Japanese Army advanced on Nanking, Rabe and the other foreign nationals, organized the International Committee for the Nanking Safety Zone and created the Nanking Safety Zone to provide Chinese refugees with food and shelter from the impending Japanese slaughter. The Nanking Safety Zone, which he helped to establish, sheltered approximately 200,000 Chinese people from slaughter during the massacre.

Rabe and his zone administrators also tried to stop the atrocities. His attempts to appeal to the Japanese by using his Nazi Party membership credentials only delayed the Japanese offensive, but that delay allowed hundreds of thousands of refugees to escape. After the war, Rabe was arrested first by the Soviet NKVD and then by the British Army. Both, however, let him go after intense interrogation. He worked but was later denounced for his Nazi Party membership by an acquaintance and lost his meager income.

In 1948, the citizens of Nanking learned of the very dire situation of the Rabe family in occupied Germany, and they quickly raised a very large sum of money, equivalent to $2000 ($20,000 in 2016). The mayor of Nanjing went to Germany, bought a large amount of food for the Rabe family, and delivered it in person. From mid-1948 until the communist takeover of China, the people of Nanking sent a food package each month to the Rabe family.

On January 5, 1950, John Heinrich Detlev Rabe died of a stroke. In 1997, his tombstone was moved from Berlin to Nanjing (as it is now) where it received a place of honor at the massacre memorial site. In 2005, Rabe's former residence in Nanking (as it then was) was renovated and now accommodates the "John Rabe and International Safety Zone Memorial Hall," which opened in 2006.

~November 24~

"Constantin Karadja"

On this day, November 24, 1889, Prince Constantin Jean Lars Anthony Démétrius Karadja was born in The Hague, Netherlands.

Prince Karadja (November 24, 1889 - December 28, 1950) was a Romanian diplomat, barrister-at-law, bibliographer, bibliophile and honorary member (1946) of the Romanian Academy. He is a descendant of a very aristocratic family having Byzantine roots in Constantinople as well as among rulers of Wallachia in the 18th and 19th centuries.

Influenced by his humanistic and juridical education, Constantin Karadja constantly followed the principles of international law respecting human rights. He did not cede in front of political pressures but engaged himself with perseverance in the protection of the rights of Romanian citizens living abroad, regardless of ethnicity or religion. He was the Romanian consul-general in Berlin from 1932 to 1941 and the head the consular department of the Romanian Foreign Ministry from June 15, 1941, to October 17, 1944. Karadja dedicated himself to save Romanian Jews.

Yosef Govrin wrote that "Tens of thousands owe their lives to his exceptional persistency, abnegation, determination, and amplitude marking his long-term engagement in favour of the Romanian Jews stranded under the Nazi regime." Govrin continued that it "required extraordinary courage to act as he did through diplomatic means" as he was putting his career in consequent jeopardy.

Shortly after his dismissal on October 17, 1944, the new foreign minister, Constantin Vişoianu, reappointed Karadja, but on September 1, 1947, he was dismissed again from the ministry permanently. Subsequently, the payment of Karadja's pension was refused, and he later died on December 28, 1950.

On September 15, 2005, Constantin Karadja posthumously received the title "Righteous Among the Nations" from the Yad Vashem Institute in Jerusalem, Israel.

~~~

"LaFarge"

On this day, November 24, 1963, John LaFarge Jr., passed away at the age of 83. LaFarge was born in Newport, Rhode Island on February 13, 1880. He was an American Jesuit priest known for his activism against racism and anti-Semitism. LaFarge did not play a major role in the civil rights movement of the late 1950s and early 1960s, in part because of his age. However, just three months before his death, LaFarge walked in the 1963 March on Washington and stood on the steps of the Lincoln Memorial behind Martin Luther King for his famous "I Have a Dream" speech, a public acknowledgment of LaFarge's early role in a movement for racial equality that was now being led by others. At his eulogy, Boston's Cardinal Richard Cushing spoke of him as a pioneer in the field of interracial justice. He died on November 24, 1963.

LaFarge Hall at Saint Joseph's University, Philadelphia, Pennsylvania, is named in honor of Fr. John LaFarge, S.J.

~November 25~

"Band Aid"

On this day, November 25, 1984, thirty-six musicians formed a supergroup and recorded "*Do They Know It's Christmas?*" for famine relief in Ethiopia. The 36 were:

Simon Le Bon (Duran Duran)
Robert "Kool" Bell (Kool & the Gang)
Bono and Adam Clayton (U2)
Pete Briquette (The Boomtown Rats)
Phil Collins (Genesis and solo artist)
Chris Cross (Ultravox)
Simon Crowe (The Boomtown Rats)
Sara Dallin (Bananarama)
Siobhan Fahey (Bananarama)
Johnny Fingers (The Boomtown Rats)
Bob Geldof (The Boomtown Rats)
Boy George (Culture Club)
Glenn Gregory (Heaven 17)
Tony Hadley (Spandau Ballet)
John Keeble (Spandau Ballet)
Gary Kemp (Spandau Ballet)
Martin Kemp (Spandau Ballet)
Marilyn
George Michael (Wham!)
Jon Moss (Culture Club)
Steve Norman (Spandau Ballet)
Rick Parfitt (Status Quo)
Nick Rhodes (Duran Duran)
Francis Rossi (Status Quo)
Sting (The Police and solo artist)
Andy Taylor (Duran Duran)
James "J.T." Taylor (Kool & the Gang)
John Taylor (Duran Duran)
Roger Taylor (Duran Duran)
Dennis Thomas (Kool & the Gang)
Midge Ure (Ultravox)
Martyn Ware (Heaven 17)
Jody Watley (Shalamar)
Paul Weller (The Style Council)
Keren Woodward (Bananarama)
Paul Young

406

~November 26~

"James P. Fleming"

On this day, November 26, 1968, United States Air Force helicopter pilot James P. Fleming rescued an Army Special Forces six-man MACV-SOG Recon Team, stranded between heavily defended enemy positions, near Đức Cơ, Vietnam. Fleming (born March 12, 1943) was later awarded the Medal of Honor. The citation reads, in part, "Despite the knowledge that 1 helicopter had been downed by intense hostile fire, Capt. Fleming descended and balanced his helicopter on a river bank with the tail boom hanging over open water. The patrol could not penetrate to the landing site, and he was forced to withdraw. Dangerously low on fuel, Capt. Fleming repeated his original landing maneuver. Disregarding his own safety, he remained in this exposed position. Hostile fire crashed through his windscreen as the patrol boarded his helicopter. Capt. Fleming made a successful takeoff through a barrage of hostile fire and recovered safely at a forward base."

~~~

"Ashtar Galactic Command"

On this day, November 26, 1977, an unidentified hijacker named Vrillon, claiming to be the representative of the "Ashtar Galactic Command," took over Britain's Southern Television for six minutes, starting at 5:12 pm. The voice of the hijacker, which was disguised and accompanied by a deep buzzing, hijacked the UHF audio signal of the early-evening news. The broadcast took over the sound only, leaving the video signal unaltered, aside from some picture distortion. The transcript of the message states:

This is the voice of Vrillon, a representative of the Ashtar Galactic Command, speaking to you. For many years you have seen us as lights in the skies. We speak to you now in peace and wisdom as we have done to your brothers and sisters all over this, your planet Earth. We come to warn you of the destiny of your race and your world so that you may communicate to your fellow beings the course you must take to avoid the disaster which threatens your world, and the beings on our worlds around you. This is in order that you may share in the great awakening, as the planet passes into the New Age of Aquarius. The New Age can be a time of great peace and evolution for your race, but only if your rulers are made aware of the evil forces that can overshadow their judgments. Be still now and listen, for your chance may not come again. All your weapons of evil must be removed. The time for conflict is now past and the race of which you are a part may proceed to the higher stages of its evolution if you show yourselves worthy to do this. You have but a short time to learn to live together in peace and goodwill. Small groups all over the planet are learning this, and exist to pass on the light of the dawning New Age to you all. You are free to accept or reject their teachings, but only those who learn to live in peace will pass to the higher realms of spiritual evolution. Hear now the voice of Vrillon, a representative of the Ashtar Galactic Command, speaking to you. Be aware also that there are many false prophets and guides at present operating on your world. They will suck your energy from you — the energy you call money and will put it to evil ends and give you worthless dross in return. Your inner divine self will protect you from this. You must learn to be sensitive to the voice within that can tell you what is truth, and what is confusion, chaos and untruth. Learn to listen to the voice of truth which is within you and you will lead yourselves onto the path of evolution. This is our message to our dear friends. We have watched you growing for many years as you too have watched our lights in your skies. You know now that we are here, and that there are more beings on and around your Earth than your scientists admit. We are deeply concerned about you and your path towards the light and will do all we can to help you. Have no fear, seek only to know yourselves, and live in harmony with the ways of your planet Earth. We of the Ashtar Galactic Command thank you for your attention. We are now leaving the planes of your existence. May you be blessed by the supreme love and truth of the cosmos.

~November 27~

"The Call for the Crusades"

On this day, November 27, 1095, at the Council of Clermont, Pope Urban II gave perhaps the most influential speech of the Middle Ages, giving rise to the Crusades by calling all Christians in Europe to war against Muslims in order to reclaim the Holy Land, with a cry of "Deus volt!" or "God wills it!"

This led to the Massacre of Jerusalem in 1099 as well as 200 years of warfare and death. (See March 31st)

~ ~ ~

"Washita River"

On this day, November 27, 1868, George Custer attacked a Cheyenne winter camp at Washita River. Estimates vary, but the death toll was between 40 and 300, with a significant number of the victims including women and children. Though called the "Battle" of Washita River, Lt. Col. George Armstrong Custer's 7th U.S. Cavalry attack was a coordinated surprise attack at dawn in which Black Kettle and his wife, Medicine Woman, were shot in the back and killed while fleeing on a pony. Black Kettle had been a survivor of the Sand Creek Massacre just four years before this massacre. Following the capture of Black Kettle's village, Custer saw large groups of mounted Indians gathering on nearby hilltops and learned that Black Kettle's village was only one of many Indian encampments along the river. Fearing an attack, he ordered some of his men to take defensive positions while the others were to seize the Indians' belongings and horses. The American soldiers destroyed what was unwanted or could not be carried, including about 675 ponies and horses. Approximately 200 horses were spared to transport the Cheyenne prisoners.

~~~

"Harvey Milk"

On this day, November 27, 1978, Dan White assassinated Harvey Bernard Milk. Milk (May 22, 1930 – November 27, 1978) was an American politician who became the first openly gay person to be elected to public office in California when he won a seat on the San Francisco Board of Supervisors.

Milk moved from New York City to settle in San Francisco in 1972 amid a migration of gay men to the Castro District. He took advantage of the growing political and economic power of the neighborhood to promote his interests, and three times ran unsuccessfully for political office. His theatrical campaigns earned him increasing popularity, and Milk won a seat as a city supervisor in 1977, his election made possible by, and a key component of, a shift in San Francisco politics.

Milk served almost 11 months in office and was responsible for passing a stringent gay rights ordinance for the city. On November 27, 1978, Milk and Mayor George Moscone were assassinated by Dan White, another city supervisor, who had recently resigned to pursue a private business enterprise but who had sought to get his position back after that endeavor had failed.

Despite his short career in politics, Milk became an icon in San Francisco and a martyr in the gay community. In 2002, Milk was called "the most famous and most significantly open LGBT official ever elected in the United States." Anne Kronenberg, his final campaign manager, wrote of him: "What set Harvey apart from you or me was that he was a visionary. He imagined a righteous world inside his head, and then he set about to create it for real, for all of us." In 2009, Harvey Bernard Milk was posthumously awarded the Presidential Medal of Freedom.

~November 28~

"Fort Rosalie"

On this day, November 28, 1729, members of the Natchez massacre most of the 300 French settlers and soldiers at Fort Rosalie, Louisiana in response to the French colonial commandant, Sieur de Chépart, demand for land from a Natchez village as his own personal plantation.

We should never forget, there is blood on all human hands, regardless of race, ethnicity, nationality, religion, or gender.

~~~

"The Velvet Revolution"

On this day, November 28, 1989, the Velvet Revolution occurred in Czechoslovakia when the Communist Party of Czechoslovakia announced it would give up its monopoly on political power.

~November 29~

"Sand Creek"

On this day, November 29, 1864, 700 European-Americans attacked and destroyed a peaceful village of Cheyenne and Arapaho in southeastern Colorado, killing and mutilating an estimated 70–163 Indians, two-thirds of whom were women and children. The attack was orchestrated by "Reverend" John M. Chivington.

According to a recent report by the University of Denver in 2014, Governor John Evans is also equally culpable as well. In Alaska, after years of calling America's highest mountain Mount McKinley, we now utilize both original indigenous name "Denali" as the co-name of the national park and geographic feature: Mt McKinley is in Denali National Park. Perhaps we could remember the Sand Creek Massacre, not just with the ceremonies at the site, but work toward the creation of a memorial at Mt Evans. Such a memorial or park would honor the Ute people, who inhabited the foothills, as well as the Cheyenne and Arapaho people who were massacred at Sand Creek.

Black Kettle survived the Sand Creek Massacre, only to be killed in the Washita River Massacre four years later. He was described by US General William Selby Harney, a key member of the Indian Peace Commission as follows: "I have worn the uniform of my country 55 years, and I know that Black Kettle was as good a friend of the United States as I am."

~November 30~

"Segregating Japanese Schoolchildren"

On this day, November 30, 1906, President Theodore Roosevelt publicly denounced the segregation of Japanese schoolchildren in San Francisco, California.

Segregation, like Apartheid, can be a step in the development of genocide. Dr. Gregory Stanton, the author of the Ten Stages of Genocide, points out the dangers of stigmatization in Classification (Step 1) & Discrimination (Stage 3).

The City of San Francisco argued such segregation was legal under *Plessy v Ferguson* (1896).

"And so, my fellow Americans: ask not what your country can do for you—ask what you can do for your country."

John F. Kennedy

~December 1~

"Rosa Parks"

On this day, December 1, 1955, Rosa Parks refused to give up her seat to a white passenger and became an international icon of resistance to racial segregation.

Rosa Parks was born on February 4, 1913, and died on October 24, 2002. When I think of the life of Rosa Parks, I often highlight a point not commonly discussed: she died in poverty. While she had collected speaker fees for her public engagements, she had donated those speaker fees to create the Rosa Parks College Fund. After being robbed and assaulted in 1995, Parks moved out of her home in Detroit and moved into a high-rise apartment. Inexplicable, her money ran out in 2002, and she was sent an eviction noticed. After a church agreed to pay her rent and publicity embarrassed the apartment complex owners, she was granted free rent for the remainder of her life.

My question is, why was it a private church congregation that had to pay her rent? Why was it that a private housing corporation had to give her free rent for life? Is she not the "First Lady of Civil Rights"? Is she not the "Mother of the Civil Rights Movement"? Would America let a former US President, Vice President or First Lady be evicted? How hard would it have been at some point between the passage of the Civil Rights Act (1964) and her death on October 24, 2005, would it have been for Congress to grant her a government pension?

I find her death in poverty a national embarrassment.

~December 2~

"The Gandhi of the Balkans"

On this day, December 2, 1944, Ibrahim Rugova, the first President of Kosovo (1992–2000; 2002-2006)) was born in what was then known as Yugoslavia. He was known as the "Gandhi of the Balkans" for his peaceful advocating for independence from Serbia. His leadership is an example that genocide can be avoided, even when lesser powers pursue self-determination if greater-powers use their power judiciously. It is also worth noting that he was a Sunni Muslim; some have questioned whether Islam and western-style democracy are compatible. Certainly, the two were compatible in Rugova.

~~~

"Devolution"

On this day, December 2, 1999, the Parliament of the United Kingdom of Great Britain and Northern Ireland devolved powers to the Northern Ireland Assembly. This step was a key element of the Good Friday Agreement, which has largely put an end to The Troubles.

While Gerry Adams was certainly the most famous of the negotiators, and it could not have been done without all parties, it was Unionist Protestant leader David Trimble who probably sacrificed the most, ultimately losing his UUP leadership post and seat in Parliament. He, as well as SDLP leader John Hume, were awarded the 1998 Nobel Peace Prize for their work.

~December 3~

"Gilbert Stuart"

On this day, December 3, 1755, Gilbert Charles Stuart (née Stewart) was born in Saunderstown, Rhode Island. Stuart's (December 3, 1755 – July 9, 1828) best-known work is the unfinished portrait of George Washington featured on the United States one-dollar bill.

~~~

"The Beginning of the End of Cherokee Nation"

On this day, December 3, 1828, a bill was introduced in the Georgia state legislature asserting the sovereignty of state government over all land and people within its geographical boundaries, including the Cherokee Tribe. The US Supreme Court skirted this issue in Cherokee v. Georgia (1831) but ultimately made the correct decision in the following year. The SCOTUS decision *Worchester v. Georgia* (1832) was subsequently ignored. US President Andrew Jackson allegedly said, "John Marshall has made his decision; now let him enforce it!" of the court's ruling. The ultimate *de facto* (not necessarily *de jure*) result of Georgia's sovereignty bill was the Indian Removal Act of 1830 and the genocidal Trail of Tears.

~~~

"Bosnia's Anne Frank"

On this day, December 3, 1980, Zlata Filipović was born in Sarajevo, Yugoslavia (present-day Bosnia and Herzegovina). Filipović is a Bosnian writer and author of *Zlata's Diary*. (See May 3rd, August 4th, and August 6th)

~December 4~

"Francisco Franco"

On this day, December 4, 1892, Francisco Franco, was born in Ferrol, Spain. Franco rose to become a general in the Spanish military and then participated in the overthrow of the government and the ensuing Spanish Civil War. The mass killings of the Loyalist and Popular Front "enemies of the state" (liberals, Socialists, Trotskyites, Stalinists, anarchists, and intellectuals) occurred from the beginning of the Spanish civil war, in July 1936, and continued until 1945, six years after the civil war had ended. Known as the White Terror, or la Represión Franquista, it is estimated that 150,000 to 400,000 Spaniards died in Franco's quest to terrify the civil population who opposed the coup d'état. He systematically repressed the people of Spain with camps, forced labor, and executions.

The Spanish Catholic Church supported the White Terror. Spanish Cardinal Gomá stated that "Jews and Masons poisoned the national soul with absurd doctrine..." Anyone who did not attend Mass faithfully was likely to be suspected of 'red' tendencies. Women could not sign a financial contract without the co-signature of their husband or father. Nor could women become judges, testify in the trial, or become professors. Until 1963, all the opponents of the dictatorship were brought before military courts. Prisoners were sent to work in militarized penal colonies and disciplinary battalions of worker-soldiers. Francoist psychiatrist Antonio Vallejo-Nájera also experimented on prisoners in the Francoist concentration camps to study the alleged bio-psych roots of Marxism. Vallejo-Nájera also said that it was necessary to remove children from Republican women and thousands of children were taken from their mothers and handed over to Francoist families. Many of the mothers were executed afterwards. Francisco Franco died on November 20, 1975.

~December 5~

"The Original Han Solo?"

On this day, December 5, 1888, Algoth Niska (December 5, 1888 – May 28, 1954) was born in Vyborg, Russia. Niska was a Finnish bootlegger, footballer, and adventurer. In 1938, prior to World War II, Niska began to smuggle something else — Jewish refugees from Germany to the relative neutrality of Finland; he estimated he saved 151 Jews using stolen and forged passports as well as various plots to get Jews from Germany through the Netherlands and Estonia. He also sometimes refused payment. When his network was exposed in 1939, he fled to Estonia but found that the Soviet Union had occupied Estonia, so he fled back to Finland in a rowboat.

~~~

"Madiba"

On this day, December 5, 2013, Nelson Rolihlahla Mandela died in Johannesburg, Gauteng, South Africa. Mandela (July 18, 1918 – December 5, 2013) was a South African anti-apartheid revolutionary. Although imprisoned for fighting apartheid, he was released and served as President of South Africa from 1994 to 1999. He was the country's first Sub-Saharan black head of state and the first elected in a fully representative democratic election. His government focused on dismantling the legacy of apartheid by tackling institutionalized racism and fostering racial reconciliation; for example, former apartheid President F.W. de Klerk served as Mandela's Deputy President. Mandela became a global symbol of goodwill and how people can make a real contribution to peace. In 1993, Mandela and F.W. de Klerk were jointly awarded Nobel Peace Prize.

~December 6~

"Philip Berrigan"

On this day, December 6, 2002, Philip Francis Berrigan died in Baltimore, Maryland. Berrigan (October 5, 1923 – December 6, 2002) was an American peace activist. Berrigan graduated with an English degree from the College of the Holy Cross, a Jesuit university in Worcester, Massachusetts. In 1950, he joined the Society of St. Joseph, better known as the Josephite Fathers, a religious society of priests and lay brothers dedicated to serving those of African descent, who were still dealing with the repercussions of slavery and daily segregation in the United States. After studying at the theological school of the Society, St. Joseph's Seminary in Washington, D.C., and was ordained a priest in 1955.

In addition to his academic responsibilities, Berrigan became active in the Civil Rights Movement. He marched for desegregation and participated in sit-ins and bus boycotts. His brother Daniel wrote of him:

> From the beginning, he stood with the urban poor. He rejected the traditional, isolated stance of the Church in black communities. He was also incurably secular; he saw the Church as one resource, bringing to bear on the squalid facts of racism the light of the Gospel, the presence of inventive courage and hope.

Berrigan was first imprisoned in 1962. During his many prison sentences, he would often hold a Bible study class and offer legal educational support to other inmates. In 1964, he co-founded the Catholic Peace Fellowship in New York City. Later he also started the Baltimore Interfaith Peace Mission in West Baltimore, Maryland. (See also April 30th)

~December 7~

"Dorie Miller"

On this day, December 7, 1941, Doris "Dorie" Miller manned a machine gun and directed fire at the attacking Japanese aircraft. Miller (October 12, 1919 – November 24, 1943) was a Messman Third Class that the United States Navy noted for his bravery during the attack on Pearl Harbor on December 7, 1941. He was the first African American to be awarded the Navy Cross, the third highest honor awarded by the US Navy at the time, after the Medal of Honor and the Navy Distinguished Service Medal (the Navy Cross now precedes the Navy Distinguished Service Medal). On May 27, 1942, Miller was personally recognized by Admiral Chester W. Nimitz, Commander in Chief, Pacific Fleet, aboard the aircraft carrier *Enterprise*. Nimitz presented Miller with the Navy Cross, at the time the third-highest Navy award for gallantry during combat. The citation reads as follows:

For distinguished devotion to duty, extraordinary courage and disregard for his own personal safety during the attack on the Fleet in Pearl Harbor, Territory of Hawaii, by Japanese forces on December 7, 1941. While at the side of his Captain on the bridge, Miller, despite enemy strafing and bombing and in the face of a serious fire, assisted in moving his Captain, who had been mortally wounded, to a place of greater safety, and later manned and operated a machine gun directed at enemy Japanese attacking aircraft until ordered to leave the bridge.

Miller became an icon for African-Americans in the World War II era. Sadly, almost two years after surviving the attack on Pearl Harbor, Miller was killed in action when the *USS Liscome Bay* was sunk by a Japanese submarine during the Battle of Makin on November 24, 1943.

~~~

"William Bulkely"

On this day, December 7, 1768, William Bulkely was born in Clonmel, County Tipperary, Ireland. In 1785, the young Bulkely emigrated to become join the Irish Brigade of France. His uncle, Richard Butler, who had been a colonel in the Irish Brigade, retain a spot for Bulkely in Walsh's Regiment. Like most of the Irish soldiers in France, and ironically, in my opinion, Bulkely opposed the French Revolution and left the army when the republicans seized power.

In 1793, he took part in the royalist insurrection, commanding the district of La Roche. He led an attack on the rebels at Les Sables, but the attack failed. Bulkely continued to fight for the royalist cause through 1793, and finally, he and his wife were captured. He was tried by a military tribunal, condemned to death, and on January 2, 1794, William Bulkely was taken to the guillotine.

~December 8 ~

"Jean Rankin"

On this day, December 8, 1941, the United States Congress declared war on Japan. Jeannette Pickering Rankin (June 11, 1880 – May 18, 1973), a lifelong pacifist, was the only member of Congress to vote against the declaration of war.

Jeannette Pickering Rankin was an American politician and women's rights advocate, and the first woman to hold national office in the United States (See also November 21st). She was elected to the U.S. House of Representatives by the state of Montana in 1916, and again in 1940.

Each of Rankin's Congressional terms coincided with the initiation of U.S. military intervention in each of the two world wars. A supporter of non-interventionism, she was one of 50 House members (total of 56 in both chambers) who opposed the declaration of war of 1917 and, as mentioned earlier, the only member of Congress to vote against declaring war on Japan after the attack on Pearl Harbor in 1941.

A Progressive Era member of the Republican Party, Rankin was also instrumental in initiating the legislation that eventually became the 19th Constitutional Amendment, granting unrestricted voting rights to women. She championed the causes of gender equality and civil rights throughout a career that spanned more than six decades.

~~~

"Sarah's Key"

On this day, December 8, 2014, France agreed to pay $60 million in restitution to those who were deported from France during WWII. The most infamous mass deportations occurred circa July 16, 1942. The Nazi government of occupied France directed raids and the mass arrest of Jews in Paris by the French police, code named Opération Vent Printanier ("Operation Spring Breeze"). The roundup was one of several aimed at eradicating the Jewish population in France. According to records of the Préfecture de Police, 13,152 Jews were arrested, including more than 4,000 children.

The French Jews were held at the Vélodrome d'Hiver in extremely crowded conditions, almost without water, food, or sanitary facilities. The innocent civilians faced similar situations at the Drancy, Pithiviers, and Beaune-la-Rolande internment camps. The French Jews were then shipped in rail cattle cars to Auschwitz for their mass murder.

In 1995, French President Jacques Chirac apologized for the complicit role that French policemen and civil servants served in the raid.

~December 9~

"Leuven"

On this day, December 9, 1425, the Catholic University of Leuven was founded in Leuven, Belgium. Several significant mentors in my life attended Leuven including Ray Collins, Joe Creedon, Ed Sirois, Bob Hawkins, Jack Lavin, and Jack Unsworth. Louven is a truly special place and both the home and school of peacemakers.

~~~

"Martin de Porres"

On this day, December 9, 1579, Martin de Porres Velázquez was born in Lima, Viceroyalty of Peru. De Porres (December 9, 1579 – November 3, 1639) was a lay brother of the Dominican Order. He was noted for work on behalf of the poor, establishing an orphanage and a children's hospital. He maintained an austere lifestyle, which included fasting and abstaining from meat. De Porres was also a friend of St. Rose of Lima. De Porres was beatified in 1837 by Pope Gregory XVI and canonized in 1962 by Pope John XXIII; he is the patron saint of mixed-race people, barbers, innkeepers, public health workers, and all those seeking racial harmony.

~~~

"UNCPPCG"

On this day, December 9, 1948, United Nations adopted the Convention on the Prevention and Punishment of the Crime of Genocide which entered into force on January 12, 1951. It defines genocide in legal terms and is the culmination of years of campaigning by lawyer Raphael Lemkin.

~December 10~

This day, December 10, is United Nations Human Rights Day.

~~~

On this day, December 10, 1978, President of Egypt Anwar Sadat and Prime Minister of Israel Menachem Begin were jointly awarded the Nobel Peace Prize. Egypt became the first country to sign a formal peace treaty recognizing the State of Israel and, thus, Israel's right to exist. Sadat was assassinated Khalid Islambouli on October 6, 1981. Islambouli stated that his primary motivation for the assassination was Sadat's signing of the Camp David Accords with the State of Israel.

~~~

"*Amistad*"

On this day, December 10, 1997, *Amistad* was released. The film historical drama directed by Steven Spielberg. The film is based on the true story of the events in 1839 aboard the slave ship *La Amistad*, during which Mende tribesmen abducted for the slave trade managed to gain control of their captors' ship off the coast of Cuba as well as the international legal battle that followed their capture by a U.S. revenue cutter. The case was ultimately resolved by the United States Supreme Court in 1841.

Filming of the exterior and interior court scenes took place at the Old Colony House in Newport, RI, and the exterior of the Rhode Island State House was used to depict the exterior of the United States Capitol.

~December 11~

"The Salvadorian Schindler"

On this day, December 11, 1901, George Mantello was born in Lekence, Transylvania, Austria-Hungary. Mantello (December 11, 1901 – April 25, 1992) was a Jewish diplomat who, while working at the Salvadoran consulate in Geneva, Switzerland from 1942 to 1945, saved thousands of Jews from the Holocaust by providing them with fictive Salvadoran citizenship papers. He was also instrumental in publicizing in mid-1944 the deportation of Hungarian Jews to the Auschwitz concentration camp.

~December 12~

"Cardinal Dulles"

On this day, December 12, 2008, Avery Robert Dulles, S.J., died in the Bronx, New York, United States. Dulles (August 24, 1918 – December 12, 2008) was a Jesuit priest, theologian, and cardinal of the Catholic Church.

Dulles was raised a Presbyterian but had become an agnostic by the time he was a student at Harvard. His religious doubts were diminished during a personally profound moment when he stepped out into a rainy day and saw a tree beginning to flower along the Charles River; after that moment, he never again "doubted the existence of an all-good and omnipotent God." He noted how his theism turned toward conversion to Catholicism: "The more I examined, the more I was impressed with the consistency and sublimity of Catholic doctrine." He converted to Catholicism in the fall of 1940. Avery Dulles entered the Society of Jesus and was ordained to the priesthood in 1956. After a year in Germany, he studied ecclesiology under the American Jesuit Francis A. Sullivan at the Gregorian University in Rome and was awarded the Doctorate of Sacred Theology in 1960.

Dulles served on the faculty of Woodstock College from 1960 to 1974, of The Catholic University of America from 1974 to 1988, and as the Laurence J. McGinley Professor of Religion and Society at Fordham University from 1988 to 2008. He was an internationally known author and lecturer. Although Jesuits make a promise against pursuing ecclesiastical dignities and do not normally accept promotions within the Church hierarchy, Dulles was created a cardinal of the Catholic Church in Rome on February 21, 2001, by Pope John Paul II. At the time of his elevation, Dulles was already over the ago to vote in the College of Cardinals, so his elevation was seen as honorary.

~~~

"Saint Finnian of Clonard and Star Wars"

This day, December 12th is the Feast of Saint Finnian of Clonard (Cluain Eraird) Finnian (c. 470 – c. 549) founded Clonard Abbey in modern-day County Meath, and the Twelve Apostles of Ireland studied under him. Saint Finnian of Clonard (along with Saint Enda of Aran) is considered one of the fathers of Irish monasticism.

Saint Fionán is claimed to have founded the monastery on Skellig Michael in the 6th century, but the first definite reference to monastic activity on the island is the death of Suibhini of Skelig dating from the 8th century. Regarless, the Gaelic Christian monastery was founded on the island at some point between the 6th and 8th century and remained continuously occupied until it was abandoned in the late 12th century.

Skellig Michael (Sceilig Mhichíl), is also known as Great Skellig (Sceilig Mhór) and is west of the Iveragh Peninsula in County Kerry, Ireland. The remains of the monastery and most of the island became a UNESCO World Heritage Site in 1996.

MOST IMPORTANLY, Skellig Michael is also the filming location for Ahch-To in both *Star Wars Episode VII: The Force Awakens* (2015) as well as *Star Wars Episode VIII: The Last Jedi* (2017).

~December 13~

"The Rape of Nanking"

On this day, December 13, 1937, the Nanking Massacre began. Also known as the Rape of Nanking (or Nanjing), it is a six-week long massacre of approximately 200,000 civilians by the Japanese Imperial Army. In addition to the gruesome murder of civilians, thousands of Chinese women were raped and survived.
John Rabe, a German businessman and member of the Nazi Party, organized a group of Westerners to create the Nanking Safety Zone to save as many civilians as possible.

As the Japanese army approached the Chinese capital of Nanking (now Nanjing) and initiated bombing raids on the city, all but 22 foreigners fled the city. On November 22, 1937, as the Japanese Army advanced on Nanking, John Rabe and the other foreign nationals, organized the International Committee for the Nanking Safety Zone and created the Nanking Safety Zone to provide Chinese refugees with food and shelter from the impending Japanese slaughter. The Nanking Safety Zone sheltered approximately 200,000 Chinese people from slaughter during the massacre.

Rabe and his zone administrators also tried to stop the atrocities. His attempts to appeal to the Japanese by using his Nazi Party membership credentials only delayed the Japanese offensive, but that delay allowed hundreds of thousands of refugees to escape.

In 1997 his tombstone was moved from Berlin to Nanjing (as it is now) where it received a place of honor at the massacre memorial site. In 2005, Rabe's former residence in Nanking (as it then was) was renovated and now accommodates the "John Rabe and International Safety Zone Memorial Hall," which opened in 2006.

~December 14~

"Andrei Sakharov"

On this day, December 14, 1989, Andrei Dmitrievich Sakharov Андре́й Дми́триевич Са́харов died in Moscow, Russian SFSR, Soviet Union.

Sakharov (May 21, 1921 – December 14, 1989) was a Russian nuclear physicist, Soviet dissident, an activist for disarmament, peace and human rights. Initially, Sakharov became renowned as the designer of the Soviet Union's RDS-37, a codename for Soviet development of thermonuclear weapons.

Sakharov later became an advocate of civil liberties and civil reforms in the Soviet Union, for which he faced state persecution; these efforts earned him the Nobel Peace Prize in 1975. The Sakharov Prize, which is awarded annually by the European Parliament for people and organizations dedicated to human rights and freedoms, is named in his honor.

~December 15~

"The Murder of Sitting Bull"

On this day, December 15, 1890, Chief Sitting Bull was murdered by an Indian Agency policeman (today the Bureau of Indian Affairs). Sitting Bull had been living in his cabin on the Standing Rock Agency (reservation). He had been living on the reservation for 4 years after returning from working on the Buffalo Bill Wild West Show. The local U.S. Indian Agent was afraid Sitting Bull was about to leave the reservation, so he ordered his arrest. At 5:30 am, Sitting Bull's house was surrounded, and he was ordered to accompany the Indian Agency policemen. His followers became enraged, and one Lakota shot the lead policeman who, in turn, turned and shot Sitting Bull point-blank in the chest. Another officer then shot Sitting Bull in the head. He was 58 or 59 years old.

~~~

"Andrzeja Górska"

On this day, December 15, 2007, Andrzeja Górska died in Warsaw, Poland. Górska (1917 – December 15, 2007) was a Polish Roman Catholic nun. During World War II the Ursuline Sisters were active in efforts to obtain "Aryan" documents for the Jewish children, protected those who looked Jewish and hid them during German raids. Górska communicated with the Zegota Council, which supplied her with documents as necessary. Górska also saved the lives of many Jewish children by smuggling them out of the ghetto and transferring them to institutions belonging to the Ursuline Sisters, which had branches throughout occupied Poland. In 1997, Yad Vashem recognized Sister Andrzeja, (Maria Górska) as Righteous Among the Nations.

~December 16~

"The Roma Porajmos"

On this day, December 16, 1942, Heinrich Himmler ordered that Roma candidates for extermination be deported to Auschwitz. More than 22,600 Roma interned in Auschwitz died. To the Roma, this genocide is known as the Porajmos. While vastly more Jews died during the German Genocide, Roma died at the highest per capita percentage of all of Hitler's targets' pre-war population.

~~~

"Right…"

On this day, December 16, 1961, Martin Luther King, Jr., was arrested at an Albany, Georgia demonstration. He was charged with obstructing the sidewalk and parading without a permit.

~~~

"About time?"

On this day, December 16, 1968, during the Second Vatican Council, the Roman Catholic Church officially revoked the Edict of Expulsion of Jews from Spain.

~December 17~

"General Order No. 11"

On this day, December 17, 1862, during the American Civil War General Ulysses S. Grant issued General Order No. 11, expelling Jews from parts of Tennessee, Mississippi, and Kentucky. The order was issued as part of a Union campaign against the black market in the war zone, which Grant thought was being run "mostly by Jews and other unprincipled traders."

Under pressure from Lincoln, the General Order was revoked a few weeks later, and, during the campaign of 1868, Grant repudiated the order, Rabbi Isaac Mayer Wise, in particular, denounced Grant and called on Jews to vote against him. In 1874, President Grant and all the members of his Cabinet attended a dedication of the Adas Israel Congregation in Washington D.C. The event was the first time an American President attended a synagogue service. Many historians have taken his action as part of his continuing effort to reconcile with the Jewish community.

~~~

"The Magnuson Act"

On this day, December 17, 1943, the *Chinese Exclusion Act* was finally repealed by the *Magnuson Act* on December 17, 1943. It had originally been passed on May 6, 1882, and was one of the most significant restrictions on free immigration in US history; it prohibited all immigration of Chinese laborers. The legislation followed revisions made in 1880 to the US-China Burlingame Treaty of 1868, revisions that allowed the US to suspend Chinese immigration. The *Chinese Exclusion Act* was the first law implemented to prevent a specific ethnic group from immigrating to the United States.

~December 18~

"Stephen Biko"

On this day, December 18, 1946, Stephen Bantu Biko was born in Ginsberg, South Africa. Biko (December 18, 1946 – September 12, 1977) was a South African anti-apartheid activist. Ideologically an African nationalist and African socialist, he was at the forefront of a grassroots anti-apartheid campaign known as the Black Consciousness Movement during the late 1960s and 1970s. For his work, he received anonymous threats and was detained by state security services on four occasions.

Following his arrest in August 1977, Biko was tortured by South African state security officers. He sustained fatal head injuries and died shortly after. Over 20,000 people attended his funeral. Many of his writings were posthumously published for a wider audience. His life was the subject of a book by his friend Donald Woods, which later became the basis for the 1987 film *Cry Freedom*.

Biko is regarded as the father of Black Consciousness and a martyr of the anti-apartheid movement. Ironically, Saint Stephen (c. ACE 5 – c. ACE 34) is traditionally venerated as the protomartyr or first martyr of Christianity according to the Acts of the Apostles.

~December 19~

"The Great Swamp Massacre"

On this day, December 19, 1675, colonists from Rhode Island, Connecticut, Massachusetts bay and the Plimouth [sic] colonies massacred a winter fort of Narragansett women, children, wounded, and elderly.

The Narragansetts had remained neutral till that point in Chief Metacomet's War (also known as King Phillip's War). Their only "crime" was caring for Wampanoag women and children as well as some Pequot and Mohican wounded.

The leader of the war party, Plimouth [sic] Colony Governor Josiah Winslow burned the camp, burned the winter food stores, and forced approximately 1000 Native Americans to flee their winter camp into the cold.

~~~

"Released"

On this day, December 19, 1986, Mikhail Gorbachev, leader of the Soviet Union, released Andrei Sakharov and his wife from exile in Gorky. Initially, Sakharov became renowned as the designer of the Soviet Union's RDS-37, a codename for Soviet development of thermonuclear weapons. Sakharov later became an advocate of civil liberties and civil reforms in the Soviet Union, for which he faced state persecution; these efforts earned him the Nobel Peace Prize in 1975.

~December 20~

"Landsberg Prison"

On this day, December 20, 1927, Adolf Hitler was released from Landsberg Prison. Hitler had spent 264 days at Landsberg following the failed Beer Hall Putsch and, during which, Hitler wrote his book, *Mein Kampf*.

~~~

"The Good Göring"

On this day, December 20, 1966, Albert Günther Göring died in Munich, Germany. Göring (March 9, 1895 – December 20, 1966) was a German businessman who helped Jews and dissidents survive Nazi Germany; His older brother was Hermann Göring, the head of the German Luftwaffe and a leading member of the Nazi Party.

~~~

"The Highwayman"

On this day, December 20, 1788, James Freney (1719–1788) was a native of County Kilkenny, Ireland. During the 1650s the Freney family lost most of their lands. In 1742, Freney opened a pub in Waterford. Unable to pay the fees charged by the town corporation, Freney fell in with the Kellymount highway gang. Proclaimed an outlaw in January 1748 (old calendar), Freney surrendered in April 1749. Freney was sentenced to emigration. During his exile, Freney wrote his autobiography, *The Life and Adventures of Mr. James Freney* in 1754. By 1776, James Freney had returned to Ireland and settled at the port of New Ross. He worked as a customs official until his death on December 20, 1788.

~December 21~

"Roger Williams"

On this day, December 21, 1603, Roger Williams was born in London, United Kingdom of Great Britain. Williams (December 21, 1603 – between January 27th and March 15th of 1683) was a Puritan, an English Reformed theologian, and later a Reformed Baptist who was expelled from the colony of Massachusetts by the Puritan leaders.

Williams fled the Massachusetts colony under the threat of impending arrest and shipment to an English prison; in 1636, he began the Providence Plantations as a refuge offering freedom of conscience. Williams was also a student of Native American languages, an early advocate for fair dealings with American Indians, and one of the first abolitionists in North America, having organized the first attempt to prohibit slavery in any of the British American colonies.

Roger Williams is best remembered as the originator of the principle of separation of church and state. Rhode Island is also the only state whose land was primarily purchased, not taken, from Native Americans.

~~~

"Sunny"

On this day, December 21, 1980, while celebrating Christmas with her family at their mansion, Clarendon Court, in Newport, Rhode Island, Sunny von Bulow again confusion and incoordination. She was put to bed by her family, but in the morning, she was discovered unconscious on the bathroom floor. She was taken to the hospital where it became clear that this time she had suffered severe enough brain injury to produce a persistent vegetative state. Although clinical features resembled a drug overdose, some of the laboratory evidence suggested hypoglycemia.

Martha Sharp Crawford von Bülow, known as Sunny von Bülow (September 1, 1932 – December 6, 2008), was an American heiress and socialite. Her husband, Claus von Bülow (b. 1926), was convicted of attempting to murder her by insulin overdose, but the conviction was overturned on appeal. A second trial found him not guilty after experts opined that there was no insulin injection and that her symptoms were attributable to over-use of prescription drugs. The story was dramatized in the book and movie, Reversal of Fortune. Sunny von Bülow lived almost 28 years in a persistent vegetative state until her death in a New York nursing home on December 6, 2008.

~December 22~

"Show me the Spot"

On this day, December 22, 1847, US Representative Abraham Lincoln (IL-7) authored the *Spot Resolution* criticizing US President James K. Polk's justification for war with Mexico. Essentially, Lincoln challenged Polk to show him the spot where American blood was shed upon American soil.

~~~

"Treason?"

On this day, December 22, 1894, Alfred Dreyfus was wrongly convicted of treason by the French courts.

This began what is known as the Dreyfus Affair and perhaps, with the exception of Vélodrone d'hiver, the most well-known example of systematic antisemitism in France.

The scandal divided France from its beginning in 1894 until it was finally resolved in 1906. In that year, the French Supreme Court unanimously cancelled the judgment of guilt. Dreyfus was reinstated in the army with the rank of artillery major by law on July 13, 1906. This reflects the rank to which he could reasonably have been expected to have risen had his career not been interrupted by the false charges against him.

However, he could never gain back the five years he spent in jail, essentially, for being Jewish.

~December 23~

"Joseph Smith"

On this day, December 23, 1805, Joseph Smith Jr. was born in Sharon, Vermont, United States. Smith (December 23, 1805 – June 27, 1844) was an American religious leader and founder of Mormonism and the Latter Day Saint movement. When he was twenty-four, Smith published the Book of Mormon. By the time of his death fourteen years later, he had attracted tens of thousands of followers and founded a religious culture that continues to the present.

~December 24~

"KKK"

On this day, December 24, 1865, the Ku Kulx Klan was founded in Pulaski, Tennessee. General Nathan Bedford Forrest is well known as an early member and, allegedly, the first Grand Master of the order. Historians and criminologists have separated the Klan's existence into three distinct manifestations. It is currently the third manifestation of Klansmen. *Virginia v. Black* (2003) discussed the role of the First Amendment in Klan activities, specifically cross-burning.

~~~

"Stille Nacht, heilige Nacht"

On this day, December 24, 1818, the first performance of "Silent Night" takes place in the church of St. Nikolaus in Oberndorf, Austria. *Stille Nacht, heilige Nacht* was composed in 1818 by Franz Xaver Gruber to lyrics by Joseph Mohr in the small town of Oberndorf bei Salzburg, Austria.

Josephus Franciscus Mohr (December 11, 1792 – December 4, 1848) was born in Salzburg to an unmarried embroiderer, Anna Schoiberin. Franz Mohr, a mercenary soldier, and deserter had abandoned Joseph's mother before the birth. Johann Nepomuk Hiernle, vicar and leader of music at Salzburg Cathedral, enabled Mohr to have an education and encouraged him in music. As a boy, Mohr would serve simultaneously as a singer and violinist in the choirs of the University Church and at the Benedictine monastery of St. Peter. Mohr entered the seminary. Having an illegitimate birth, Mohr needed a special dispensation for him to attend seminary. Mohr graduated and was ordained as a priest.

~December 25~

"The Christmas Truce"

On this day, December 25, 1914, a series of widespread but unofficial ceasefires along the Western Front known as The Christmas truce (German: Weihnachtsfrieden; French: Trêve de Noël).

In the week leading up to the holiday, German and British soldiers crossed trenches to exchange seasonal greetings and talk. In areas, men from both sides ventured into no man's land on Christmas Eve and Christmas Day to mingle and exchange food and souvenirs. There were joint burial ceremonies and prisoner swaps, while several meetings ended in carol-singing. Men played games of football with one another, giving one of the most enduring images of the truce. However, the peaceful behavior was not ubiquitous; fighting continued in some sectors, while in others the sides settled on little more than arrangements to recover bodies.

~December 26~

"Mankato Mass-Hanging"

On this day, December 26, 1862, the largest mass-hanging in US history took place in Mankato, Minnesota, when 38 Native Americans were executed. Official history often points out the Dakota insurrection but glosses over the failure of the US to abide by its treaty obligations. Throughout the late 1850s, the US failed to make full or timely annuity payments, causing increased hunger and hardship among the very same Dakota who had helped Europeans to settle Mankato in 1852. On August 17, 1862, one young and exasperated Dakota killed five settlers and started the Dakota War of 1862. As a result of this war, the Dakota were expelled from Minnesota, their reservations were abolished, and these 38 Dakota were executed.

~~~

"Cardinal Mindszenty"

On this day, December 26, 1948, József Mindszenty was arrested in Hungary and accused of treason and conspiracy. Mindszenty (March 29, 1892 – May 6, 1975) was the Prince Primate, Archbishop of Esztergom, Prince Cardinal, and leader of the Catholic Church in Hungary from October 2, 1945, to December 18, 1973. During WWII, he was imprisoned by the pro-Nazi Arrow Cross Party and later also opposed communism; For five decades "he personified uncompromising opposition to fascism and communism in Hungary." After being tortured, he was given a life sentence in a 1949 show trial but was freed in the Hungarian Revolution of 1956 and granted political asylum in the US Embassy in Budapest. Mindszenty lived for fifteen years in the US Embassy before he was allowed to leave the country in 1971. Cardinal József Mindszenty died in exile in Vienna, Austria.

~December 27~

"The First 'Nuremberg Laws'?"

On this day, December 27, 1512, the Laws of Burgos were issued by the crown of Spain in Burgos, Kingdom of Castile (Spain). These laws were the first codified set of laws governing the behavior of Spaniards in the Americas, particularly with regards to the Indigenous peoples of the Americas ('native Caribbean Indians').

These laws authorized and legalized the colonial practice of creating Encomiendas, where Native Americans were forcibly grouped together to work under colonial masters. It also ordered that the Indians be catechized, outlawed bigamy, and required that the huts and cabins of the Indians be built together with those of the Spanish.

Nominally, there were positive aspects of the Burgos laws, such as respect for native sacred dance, hygiene, and literacy of the children of chiefs, but these laws were poorly enacted and resulted in the grave mistreatment of Native Americans.

Today, there are no Taino people left. They were eliminated by systematic slavery, destruction of language and culture, forced conversion and the abundance of Euro-African disease.

~~~

"Who Does *THAT*?"

On this day, December 27, 1983, Pope John Paul II visited Mehmet Ali Ağca in Rebibbia's prison and personally forgave him for the 1981 attempted assassination in St. Peter's Square.

~December 28~

"A Freed Freeman"

On this day, December 28, 1829, Elizabeth Freeman died in Stockbridge, Massachusetts. Freeman (c.1744—December 28, 1829), also known as Bet or Mum Bett, was the first black slave to file and win a freedom suit in Massachusetts. The Massachusetts Supreme Judicial Court ruling, in Freeman's favor, found slavery to be inconsistent with the 1780 Massachusetts State Constitution. Her suit, *Brom and Bett v. Ashley* (1781), was cited in the Massachusetts Supreme Judicial Court appellate review of Quock Walker's freedom suit. When the court upheld Walker's freedom under the state's constitution, the ruling was considered to have implicitly ended slavery in Massachusetts.

Any time, any time while I was a slave, if one minute's freedom had been offered to me, and I had been told I must die at the end of that minute, I would have taken it—just to stand one minute on God's airth [sic] a free woman— I would.

~Elizabeth Freeman~

~~~

~December 29~

"The Forgettable Andrew Johnson"

On this day, December 29, 1908, Andrew Johnson was born in Raleigh, North Carolina. Andrew Johnson (December 29, 1808 – July 31, 1875) was the 17th President of the United States of America. Controversial to say the least. He was merciful to the South in the face of the Radical Republicans, and even "lost guns" near the southern border to protect Mexican sovereignty from the French-Austrian invasion by Maximillian of Austrian.

~~~

"Wounded Knee"

On this day, December 29, 1890, hundreds of Lakota were massacred by the US 7th Cavalry at Wounded Knee, Pine Ridge Indian Reservation, South Dakota. The encamped Lakota were of members of Spotted Elk's band as well as the Hunkpapa followers of the recently murdered Chief Sitting Bull. The band had camped at Wounded Knee after being intercepted by US Cavalry for leaving the reservation without permission. The catalyst for the massacre was apparently the disarming of Black Coyote, who was deaf and didn't completely understand the disarming. For an unknown reason, his rifle discharged in a scuffle with US soldiers, and the slaughter began. While official US records state 300 Lakota were killed, Native Americans state that many more were killed. Most of the Lakota were disarmed, and the US military had established positions on neighboring hills with four Hotchkiss guns, thus creating kill zones. Today, many believe the massacre was revenge for the losses of the US 7th Cavalry at the Battle of Little Big Horn. Lost Bird, an infant and the lone survivor, was taken by Leonard Colby as a war trophy.

~December 30~

"Grigori Yefimovich Rasputin"

On this day, December 30, 1916, Grigori Rasputin took a knife to the abdomen and had his entrails hung out, was fed cakes and red wine laced with a massive amount of cyanide, and was shot through the back, but did not die. Then Rasputin was shot three more times but did not die. He was then clubbed and castrated; Then his body tied-up, wrapped in a carpet, thrown into the icy Neva River... He drowned...

~December 31~

"The Nazi Hunter"

On this day, December 31, 1908, The Nazi Hunter was born.
Simon Wiesenthal was born in the Kingdom of Galicia and
Lodomeria, then part of the Austro-Hungarian Empire and now
part of Ukraine.

During WWII, he was a slave laborer in Nazi concentration
camps, including Janowska, Plaszow, and Mauthausen.
He is most known for the part he played in locating Adolf
Eichmann, who was captured in Buenos Aires in 1960, as well as
the Simon Wiesenthal Center that bears his name.

Wiesenthal died in his sleep at age 96 in Vienna, Austria, on
September 20, 2005, and was buried in the city of Herzliya in
Israel.

~~~

"Amasa Sprague"

On this day, December 31, 1843, Amasa Sprague was beaten to
death in what is now considered an unsolved crime. Sprague, a
Cranston textile factory owner, was a member of a prominent
Rhode Island family. Allegedly the beating was revenge for
Sprague effort to have a liquor license repealed for the Gordon
Brothers' bar. Nicholas Gordon and his brother John Gordon
were Roman Catholic immigrants from Ireland and anti-
immigrant and anti-Catholic bias is considered to have tainted the
legal process.

Nicholas, John, and William Gordon (another brother) were all tried for murder, but only John was convicted, a conviction based on contradictory circumstantial evidence. William was found not guilty and in Nicholas's case, held after John's execution, the jury was hung. The murder was considered a major event of the period, and the trial of accused killer John Gordon was marked by anti-Irish bigotry; Gordon was subsequently found guilty and executed. It was the last execution in Rhode Island history.

~~~

Conclusion

Perhaps it is appropriate that we end with the Nazi Hunter and excessive misjustice. After all, it is the hunting of others to whom we ascribe guilt that perpetuates the cycle of violence. Peace comes from acknowledgement, ownership, and awareness, and not vengeance. Justice is not blood-thirsty, she is curious and forgiving.

Do not forget to show hospitality to strangers, for by so doing some people have shown hospitality to angels without knowing it. Continue to remember those in prison as if you were together with them in prison and those who are mistreated as if you yourselves were suffering.

~Hebrews 13: 2-3~

Whoever destroys a soul, it is considered as if he destroyed an entire world. And whoever saves a life, it is considered as if he saved an entire world.

Mishnah Sanhedrin 4:5; Yerushalmi Talmud 4:9, and Babylonian Talmud Sanhedrin 37a

The hour of departure has arrived, and we go our ways — I to die, and you to live. Which is better God only knows.

Socrates

Apology, 4th century B.C.E.

Index

Heroes

February 15, 2011	Mohamed Shalgham
February 17, 1876	Luiz Martins de Souza Dantas
February 20, 1895	Frederick Douglass
February 20, 1973	Dimitar Peshev
February 22, 1972	Paul Grüninger
February 25, 2005	Peter Benenson
February 26, 2017	Gerald Bernard Kaufman
February 28, 2015	Yaşar Kemal
February 29, 1988	Desmond Tutu
March 2, 1931	Mikhail Sergeyevich Gorbachev
March 2, 1953	Russ Feingold
March 6, 1984	Martin Niemöller
March 12, 1991	LeRoy Collins
March 12, 2000	Pope John Paul II
March 15, 1965	Lyndon B. Johnson
March 17, 1907	John Orlando Pastore
March 17, 1965	Judge Frank Johnson
March 20, 1903	Edward E. Swanstrom
March 23, 1775	Patrick Henry
March 23, 1919	Desmond Thomas Doss
March 23, 1943	Archbishop Damaskinos Papandreou
March 24, 1980	Óscar Arnulfo Romero y Galdámez
March 26, 1964	Malcolm X and MLK, Jr.
March 27, 2006	Rudolf Vrba
March 30, 2005	Fred Korematsu
April 2, 1939	Anthony Lake
April 3, 1873	Susan B. Anthony
April 5, 1883	Carlos de Almeida Fonseca Sampaio
April 9, 1947	The Journey of Reconciliation
April 9, 1961	Zog
April 10, 1998	The Good Friday Agreement
April 12, 1912	Clarissa Harlowe Barton
April 12, 2016	Christopher John Antal
April 14, 1866	Johanna Mansfield Sullivan Macy
April 14, 1954	Luiz Martins de Souza Dantas
April 15, 1935	The Roerich Pact
April 21, 1903	Hans Hedtoft Hansen
April 25, 1992	George Mantello
April 25, 2003	Maurice Cheeks
April 26, 1895	Oscar Wilde
April 26, 2008	Mallory Holtman and Liz Wallace
April 28, 1908	Oskar Schindler
April 30, 1947	Geralyn Wolf

April 30, 2016	Daniel Joseph Berrigan
May 2, 1895	Wilhelm Adalbert Hosenfeld
May 4, 1938	Carl von Ossietzky
May 4, 1994	Yitzhak Rabin and Yasser Arafat
May 5, 2000	Gino Bartali
May 6, 1527	The Last Stand Battle
May 6, 2001	Pope John Paul II
May 8, 1956	The Szczurowa Massacre Memorial
May 10, 1902	Joachim Prinz
May 10, 1960	Paul David Hewson
May 10, 1994	Nelson Mandela
May 11, 1973	Daniel Ellsberg
May 12, 2008	Irena Sendlerowa
May 12, 2002	Jimmy Carter
May 13, 1940	"Blood, toil, tears, and sweat"
May 17, 1954	*Brown v. Board of Education of Topeka, KS*
May 19, 1909	Nicholas George Winton
May 19, 1921	Seiichi Nakahara and Yuri Kochiyama
May 22, 1942	Richard Oakes
May 22, 1943	Betty Williams
May 23, 1820	William Drennan
May 24, 1991	Operation Solomon
May 26, 1868	Edmund G. Ross
May 26, 2017	Ricky John Best, Taliesin Myrddin, Namkai-Meche, and Micah Fletcher
May 30, 1941	Manolis Glezos and Apostolos Santas
June 1, 1843	Isabella Baumfree
June 2, 1969	Joseph Guy LaPointe Jr.
June 4, 1940	"We shall fight on the beaches…"
June 5, 1984	Tank Man
June 9, 1954	Joseph Welch
June 12, 1987	Ronald Reagan
June 13, 1936	August Landmesser
June 16, 1981	Ken Taylor
June 18, 1940	"This was their finest hour"
June 18, 1964	Israel Dresner
June 20, 1789	The Serment du Jeu de Paume
June 22, 2010	Armando Galarraga
June 22, 1988	Leonard P. Matlovich
June 23, 1937	Martti Ahtisaari
June 24, 1900	Raphael Lemkin
June 25, 1976	Missouri Governor Kit Bond
June 26, 1963	John F. Kennedy
June 26, 2016	Pope Francis

June 27, 1844	Thomas Wilson Dorr
June 30, 2007	Peter Rometti
July 1, 2015	Nicholas Winton
July 2, 2016	Elie Wiesel
July 4, 1939	Henry Louis Gehrig
July 4, 1946	Ronald Kovic
July 6, 1935	Lhamo Thondup
July 6, 1944	Second Lieutenant Jackie Robinson
July 6, 1971	Louis Armstrong
July 7, 1983	Samantha Reed Smith
July 8, 1942	Brother Álvaro
July 9, 1974	Earl Warren
July 10, 1807	Solomon Northup
July 12, 1997	Malala Yousafzai
July 13, 2000	Seretse Goitsebeng Maphiri Khama
July 14, 1960	Jane Goodall
July 16, 1894	Henryk Sławik
July 17, 1903	Hiram "Harry" Bingham IV
July 18, 1914	Gino Bartali
July 18, 1918	Nelson Rolihlahla Mandela
July 18, 1977	Josef Korbel
July 18, 2007	The Elders
July 19, 1885	Aristides de Sousa Mendes do Amaral e Abranches
July 21, 1967	Albert John Lutuli
July 24, 1750	John Philpot Curran
July 26, 1948	Executive Order 9981
July 27, 2004	Barrack Obama
July 29, 1905	Dag Hammarskjöld
July 30, 1718	William Penn
July 31, 1947	Raoul Gustaf Wallenberg
July 31, 1986	Chiune Sugihara
August 1, 1993	William J. Clinton
August 2, 1923	Shimon Peres
August 3, 1940	Ramón Antonio Gerardo Estévez
August 3, 1936	Jesse Owens
August 4, 1936	Jesse Owens
August 7, 1927	Ralph Johnson Bunche
August 10, 1951	Juan Manuel Santos Calderón
August 15, 1992	Giorgio Perlasca
August 16, 1913	Menachem Begin
August 18, 1991	Boris Yeltsin
August 22, 1893	Dorothy Parker
August 24, 1900	Raphael Lemkin
August 24, 2015	Tony Abbott
August 25, 1985	Samantha Reed Smith
August 27, 2008	Avraham Nathan
August 28, 1963	*I Have a Dream*
September 1, 1604	Adi Granth

September 4, 2016	Anjezë Gonxhe Bojaxhiu
September 6, 2008	Abdullah Gül
September 8, 1993	The San Miguel School
September 13, 1967	Varian Mackey Fry
September 13, 1989	Desmond Tutu
September 17, 1978	The Camp David Accords
September 19, 1940	Witold Pilecki
September 22, 1948	Gail Halvorsen
September 24, 1957	Little Rock
September 24, 1962	James Meredith
September 25, 2011	Wangari Muta Maathai
September 27, 1540	The Society of Jesus
September 28, 1997	Ángel Sanz-Briz
September 28, 1997	Fengshan
September 29, 2015	The Redemption of Dachau
October 1, 1924	James Earl Carter, Jr.
October 2, 2006	West Nickel Mines School
October 3, 1958	George Kennedy Allen Bell
October 5, 1936	Václav Havel
October 6, 2015	Árpád Göncz
October 7, 1931	Desmond Mpilo Tutu
October 7, 1998	Matthew Shepard
October 9, 1974	Oskar Schindler
October 9, 1950	Jody Williams
October 11, 1926	Thích Nhất Hạnh
October 13, 1925	Marc H. Tanenbaum
October 14, 1843	Daniel O'Connell
October 16, 1978	Karol Wojtyla
October 17, 1933	Albert Einstein
October 18, 1944	Gisi Fleischmann
October 19, 1943	Albert Schatz
October 19, 2003	Alija Izetbegović
October 21, 1833	Alfred Bernhard Nobel
October 23, 1956	The Hungarian Uprising
October 25, 1955	Sadako Sasaki
October 27, 1891	Paul Grüninger
October 27, 1992	Allen R. Schindler, Jr.
October 28, 1914	Jonas Edward Salk
October 29, 1933	Richard Perry Loving
October 29, 1938	Ellen Johnson Sirleaf
October 29, 1998	Truth and Reconciliation
October 30, 1735	John Adams
October 30, 1945	Jackie Robinson
November 1, 1878	Carlos Saavedra Lamas
November 2, 2002	Sciullo, Perretta, and Leftwich
November 3, 1942	Tadatoshi Akiba
November 4, 1908	Joseph Rotblat
November 5, 1805	Thomas Wilson Dorr
November 5, 1991	Pedro Arrupe, S.J.

November 6, 1913	Mohandas Gandhi
November 6, 1965	Cornell, Edelman, and Lisker
November 7, 1854	Francisco Luis Febres-Cordero y Muñoz
November 8, 1897	Dorothy Day
November 9, 1965	Roger Allen LaPorte
November 9, 1989	Harald Jäger
November 12, 2015	Adel Termos
November 13, 1956	The Montgomery Bus Boycott
November 14, 1960	Ruby Bridges
November 19, 1863	Abraham Lincoln
November 20, 1957	Goodluck Ebele Azikiwe Jonathan
November 22, 2004	The Orange Revolution
November 22, 2005	Yona Metzger
November 23, 1882	John Heinrich Detlev Rabe
November 24, 1889	Prince Constantin Karadja
November 24, 1963	John LaFarge Jr.
November 25, 1984	*"Do They Know It's Christmas?"*
November 26, 1968	James P. Fleming
November 28, 1989	The Velvet Revolution
November 30, 1906	Theodore Roosevelt
December 1, 1955	Rosa Parks
December 2, 1944	Ibrahim Rugova
December 5, 1888	Algoth Niska
December 5, 2013	Nelson Rolihlahla Mandela
December 6, 2002	Philip Francis Berrigan
December 7, 1941	Doris "Dorie" Miller
December 9, 1579	Martin de Porres Velázquez
December 10, 1978	Sadat and Begin
December 11, 1901	George Mantello
December 12, 2008	Avery Robert Dulles, S.J.
December 14, 1989	Andrei Dmitrievich Sakharov
December 15, 2007	Andrzeja Górska
December 19, 1986	Mikhail Gorbachev
December 20, 1966	Albert Günther Göring
December 21, 1603	Roger Williams
December 22, 1847	Abraham Lincoln (IL-7)
December 25, 1914	The Christmas Truce
December 26, 1948	József Mindszenty
December 27, 1983	Pope John Paul II
December 28, 1829	Elizabeth Freeman
December 31, 1908	The Nazi Hunter

Horrors

January 5, 1527	Felix Manz
January 10, 1912	Maria Mandl
January 15, 1951	Ilse Koch
January 17, 1893	Lorrin Thurston
January 17, 1892	Mercy L. Brown
January 19, 1983	Klaus Barbie
January 24, 2015	Trace O'Connell
January 25, 1945	The March to the Sea
January 23, 1870	The Piegan Massacre
January 28, 1986	Space Shuttle Challenger
January 29, 1863	The Bear Creek Massacre
January 30, 1972	Bloody Sunday (Ireland)
February 1, 1902	Therese Brandl
February 1, 1968	Nguyễn Văn Lém/Nguyễn Ngọc Loan
February 4, 1997	Slobodan Milošević
February 15, 1909	George Spencer Millet
February 15, 1952	Tomislav Nikolić
February 16, 1987	John Demjanjuk
February 17, 2016	Ammon Bundy
February 18, 1942	Sook Ching Massacres
February 19, 1942	Executive Order 9066
February 23,1898	Émile Zola Convicted
February 23, 1944	Operation Lentil ("Chechevitsa")
February 24, 1831	The Treaty of Dancing Rabbit
February 25, 1915	Demobilization of the Armenians
February 26, 2012	Trayvon Benjamin Martin
February 27, 1944	Khaibakh Massacre
February 28, 2002	The Gulbarg Society Massacre
March 1, 1562	The Wassy Massacre
March 4, 2009	Omar Hassan al-Bashir
March 5, 1940	The Katyn Massacre
March 7, 1965	"Bloody Sunday" (Selma, Alabama)
March 8, 1782	The Gnadenhutten Massacre
March 9, 1956	The March Incident
March 11, 1879	The Ryukyu Kingdom
March 12, 1942	Czeslawa Kwoka
March 12, 1943	Ratko Mladić
March 13, 1943	Krakow Ghetto
March 14, 1984	John Gregg
March 20, 1990	Mihăilă Cofariu
March 21, 1933	Dachau

March 21, 1937	The Winship Massacre
March 21, 1960	The Sharpeville Massacre
March 23, 1933	Ermächtigungsgesetz
March 24, 1832	Hiram, Ohio
March 25, 1710	The Priest Hunter
March 28, 1959	Tibet
March 31, 1146	St. Bernard of Clairvaux
April 1, 1924	Adolf Hitler
April 5, 1968	The Assassination of MLK, Jr.
April 6, 1994	The Shot Heard Round Rwanda
April 7, 1994	The Rwandan Genocide
April 11, 1979	Idi Amin
April 12, 1864	The Fort Pillow Massacre
April 12, 1927	The Shanghai Massacre
April 13, 1948	The Haganah Massacre
April 15, 1395	Timur
April 17, 1521	The Trial of Martin Luther
April 19, 1995	The Oklahoma City Bombing
April 19, 2014	David Ead
April 20, 1945	The Bullenhuser Damm School
April 22, 2017	The 101st Anniversary of the Armenian Genocide
April 23, 1993	Joe Mollicone
April 24, 1915	The Armenian Genocide
April 26, 1937	Guernica
April 29, 1946	Hideki Tojo
May 1, 1945	Adolf Hitler
May 4, 1963	Walter Gadsden
May 6, 1882	*The Chinese Exclusion Act*
May 7, 2016	Islamic State (IS)
May 14, 1922	Franjo Tuđman
May 14, 1948	The Palestinian Diaspora
May 18, 1975	Michael Woodmansee
May 21, 1864	The Circassian Genocide
May 23, 1945	Heinrich Himmler
May 25, 1915	Mehmed Talat
May 26, 1637	The Mystic Massacre
May 28, 1948	DF Malan
May 28, 1948	Ceausescu and Pot
May 31, 1909	Giovanni Palatucci
June 1, 1962	Adolf Eichmann
June 3, 1940	Franz Rademacher
June 4, 2000	Amadou Diallo
June 5, 1968	Robert F. Kennedy

June 5, 1984	Indira Gandhi
June 6, 1889	Jonathan Edward Back
June 6, 1985	Wolfgang Gerhard
June 7, 1892	Homer Plessy
June 7, 1998	James Byrd
June 8, 1967	The *USS Liberty*
June 10, 1942	Lidice
June 10, 1986	Patrick Joseph Magee
June 17, 1964	Jimmy Brock
June 17, 2012	Rodney Glen King
June 19, 1945	Radovan Karadžić,
June 19, 1964	U.S. Senator Strom Thurmond (R-SC)
June 20, 1893	Lizzie Borden
June 21, 1964	Mississippi Burning
June 24, 1942	Ležáky
June 26, 1953	Lavrentiy Beria
June 26, 2018	*Trump v. Hawaii*
July 5, 2013	Jorge Rafael Videla
July 6, 1995	Srebrenica
July 15, 1834	The Spanish Inquisition
July 16, 1942	Opération Vent Printanier
July 17, 2014	Daniel Pantaleo
July 25, 1755	The Expulsion of the Acadians
July 25, 1956	*SS Andrea Doria*
July 28, 1932	Herbert Hoover
August 4, 1944	Anne Frank
August 4, 1964	Mississippi Burning
August 5, 1962	Nelson Mandela
August 6, 1945	Hiroshima
August 7, 1930	Thomas Shipp and Abram Smith
August 9, 1997	Albner Louima
August 9, 2014	Darren Wilson
August 10, 1948	Maria Mandl
August 12, 1676	"Praying Indian" John Alderman
August 12, 1898	Hawaii
August 13, 1906	The Brownsville Affair
August 15, 1928	Czeslawa Kwoka
August 17, 1915	Leo Frank
August 19, 1854	Conquering Bear
August 20, 1191	The Massacre of Ayyadieh
August 28, 1955	Emmett Till
August 28, 1957	U.S. Senator Strom Thurmond
August 29, 587 BCE	Solomon's Temple
August 29, 1758	Indian Mills, New Jersey
September 1, 1939	Adolf Hitler
September 3, 2001	Holy Cross
September 7, 70	The Destruction of the Temple
September 9, 1922	Smyrna

September 9, 1940	The Treznea Massacre
September 11, 1609	The (first) Expulsion Order
September 12, 1919	German Workers' Party
September 12, 1938	Sudetenland Crisis
September 14, 1940	The Ip Massacre
September 15, 1935	The Nuremberg Laws
September 15, 1935	The Swastika
September 16, 1936	Suzanne Mol
September 17, 1948	Folke Bernadotte
September 18, 1943	Sobibór
September 20, 1737	The Walking Purchase
September 26, 1493	Pope Alexander VI
September 26, 1468	Juan de Torquemada
October 4, 1940	Hitler and Mussolini
October 11, 1973	Craig Chandler Price
October 12, 1998	Matthew Shepherd
October 15, 1894	The Dreyfus Affair
October 15, 1944	The Arrow Cross Party
October 16, 2015	The Hungarian Border Barrier
October 20, 1951	The Johnny Bright Incident
October 22, 362	The Oracle of Apollo at Daphne
October 27, 1838	The Mormon Extermination Order
November 2, 1675	Josiah Winslow
November 5, 1805	Guy Fawkes
November 9, 1938	Kristallnacht
November 10, 1865	Heinrich Hartmann Wirz
November 11, 2017	Caesar Goodson
November 13, 1002	The St. Brice's Day Massacre
November 15, 1943	The Roma Pogroms
November 16, 1688	"Goody" Ann Glover
November 16, 1989	El Salvadoran Death Squad
November 17, 1894	H. H. Holmes
November 18, 1978	Jerry Bibb Balisok
November 21, 1922	Rebecca Latimer Felton
November 22, 1963	John F. Kennedy
November 27, 1095	Pope Urban II
November 27, 1868	Washita River Massacre
November 27, 1978	Harvey Bernard Milk
November 28, 1729	Fort Rosalie Massacre
November 29, 1864	The Sand Creek Massacre
December 3, 1828	The Cherokee Tribe
December 4, 1892	Francisco Franco
December 13, 1937	The Nanking Massacre
December 15, 1890	The Murder of Sitting Bull
December 16, 1942	The Roma Porajmos
December 16, 1961	Martin Luther King, Jr.
December 17, 1862	General Order No. 11
December 18, 1946	Stephen Bantu Biko
December 19, 1675	The Great Swamp Massacre

December 20, 1927	Landsberg Prison
December 22, 1894	The Dreyfus Affair
December 24, 1865	The Ku Kulx Klan
December 26, 1862	The Mankato Hangings
December 27, 1512	The Laws of Burgos
December 29, 1890	Wounded Knee
December 30, 1916	Grigori Rasputin
December 31, 1843	Amasa Sprague

Happenstances

January 2, 1492	The Reconquista
January 3, 1624	William Tucker
January 5, 1527	Felix Manz
January 7, 1979	Vietnam ended the Cambodian Genocide
January 11, 2003	George Ryan
January 12, 1958	Christiane Amanpour
January 14, 1917	Elisha Hunt Rhodes
January 15, 1919	The Great Molasses Flood
January 16, 1786	The Statute for Religious Freedom
January 16, 1969	Jan Palach
January 16, 2006	Ellen Johnson Sirleaf
January 17, 1893	Lorrin Thurston
January 18, 1788	The First Fleet
January 19, 1924	Nicholas Colasanto
January 20, 1925	William Herrell Kugle, Jr.
January 21, 1878	The Providence Grays
January 22, 2006	Evo Morales
January 23, 1879	The Battle of Rorke's Drift
January 28, 1540	Ludolph van Ceulen
January 28, 1985	"We Are the World"
January 28, 2016	Vincent Albert "Buddy" Cianci
January 30th	Fred Korematsu Day
January 31, 1999	*Family Guy*
February 2, 1793	Samuel Whittemore
February 5, 1576	Henry of Navarre
February 8, 1887	The Dawes Allotment Act
February 9, 1957	Miklós Horthy
February 13, 858	Kenneth MacAlpin
February 15, 1898	The *USS Maine*
February 18, 1885	Mark Twain
February 21, 1952	The Language Movement
February 22, 1943	The White Rose
February 22, 1980	The Miracle on Ice
February 29, 1988	Desmond Tutu
March 5, 1976	*Lynch v. Donnelly* (1984)
March 6, 2011	Herman Harband
March 7, 1707	Stephen Hopkins
March 8, 1937	Juvénal Habyarimana
March 10, 1959	The Dalai Lama
March 13, 1943	Fran Dederich Thatcher
March 15, 2006	The New America?

March 16, 2003	Rachel Corrie
March 18, 1869	Neville Chamberlain
March 19th	The U.S. Constitution/The Bible
March 19, 2017	St. Joseph's Day
March 19, 2017	JK Rowling
March 21, 1773	David Melville
March 21, 1806	Benito Pablo Juárez García
March 21, 1842	Elisha Hunt Rhodes
March 22, 1991	Edith Christine Jackson Barlow
March 25, 1916	Ishi
March 27, 1997	Dexter Scott King
March 27, 2009	Irving Raskin Levine
March 29, 1990	The Hyphen War
March 29, 1901	James Stephens
April 1, 2005	Serbian Srebrenica Apology
April 3, 1968	"I've Been to the Mountaintop"
April 7, 1963	The Birmingham March
April 8, 1730	Shearith Israel
April 10, 1794	Matthew Calbraith Perry
April 13, 1742	Handel's *Messiah*
April 14, 70	The Siege of Jerusalem
April 15, 1776	George Washington
April 16, 1890	Nathaniel Grigsby
April 17, 1949	The Republic of Ireland
April 18, 1981	The Longest Game in History
April 18, 2007	K-77
April 20, 2013	*A Pug's Life*
April 23, 1014	The Battle of Clontarf
April 23, 1675	Charles Spencer
April 24, 1916	The Easter Rising
April 25, 1707	Battle of Almansa
April 27, 1653	Philip O'Reilly
April 27, 1987	Kurt Waldheim
April 28, 1952	The End of WWII
April 29, 1975	The Fall of Saigon
April 29, 2015	Shinzo Abe
April 30, 1952	Mr. Potato Head
May 3, 1960	The Anne Frank House Museum
May 3, 1920	*The Government of Ireland Act* (1920)
May 4, 1776	The Republic of Rhode Island
May 8, 1945	Alfred Jodl and Karl Dönitz
May 9, 1926	Richard E. Byrd and Floyd Bennett
May 9, 1926	The Vast Wasteland

May 11, 1976	The Arcade in Providence
May 14, 1948	Israeli Independence
May 15, 1945	Bernard Herzog
May 16, 1843	The Oregon Trail
May 17, 1892	George Brown
May 19th	The Pontic Genocide
May 19, 1795	Josiah Bartlett
May 20th	The Day of Remembrance
May 20, 1899	Jacob German
May 20, 2002	East Timor
May 22, 1973	The Windmill Cottage
May 23, 1824	Ambrose Everett Burnside
May 24, 1798	The Irish Rebellion of 1798
May 25, 2000	Liberation Day
May 28, 2016	Barack Obama
May 29, 1982	Pope John Paul II
May 29, 2011	"Hands Across Hawthorne"
May 31, 1857	Pope Pius XI
June 2, 1924	The Indian Citizenship Act
June 7, 1917	The Mines at Messines
June 8, 632	Muhammed
June 11, 1963	Thích Quảng Đức
June 14, 1789	*HMS Bounty*
June 14, 1954	"Under God"
June 15, 1888	Frederick III
June 23, 2018	Donald Hall
June 25, 1876	The Battle of the Little Bighorn
June 27, 2001	Jack Lemmon
June 28, 1914	Franz Ferdinand
June 28, 2001	Slobodan Milošević
June 29, 2011	John Gordon
June 30, 1934	The Night of the Long Knives
July 1, 1520	Moctezuma II
July 1, 1991	Clarence Thomas
July 2, 2016	Bono and Adam Bevell
July 3, 1970	The Falls Curfew
July 8, 1663	John Clarke
July 10, 1989	Melvin Jerome Blanc
July 11, 1898	Miklós Voglhut
July 14, 1771	Junípero Serra
July 20, 1944	Claus von Stauffenberg
July 20, 1969	Apollo 11
July 21, 1721	Walter Kennedy
July 22, 1499	The Battle of Dornach
July 22, 1937	The Attempted Court-Packing
July 23, 1992	Joseph Ratzinger

July 25, 1861	The Crittenden–Johnson
July 28, 1868	The 14th Amendment
July 28, 1915	Republic of Haiti
July 28, 1917	The Silent Parade
August 1, 2004	Lawrence Cook
August 6, 1945	Yoko Moriwaki
August 8, 1942	The Quit India Movement
August 9, 1965	Singapore
August 11, 1975	Anthony McAuliffe
August 11, 1947	Muhammad Ali Jinnah
August 12, 1898	Mervyn Edward Griffin Jr.
August 13, 1831	Nat Turner
August 14, 1945	*V-J Day in Times Square*
August 14, 2015	The US Embassy in Havana
August 16, 1946	Masoud Barzani
August 17, 1585	Roanoke Colony
August 18, 1587	Virginia Dare
August 19, 1991	Mikhail Gorbachev
August 21, 2001	Macedonia
August 22, 1831	Nat Turner's Rebellion
August 23, 1785	Oliver Hazard Perry
August 26, 1920	The 19th Amendment
August 29, 1911	Ishi
August 30, 1999	East Timor
August 31, 1997	Diana Spencer
September 1, 1864	Roger David Casement
September 2, 1841	Robert Clay Allison
September 2, 2005	George W. Bush
September 5, 1874	Napoléon "Nap" Lajoie
September 8, 2002	Helen Herczberg Gawara
September 10, 1979	António Agostinho Neto
September 15, 2005	The Cohen Rule
September 21, 1745	Battle of Prestonpans
September 21, 1937	J. R. R. Tolkien's *The Hobbit*
September 21, 1976	Orlando Letelier
September 21, 1981	Sandra Day O'Connor
September 22, 1914	Ellison Myers Brown, Sr.
September 23, 1939	Sigmund Freud
September 23, 1968	Francesco Forgione
September 24, 1906	Devils Tower
September 30, 1862	Isaac Peace Rodman
October 1, 1946	The Nuremburg Trials
October 5, 2004	Rodney Dangerfield
October 6, 1849	The 13 Martyrs of Arad
October 6, 1908	Austria-Hungary annexed Bosnia
October 8, 2008	Piomingo Day
October 10, 1967	Frank William "Menty" Keaney
October 12, 1492	Christopher Columbus
October 24, 2002	*Gorman v. St. Raphael's Academy*

October 26, 1956	Godwin's Law
October 29, 539 BCE	Cyrus the Great
October 30, 1773	Hannah Robinson
October 31, 1517	The 95 Theses
November 4, 1948	Resolution 61
November 7, 1941	*Armenia*
November 9, 1791	Napper Tandy
November 9, 1989	Mary Dolencie
November 10, 1956	"Seven Days of Freedom"
November 15, 1985	The Anglo-Irish Agreement
November 17, 1953	The Blasket Islands
November 17, 1973	Richard Nixon
November 17, 1978	The *Star Wars Holiday Special*
November 20, 1945	The Nuremburg Trials
November 26, 1977	"Ashtar Galactic Command"
December 2, 1999	Devolution
December 3, 1755	Gilbert Charles Stuart
December 3, 1980	Zlata Filipović
December 7, 1768	William Bulkely
December 8, 1941	Jeannette Pickering Rankin
December 8, 2014	Restitution
December 9, 1425	Leuven
December 9, 1948	UNCPPCG
December 10th	UN Human Rights Day
December 10, 1997	*Amistad*
December 12th	Saint Finnian of Clonard
December 17, 1943	*The Magnuson Act*
December 20, 1788	James Freney
December 21, 1980	Sunny von Bulow
December 23, 1805	Joseph Smith Jr.
December 24, 1818	*Stille Nacht, heilige Nacht*
December 29, 1908	Andrew Johnson
December 16, 1968	Revoked the Edict of Expulsion

Made in the USA
Columbia, SC
12 July 2018